IMAGES
of America

WINNSBORO

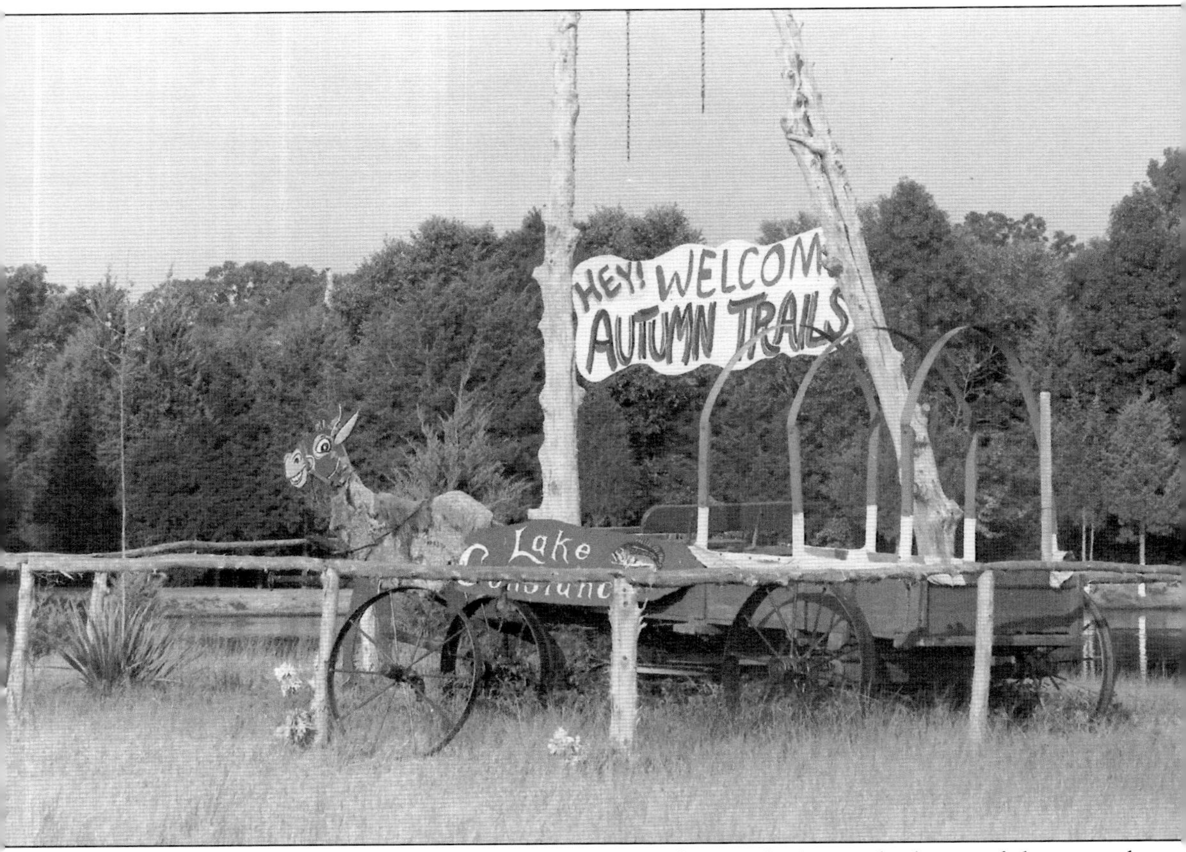

In the last half a century, Winnsboro has become known for being the home of the annual Autumn Trails Festival, held each October. For a number of years, starting in the late 1950s, this sign greeted visitors as they arrived along Highway 11, headed toward the campgrounds at City Park. (Courtesy of the *Winnsboro News*.)

On the Cover: In 1913, the first sweet potato processing plant in Texas was built in Winnsboro. Wood stoves burned inside the plant to dry the potatoes and preserve them. Between Winnsboro and Pittsburg, farmers grew thousands of bushels of potatoes each year that were shipped to markets in the West. (Courtesy of the *Winnsboro News*.)

IMAGES
of America

WINNSBORO

Maryann Miller and Bill Jones

ARCADIA
PUBLISHING

ISBN 978-0-7385-9967-0

Published by Arcadia Publishing
Charleston, South Carolina

Printed in the United States of America

Library of Congress Control Number: 2013931119

For all general information, please contact Arcadia Publishing:
Telephone 843-853-2070
Fax 843-853-0044
E-mail sales@arcadiapublishing.com
For customer service and orders:
Toll-Free 1-888-313-2665

Visit us on the Internet at www.arcadiapublishing.com

To the people of Winnsboro

Contents

ACKNOWLEDGMENTS

Many people assisted with compiling this book, and the authors want to thank everyone who shared stories and pictures. Special thanks go to the *Winnsboro News*, where Bill Jones's weekly column, "Historical Reflections," has been published for many years. The newspaper owners were also gracious in sharing pictures from their archives.

The authors also want to thank local photographer Bob Williams, who was a tremendous help in capturing images for the book and allowing us to share them.

There were many other people who helped by sharing pictures and historical information, including the following: Winnsboro mayor Carolyn Jones; Vickie Friday Martin, librarian at the Gilbreath Memorial Library; the Winnsboro Chamber of Commerce; Bonnie Sir Kigian White, artist; Anita Williams; Bea Lestage; and Sue Hamm.

Maryann would like to thank Bill Jones for being such a wonderful partner in writing this book. He is like a walking history book of Winnsboro and that made the research so much easier.

As a member of the Winnsboro Preservation League and the Winnsboro Heritage Society, Bill Jones would like to thank members of both organizations for their support through the years as he documented and preserved the history of Winnsboro.

Introduction

Winnsboro, like so many other small towns across America, has had a varied and interesting history and it continues to be a destination for tourists and people looking for a nice place to retire. The town sits in the heart of the beautiful Piney Woods of East Texas, just 90 miles east of Dallas and 100 miles west of Shreveport, Louisiana.

By the beginning of the 16th century, all of East Texas was a giant forest inhabited by mostly friendly Caddo Indians. Spring-fed streams were abundant with fish, and game such as deer, wild turkey, and bear roamed the countryside.

European explorers made successful expeditions through the area in the 17th and 18th centuries, and both France and Spain considered this part of East Texas their "sphere of influence." In 1821, Mexico gained its independence from Spain and made land available for colonization. However, until 1836, when Texas won its independence, migration from the United States was not significant.

In the summer of 1854, William Rile McMillan and John Elliott Winn left Belleview, near Henderson, in search of a new location for their business. They traveled north to Gilmer, then followed the Jefferson Road northwest toward Greenville.

Late one afternoon, the adventuresome pair reached a crossroads—the road to the north pointed to Clarksville and the Jonesboro Crossing on the Red River, the south trail to the water port on the Sabine River, three miles south of present-day Hawkins. The traveled path to the west pointed to Reilly Springs and Greenville. The east route extended to the port city of Jefferson, second only to Galveston as the state's most important water port.

McMillan and Winn made camp for the night on a rolling slope covered by huge oak trees near the crossroads. Next morning, they decided to inspect the countryside. The soil was excellent for agriculture, game was plentiful, and there was a good supply of water at the old city waterworks.

The nearest settlement, Cornersville, was two miles to the west. In 1861, Rev E.H. Green of Greenhill, a community northwest of Mount Pleasant, established one of the early Presbyterian churches in Texas. The church was located in Webster, another nearby community, and it is believed to be the first Presbyterian church to receive sanction west of the Mississippi. In 1871, eleven members of the congregation joined Presbyterians of Winnsboro and built a small white sanctuary at what is now 400 Church Street in Winnsboro.

McMillan and Winn were impressed with business prospects at the crossroads, today the intersection of North Main and Pine Streets. They were successful in acquiring 361 acres of land out of the Gray B. King survey from the William Logan estate with the crossroads being near the center of the tract.

They named the settlement "Crossroads." The first structure, a mercantile business, constructed by McMillan and Winn, was 20 by 40 feet, with a porch across the entire front and a sign above the porch that read "Cheap Cash Store." This store is believed to be Wood County's first business.

Across the road, to the southwest of the store, was an excellent water well frequently used by travelers and passing teamsters transporting goods to the West.

Dr. Joseph McGee and Andrew Vannoy operated the first sawmill and constructed a commissary store at the southwest corner of the crossroads. The first residence, a two-room cabin, was built at the northeast corner of the crossroads by W.R. McMillan, and then John Winn constructed a one-room bungalow about 200 to 300 feet west of the McMillan dwelling.

Next, business lots were laid out on either side of West Pine Street. The settlement required a new name, as Texas had another community called Crossroads. The name chosen was Winnsborough in honor of McMillan's stepfather, Capt. John Elliott Winn. With the new name, the post office opened March 6, 1855.

James and Nancy Cook arrived at the new town of Winnsborough in 1859. They purchased the east 200 acres out of the McMillan-Winn tract, including the two-room McMillan residence, and proceeded to expand the structure to a two-story building, sporting a mixture of early Texas and Victorian architecture.

The detached kitchen received the name "Cook Tavern;" here, travelers and locals enjoyed delicious food at a large kitchen table. Cook Tavern was the only place in the frontier town to acquire news, as passengers from the Jefferson-McKinney stagecoach were patrons at the Cook Tavern and would relate news from the East.

By 1860, Winnsborough had a number of business establishments. The first Jewish merchant in Wood County was Isaac Farber, who owned the Cheap Cash Store. Drury Connally opened a mercantile business, and two Germans named Miller and Hekel put in a successful blacksmith and woodworking shop. Vannoy and McGee sold their commissary store to James and Nancy Cook in 1859, and W.R. McMillan returned from medical school in New Orleans and opened a drugstore. The first grocery store was owned by Ellbert Moore, and Tom Ferris was proprietor of the gristmill at Tanyard Springs.

In the next 20 years, the town grew to include three churches, schools, eight steam gristmills and cotton gins, an opera house, and a weekly newspaper, the *Sentinel*; and it boasted 700 inhabitants.

Winnsboro is a charming small town surrounded by beautiful countryside. The city has now grown to a population of 3,584, with about 33,000 residents in a 12-mile radius around the town who live near one of the many area lakes. Winnsboro is a Main Street City, a Certified Retirement Community, and the location of a State Certified Arts District—the only small town to have that designation. It is the home of Autumn Trails, the Winnsboro Center for the Arts, Crossroads Music Company, popular restaurants for fine dining, antique shops, a coffee shop, two general stores, a day spa, an upscale kitchen store, and many other places to visit and enjoy.

Creativity abounds in and around Winnsboro, with many fine artists, professional musicians, writers, actors, and entertainers who make their home here. There are a number of venues for live music, theater, and art exhibits, as well as a several artists' studios scattered throughout the area.

One

From Wilderness to a Thriving Community

The Winnsboro area of East Texas first belonged to Native Americans. A community of Caddo Indians known as Nandacao settled at the site where Winnsboro was later founded. An Indian trail passed through the site, originating from the east and heading to the headwaters of the Sabine River near what is now Greenville, Texas. This trail was known as the Caddo Trace.

The Native Americans were here from around 700 AD until the 1840s. They raised families, played games, taught their children the Caddo way of life, conducted religious ceremonies, grew old, and buried their loved ones in sacred burial grounds for over 1,100 years. The Indians were primarily farmers and had two major tribes. The Kadohadacho lived in large villages along the Red River near the present-day Oklahoma-Arkansas border. The other was the Tejas or Hasinai Caddo, who lived farther southeast.

The Caddo Indians of East Texas formed the Hasinai Confederacy, which extended north to the Red River, west to the Trinity River, south to near the headwaters of the Neches and Angelina Rivers, and east to what is now Shreveport, Louisiana. The Caddos developed a superior form of government, trade with the Plains Indians, and a network of trails to all sections of their confederacy.

In 1845, when Texas was admitted to the Union, the federal government forced the relocation of both the Hasinai and the Kadohadacho onto the Brazos Reservation. In 1859, many of the Caddo were relocated to Indian Territory west of the Mississippi River. After the Civil War, the Caddo were concentrated on a reservation located between the Washita and Canadian Rivers.

After the Civil War, Winnsboro almost died. The town was one of the strongest advocates for secession in the area, and many local young men had been casualties of the war. Other young people left because of the constant demands of Reconstruction authorities. The Winnsboro Post Office closed in 1868 and did not reopen until 1874. This was when the community of Webster began to thrive.

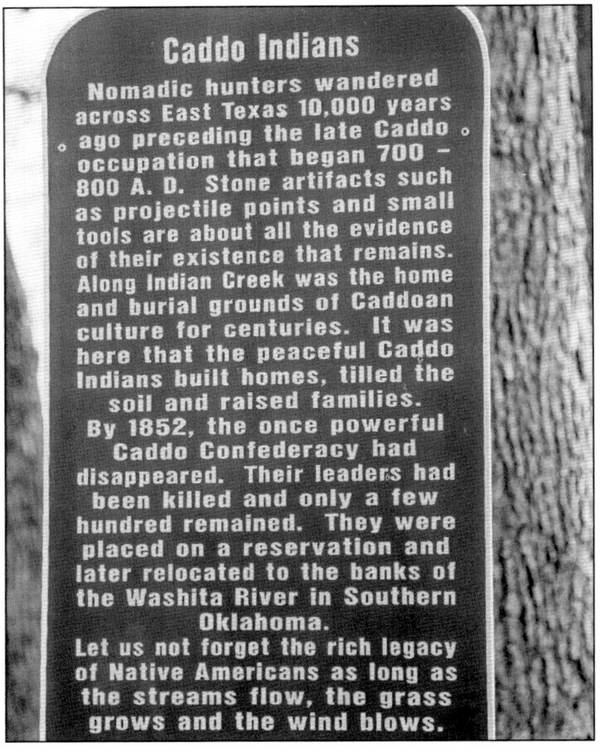

All that is left of the Caddo Indian influence in the area are some artifacts found along the creek in what is now City Park. The Winnsboro Preservation League erected this historical marker to acknowledge the legacy that the Indians left. (Courtesy of Bob Williams.)

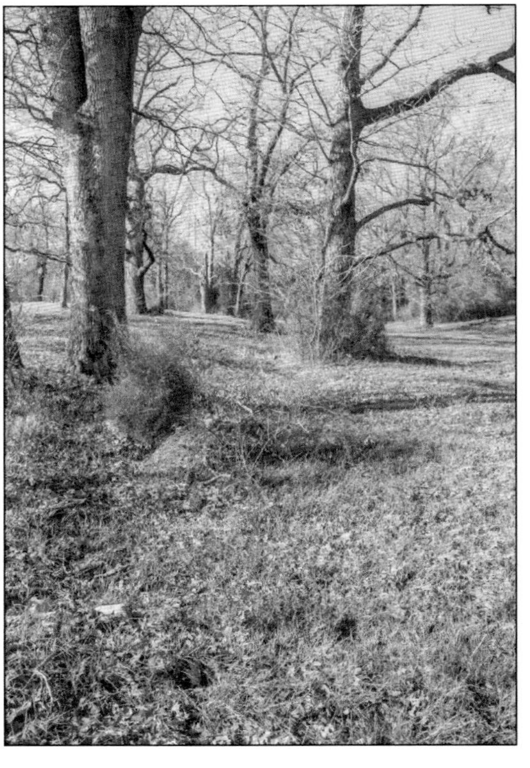

A faint trail, which is all that is left of the Old Jefferson Trace Roadway, passes through the original Craddock homestead. In the late 1830s, steamboats would come up the Mississippi River to Jefferson, where goods would be unloaded and then carried by wagon to points west. This trail left Jefferson and headed toward Gilmer, then on to Webster. It was considered one of the main trails out of Jefferson and was called the Jefferson-Dallas Wagon Road. (Courtesy of Bob Williams.)

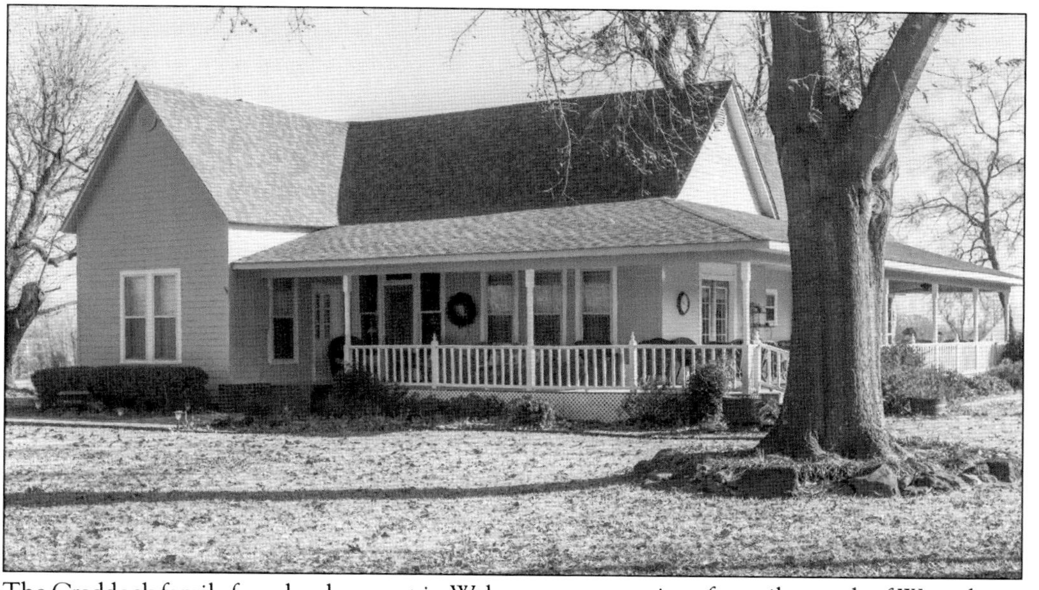

The Craddock family farm has been out in Webster, a community a few miles south of Winnsboro, since 1858. Webster was a thriving community at the time, and in 1856, it was said that the community of Webster was larger than Dallas, with a population of 850 people. Two Jewish merchants owned warehouses where they would receive goods that came from Jefferson. Those goods would then be dispersed to Dallas and other points west. (Courtesy of Bob Williams.)

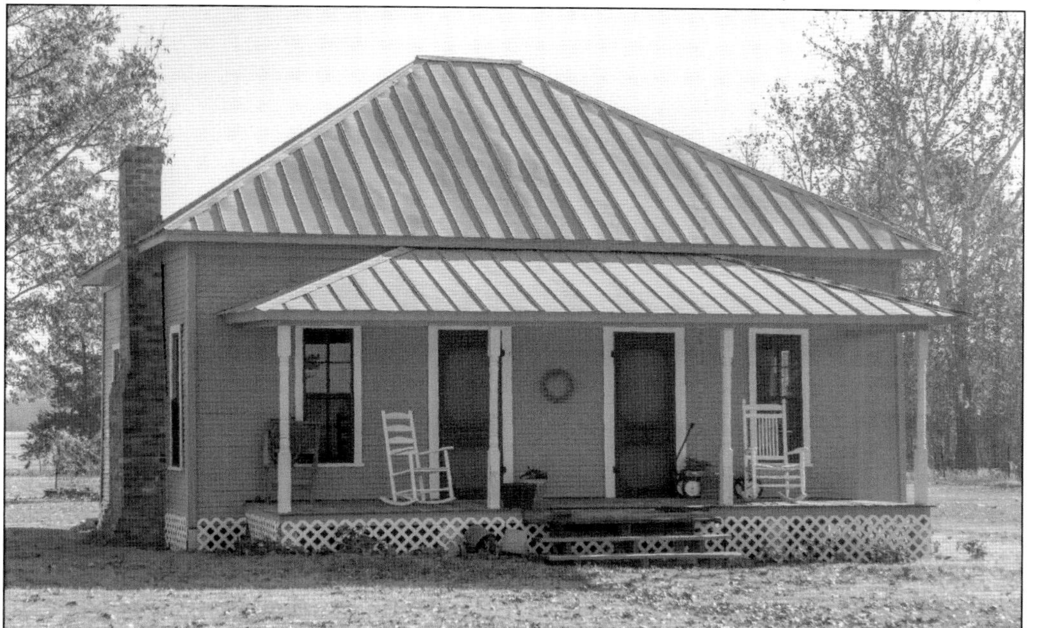

This home on the property now owned by Jimmy and Sue Craddock Hamm was once the home of Sarah Jane "Granny" Craddock, who came to East Texas from North Carolina. The building, a California bungalow with four rooms and a porch, has been restored and turned into a museum. (Courtesy of Bob Williams.)

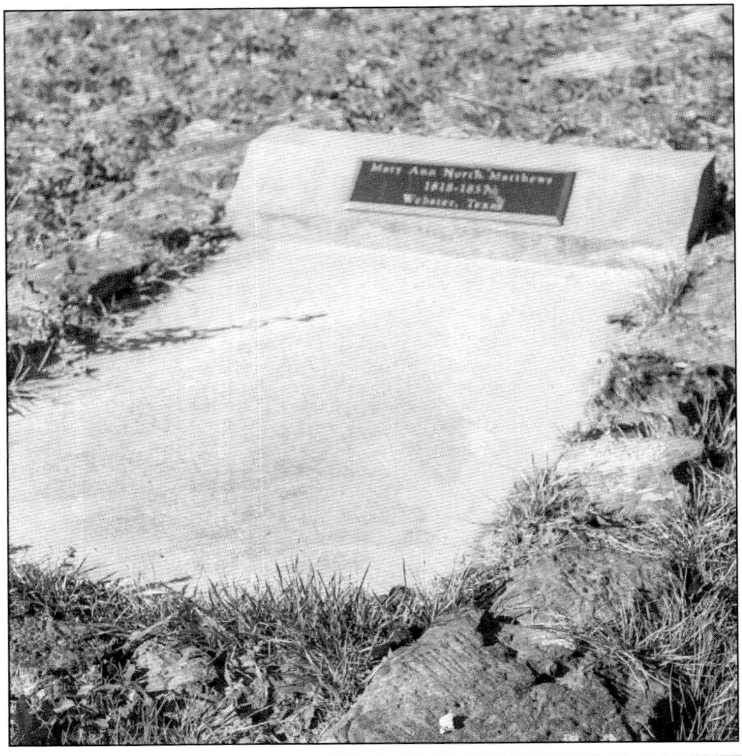

The only visible grave marker in the Old Webster Cemetery is that of Mary Ann North Clements Matthews (1818–1857). She was the daughter of David Clements, brother of Samuel Clements. Her husband, Gilbert Matthews, was instrumental in developing the village into a trade center. He built a fashionable home and a large commissary store that also served as a post office. He was also a Wood County judge. (Courtesy of Bob Williams.)

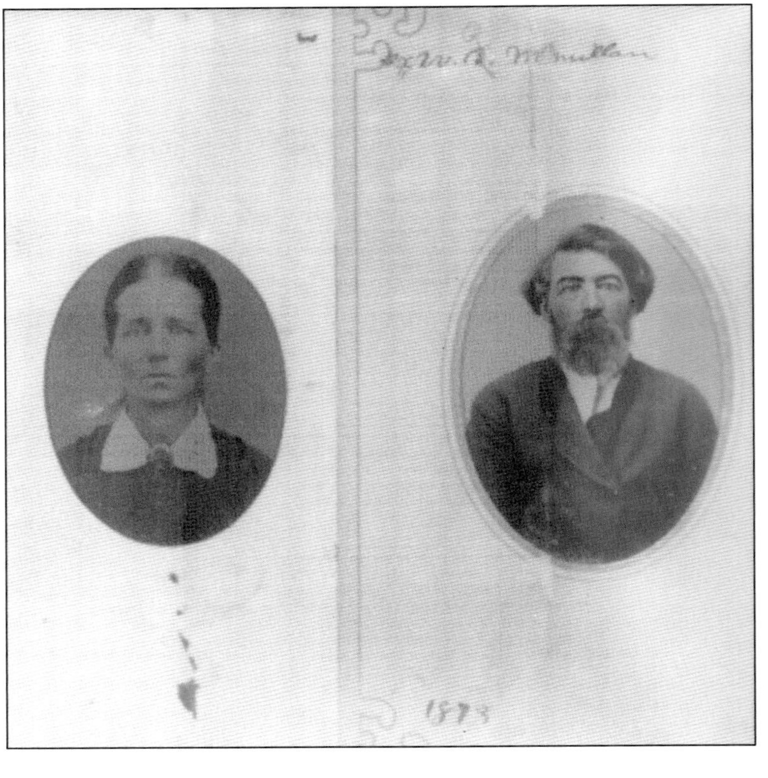

William Rile McMillan (right) and John Elliot Winn came to the area in 1854 and considered the land that became Winnsboro one of the prettiest places in East Texas. They decided to move their business here and established a community called Crossroads. (Courtesy of Bill Jones.)

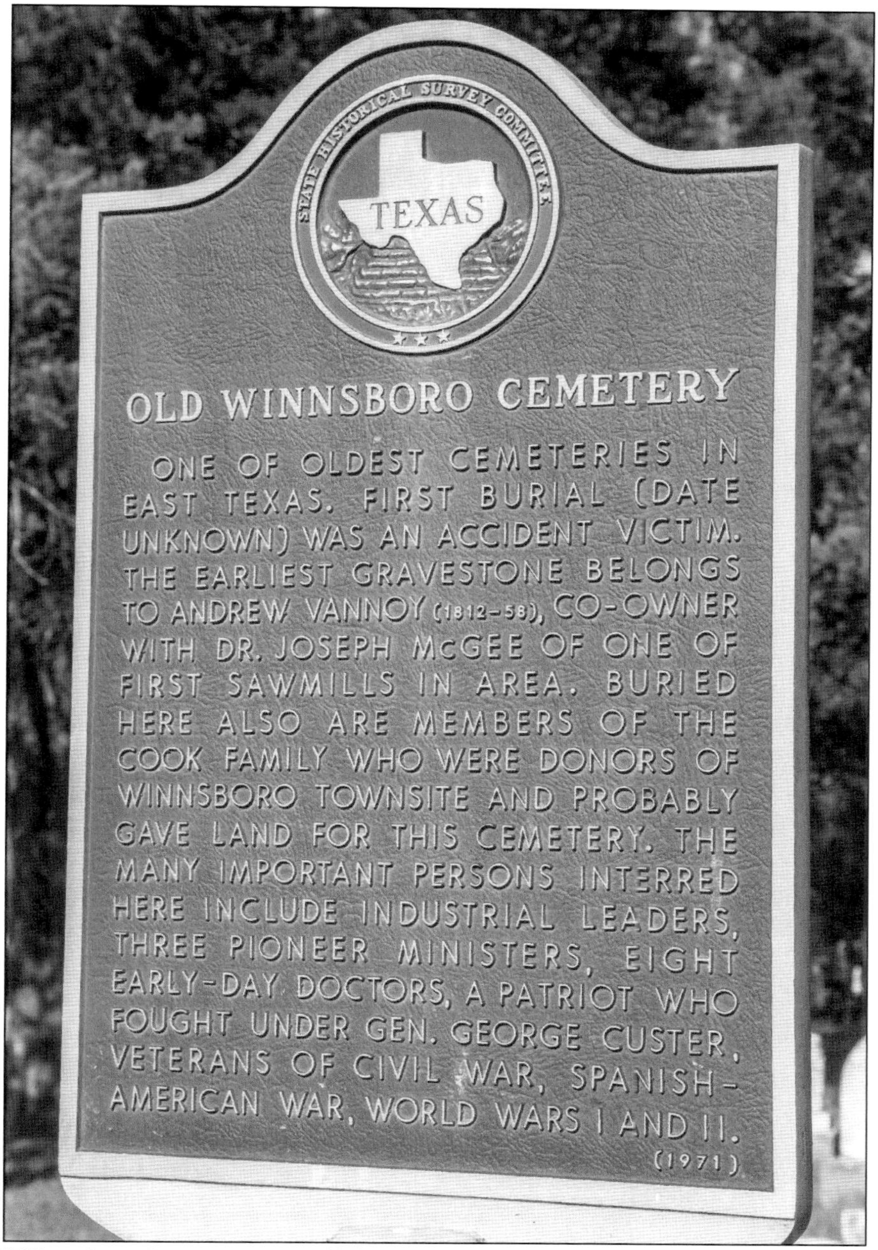

The Old Winnsboro Cemetery, now called City Cemetery, was established in 1855 on land believed to have been donated by the Cook family. The earliest gravestone marks the burial spot of Andrew Vannoy (1812–1858) who, with Dr. McGee, owned the first sawmill in Winnsboro. The oldest birth date on any marker in the City Cemetery is that of David White: July 28, 1788. At least one Spanish-American War veteran, Cpl. Wesley Douglas, who was with the 1st Texas Infantry, is buried there, as are a number of Civil War soldiers, including Dr T.N. Skeen (1843–1919), J.R. Wright Sr. (1830–1911), E.C. Mitchell (1843–1923), Dr. W.S. Mims (1341–1913), Charles B. Gorman (1841–1922), and R.J. Cook (no dates). Members of the Cook family are also buried in the City Cemetery as well as other important early settlers. (Courtesy of Bob Williams.)

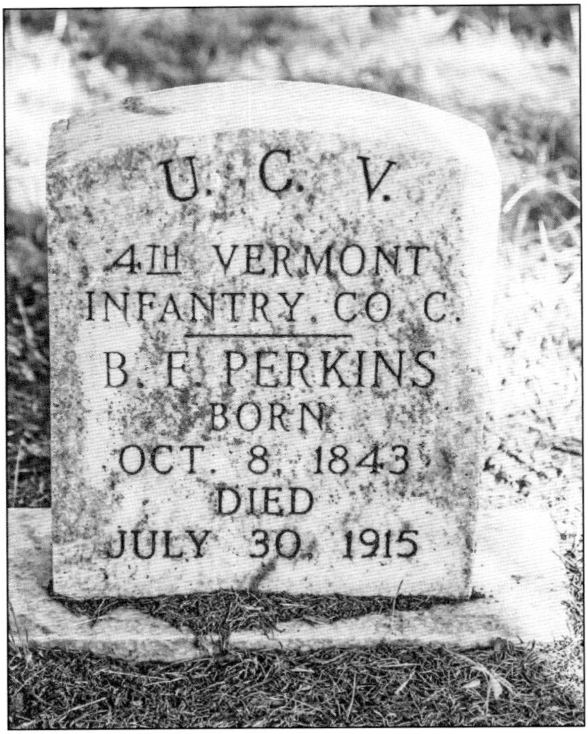

Thirty-five Confederate soldiers are buried in the City Cemetery along with one Union soldier, B.F. Perkins from New Hampshire. He was part of the migration to the West after the Civil War. Settlers were on their way West but stopped here because of the Indian uprisings on other side of McKinney. Many people left the South because of malaria and black fever, and they would stay here for a year or two and then move farther West when the Indians were pushed out. (Courtesy of Bob Williams.)

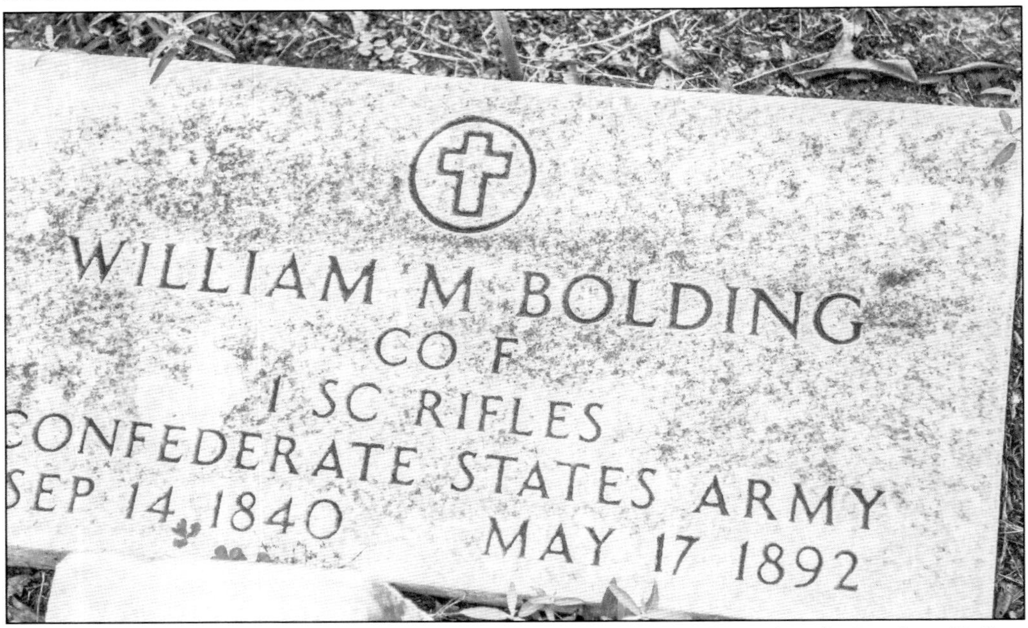

A Confederate soldier, William M. Bolding was in Company F, 1st South Carolina Rifles, Confederate States Army. He was born on September 14, 1840, and died on May 17, 1892. During the Civil War, this area was a haven for wounded Confederate soldiers. Many came here to heal from wounds suffered in battle. Others came from the East and South to escape sickness and reconstruction in the Deep South following the war. (Courtesy of Bob Williams.)

James Floyd Embry was the great-great-grandfather of Vickie Friday Martin, current librarian in Winnsboro. He enlisted in the Confederate army on December 28, 1862. He was with Company A, 1st Regiment, Georgia State Troops. The family owned the Hiram Embry Plantation in Georgia, where an historical marker recounts the battle of Peachtree Creek, which occurred on the plantation in July 1864. (Courtesy of Vickie Friday Martin.)

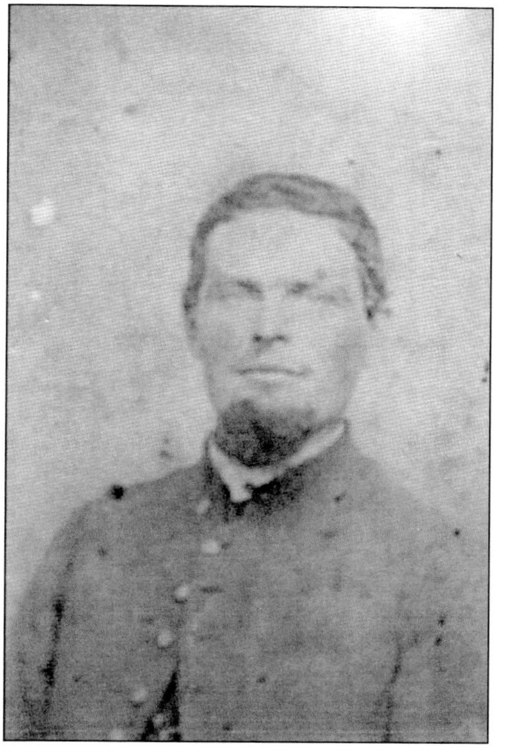

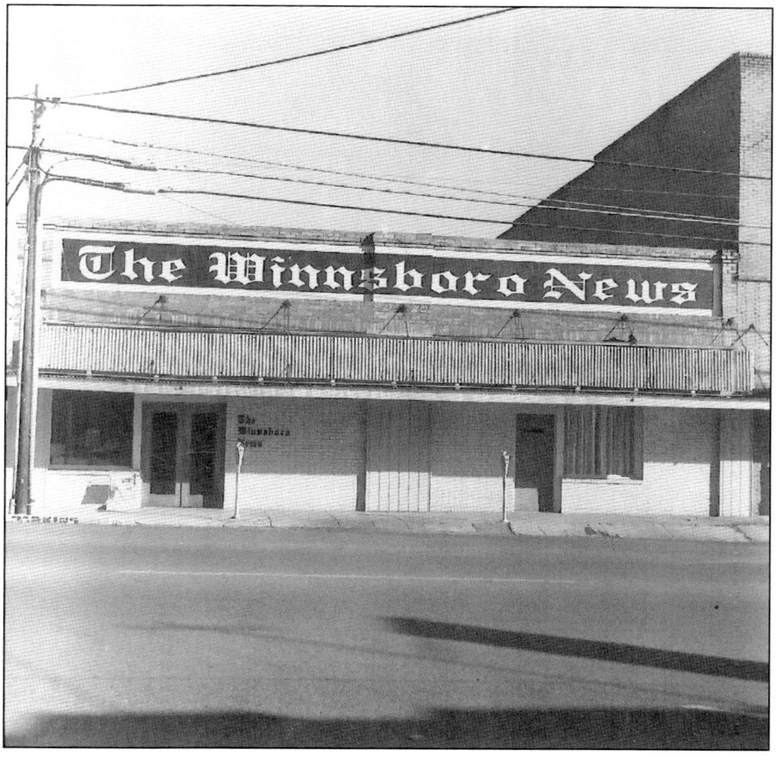

The *Winnsboro News*, the current weekly newspaper, can trace its origin to the first newspaper established in the town in 1878. R.L. Hayes, who came here from the East, liked what he saw, and decided to stay, established the *Winnsboro Sentinel*. He rented a shanty building near the railroad depot and, with limited funds, started the weekly publication. (Courtesy of the *Winnsboro News*.)

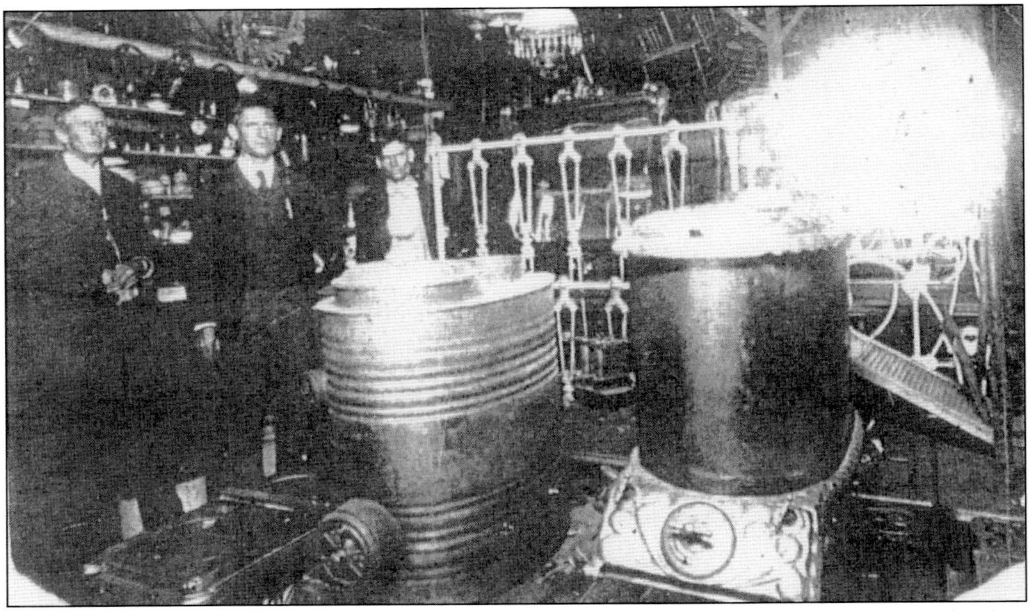

Andrew Vannoy and Dr. Joseph McGee came to Winnsboro in 1855 and established the first sawmill in East Winnsboro. They built a commissary store on the southwest corner of Main and Pine Streets; they called it the Cheap Cash Store. They also set aside land in East Winnsboro for the McGee Black Cemetery after two little girls burned in a fire; because blacks could not be buried in the City Cemetery, there was no place to put their remains. (Courtesy of the *Winnsboro News*.)

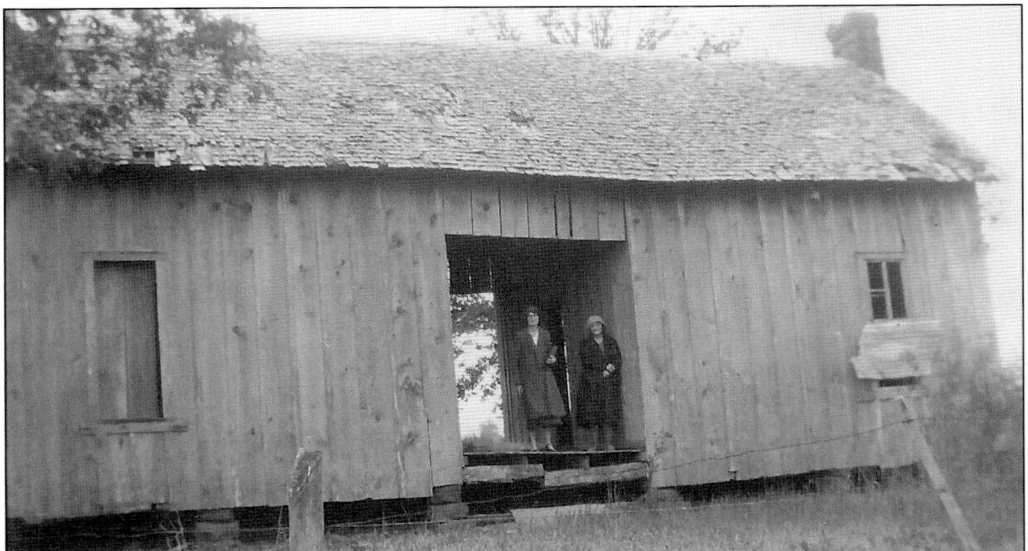

This dogtrot house is typical of the style of homes built in the 1800s. This one was built on property owned by Jason Rushing and his wife, Lucy Ross Rushing, daughter of A.J. Rushing. It was deeded to Lucy Ross Rushing by either T.H. Ross in 1900 or A.J. Ross Jr. in 1902 in the Cornersville community. It was later replaced by a farmhouse that was built in the 1930s. (Courtesy of Bonnie Sir Kigian White.)

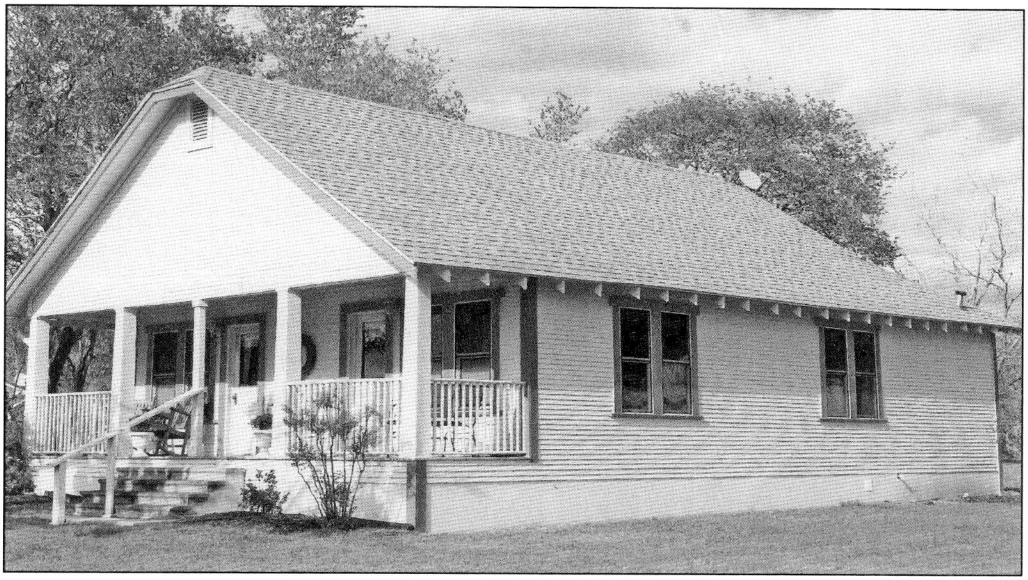

Hunter's Moon Studio is currently the home of artist Bonnie Sir Kigian White. The land was purchased in 1862 by her great-great-grandfather A.J. Ross in an area known as Cornersville. This is the farmhouse that was built in the 1930s, and it has been fully restored. Bonnie is proud of the legacy her grandparents and their parents left to the area. A.J. Ross gave property for a small country school, and J. R. Rushing donated land where Mount Zion Church was built. The Cornersville School was deeded to the Cornersville community by A.J. Ross and his wife, E.H. Ross, on July 27, 1878, for use as a school and place of worship for all "Orthodox denominations." This photograph was taken around 1910, and the child in the bottom row at far left is Alta Maye Horne, great-granddaughter of A.J. Ross and mother of Bonnie Sir Kigian White. (Both, courtesy of Bonnie Sir Kigian White.)

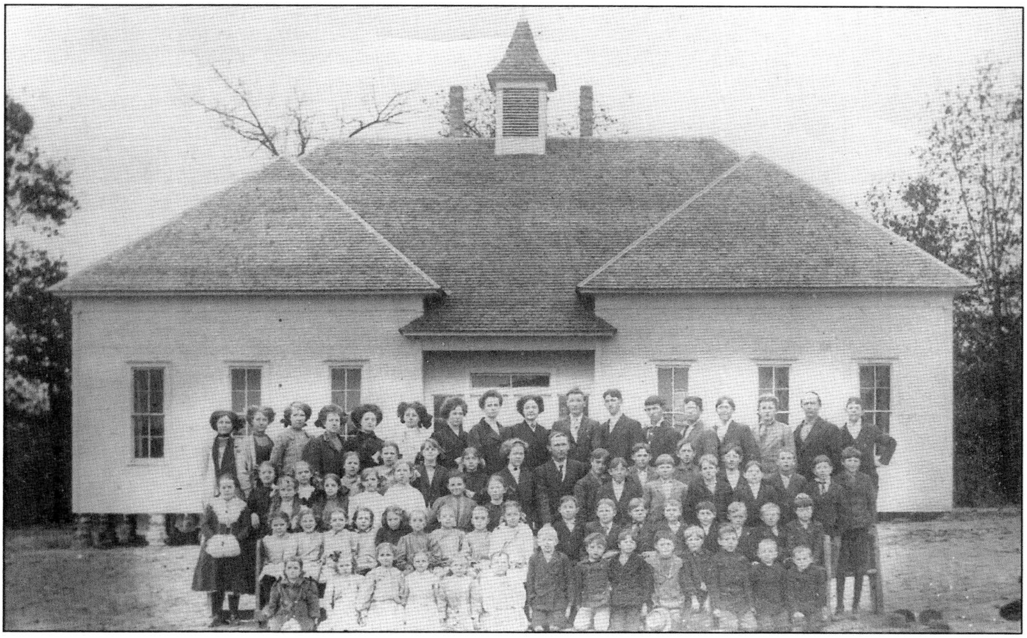

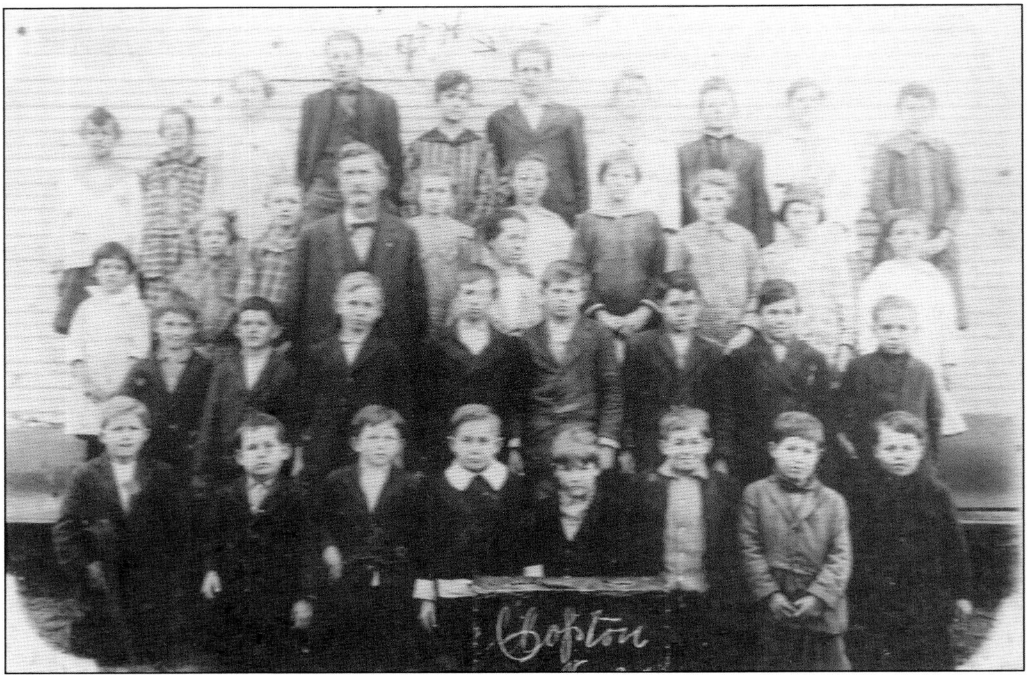

It was common for small communities to get established near a larger town like Winnsboro, and Clopton was one of those communities. These children are posed in front of the school but are not identified. Like most of the small communities in the area, Clopton also had a church and a general store. (Courtesy of the *Winnsboro News*.)

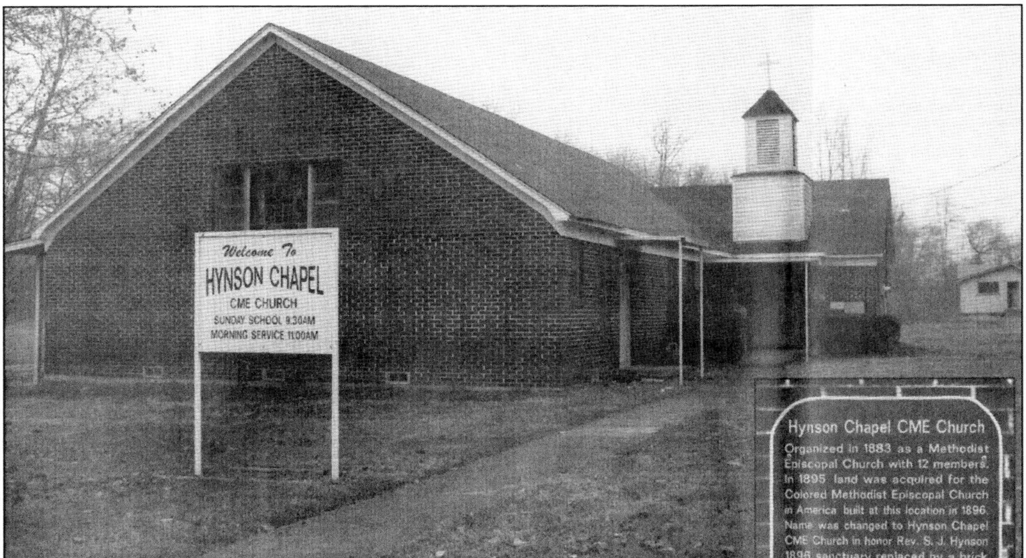

Hynson Chapel CME Church was first organized in 1883 and was a member of the Colored Methodist Episcopal Church in America. Later, the name was changed to Hynson Chapel CME Church, honoring S.J. Hynson, pastor during construction of the new brick sanctuary in 1957. (Courtesy of the *Winnsboro News*.)

Two

The Coming of the Railroad

In 1876, Nancy Cook convinced the East Line & Red River Railroad to come to Winnsboro. As soon as the depot was built and the trains started coming in 1878, all the businesses on North Main and Pine Streets relocated, quickly building little wooden shanties near the railroad tracks. Winnsboro soon became a major shipping center, and farmers would bring their products to be shipped west. Prior to the coming of the railroad, it would take two weeks to transport bales of cotton by oxcart to Jefferson, Texas, which was the second largest port in Texas at the time.

At one time, at least 25 carloads of lumber would leave Winnsboro every day to go west for building needs in Dallas. The largest lumber mill in the state of Texas was Ragley Lumber Mill, owned by Wolfgang Ragley, who came to Texas from Pennsylvania after fighting in the Union army. Later, he moved to Dallas, where the Ragley family became very prominent residents.

While still doing business in Winnsboro, Wolfgang Ragley had a railroad tram that brought lumber from his mill to town. In 1896, he sold the tram to Schluter and Whiteman, who then sold it to Texas Southern Railroad Company in 1902. At that time, the tram carried peaches from the community of Peach, which was the largest peach producing center in Texas. Later, the Texas Southern became the Marshall & East Texas Railroad (M&ET). It went from Winnsboro to Marshall and operated until 1917.

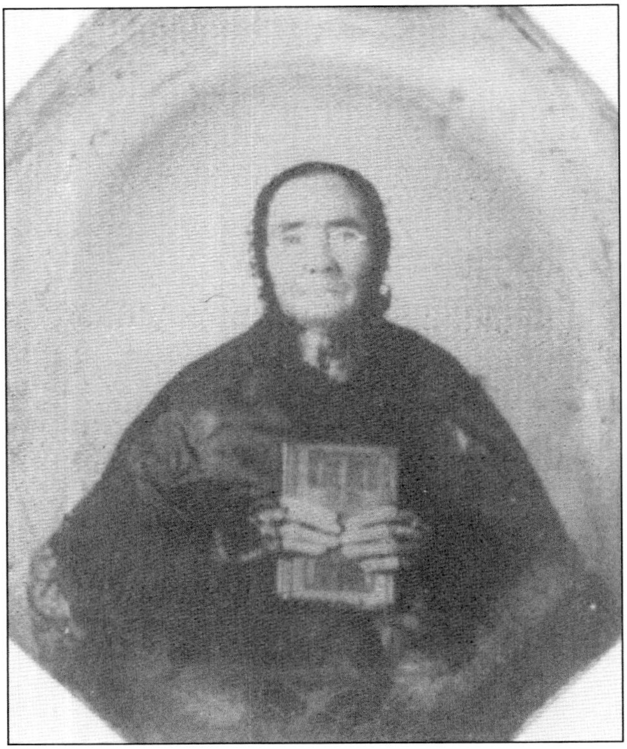

James and Nancy Cook came to Winnsboro in 1859 and bought 200 acres in the area where North Pine Street connects with North Main Street now. That area was known as Cook's Town, and it became the information center of Winnsboro. In 1876, when there was talk of building a railroad from Jefferson, Nancy Cook went to railroad officials and made the offer to give them right-of-way to bring railroad to Winnsboro instead of Webster if they would allow her to determine where the depot would be built. Also part of the deal was an offer of a half interest in 100 acres to be developed as a town. Left and below are images of what the depot looked like when built and today. It has been restored to house the chamber of commerce offices, as well as other city offices. (Left, courtesy of Bill Jones; below, courtesy of Maryann Miller.)

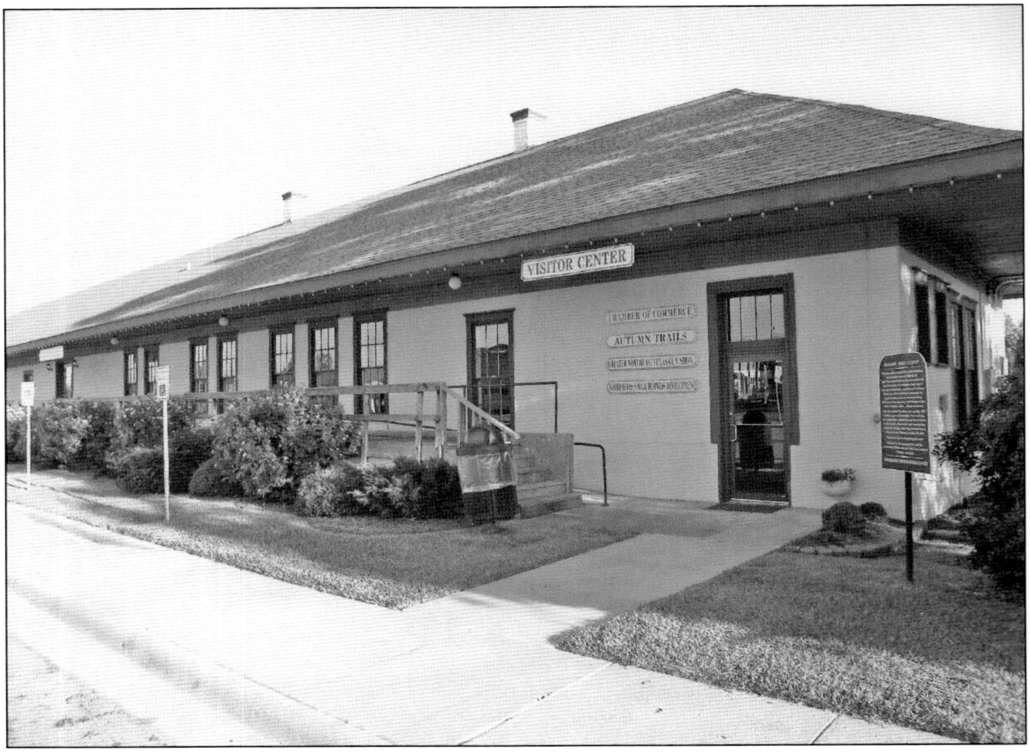

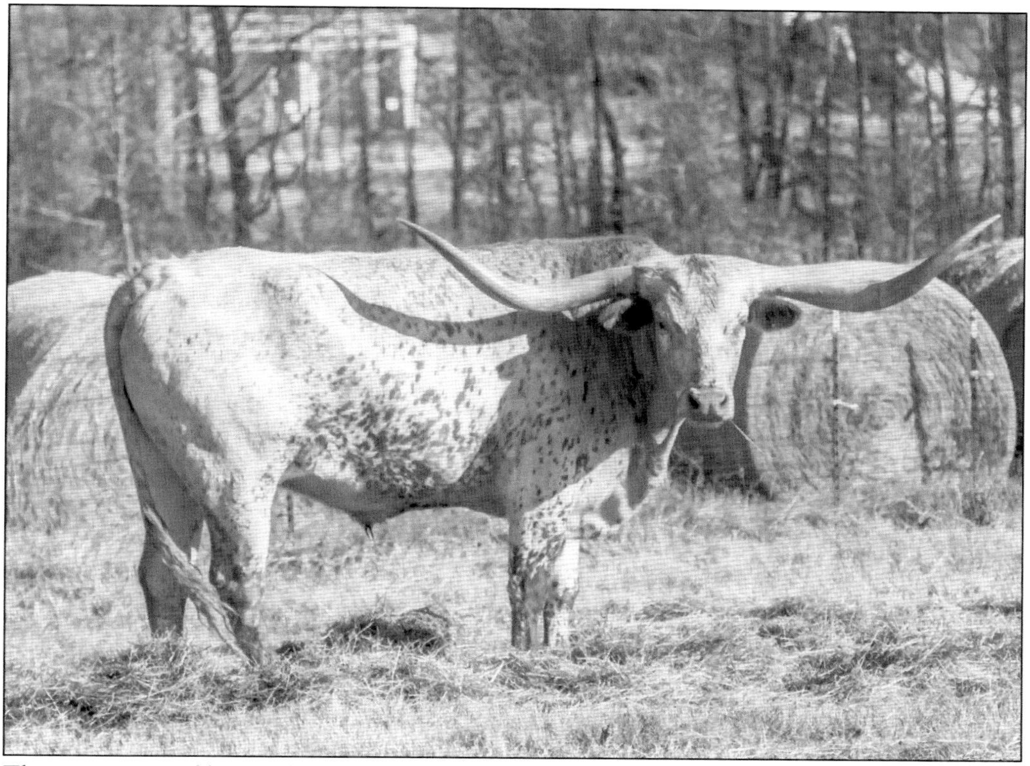

The emergence of livestock as an important industry, along with row crops and timber, began in Winnsboro around 1878. The railroad allowed the shipping of livestock to distant markets, where prices were higher than what was offered locally. Texas Longhorns were a popular breed at the time, and some local ranchers still raise them. This steer is part of a small herd on Jimmy and Sue Hamm's ranch, a legacy from the Craddocks. (Courtesy of Bob Williams.)

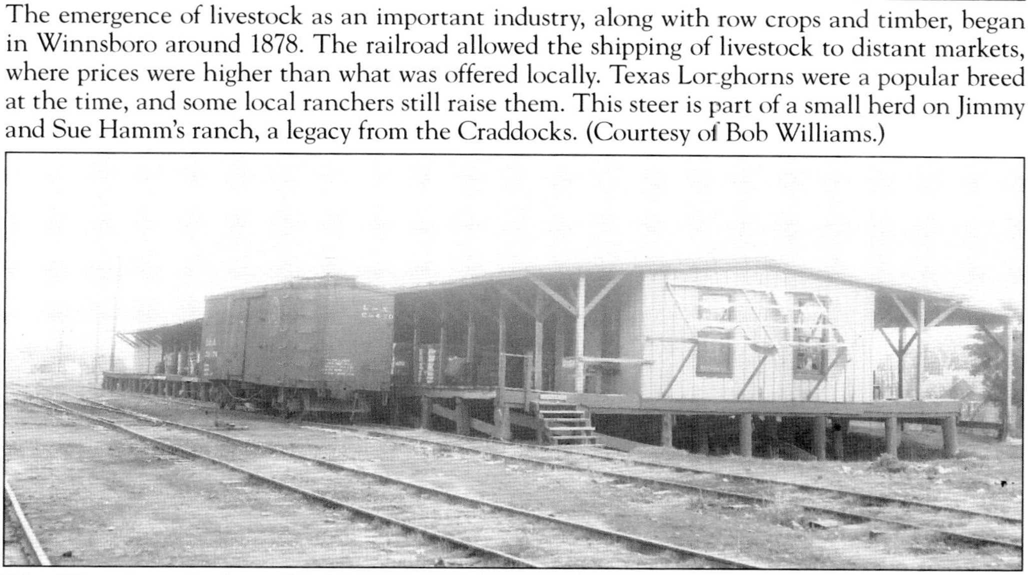

The Winnsboro Packing Shed is where produce would be brought to be shipped in baskets or crates. Perishables, such as potatoes, squash, cucumbers, and strawberries, would be packed here. Gallon buckets of syrup would also be shipped from here in the fall. Goods were first transported by wagon and later by motor vehicle. This building was used by W.A. Nabors and E.R. Crone in the early 1900s and was located on the south side of the railroad tracks at the corner of Walnut and Carnegie Streets. (Courtesy of the *Winnsboro News*.)

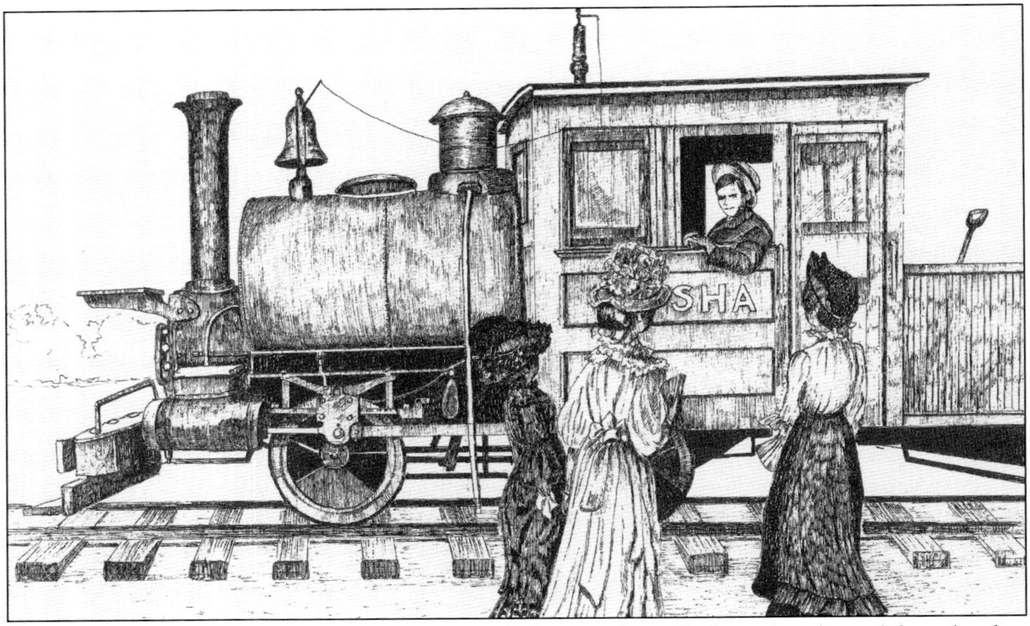

The Ragley Mill log engine, known as the "Ethyl Ann," brought huge logs by rail from lumber camps at Merrimac, Jim Hogg (Ogburn), and Peach to the mill in east Winnsboro from 1890 to 1902. The narrow-gauge steam engine was powerful but slow, powered by a piston drive for each wheel. Locals referred to the engine as the "Shay." On a Sunday afternoon in 1900, Myrtle Moore, in the white dress, and a friend stopped to chat by the Shay. (Courtesy of Peggy Thomas.)

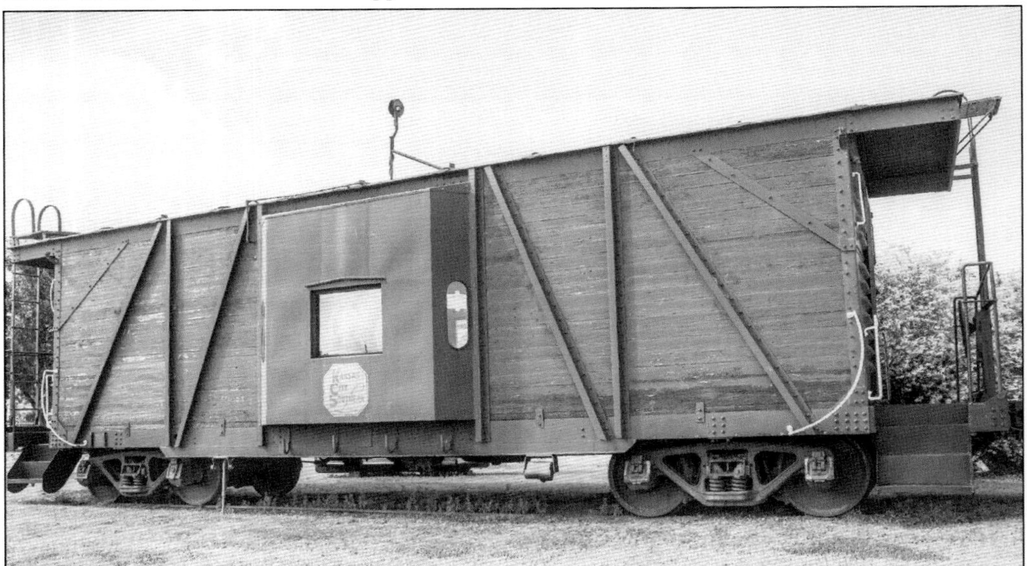

The caboose, which sits next to the depot in the original depot area, has been restored and will be used as a historical museum by the City of Winnsboro. The depot is still a gathering spot for community events and is an active visitor's center. (Courtesy of Bob Williams.)

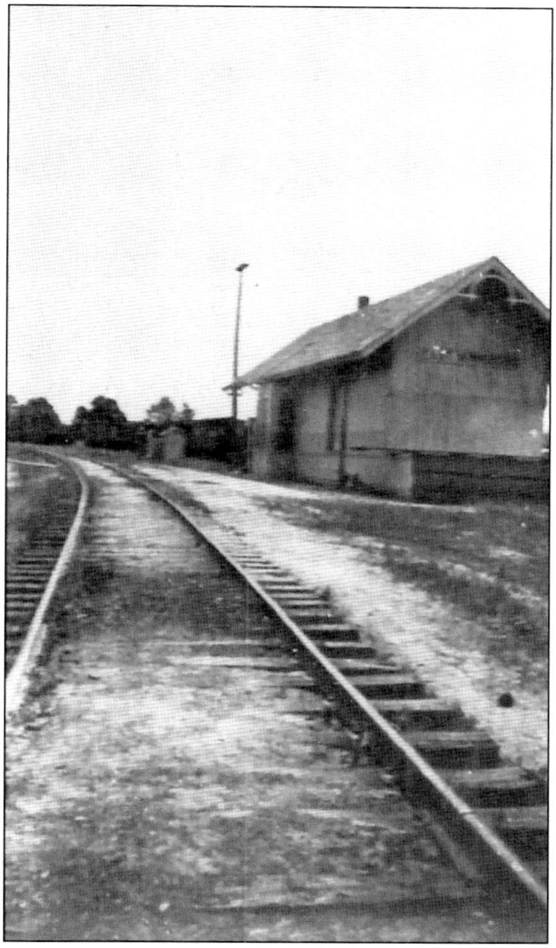

Every morning except Sunday, a passenger train left Marshall at 8:00 a.m. for Winnsboro and stopped at this depot east of town. The train consisted of a combination baggage-and-mail car, passenger car, and day coach and had a seating capacity of 70. There were 24 stops between Marshall and Winnsboro, but the train always stopped here, because Winnsboro had a reputation up and down the line for fine food. On October 15, 1915, the M&ET suffered a disastrous passenger train wreck in which several people were killed and a number injured. Damage settlements and court costs were over $250,000, which put the railroad into receivership. In later years, the trains did not run on schedule, due to a number of problems, including bridges that would burn down, making it impossible for the trains to pass. Locals started referring to the M&ET as the Misery & Eternal Torment Railroad. (Both, courtesy of the *Winnsboro News*.)

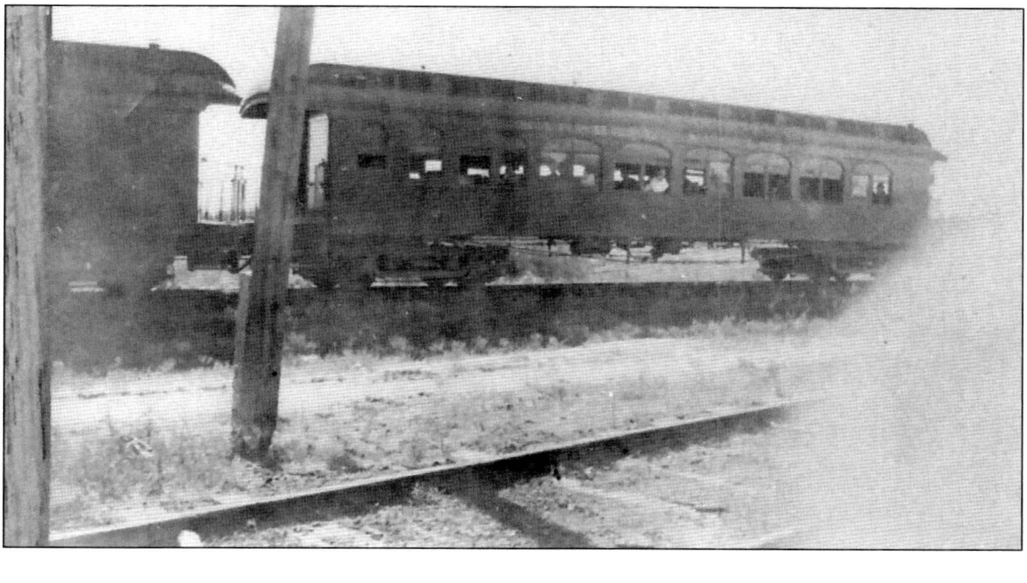

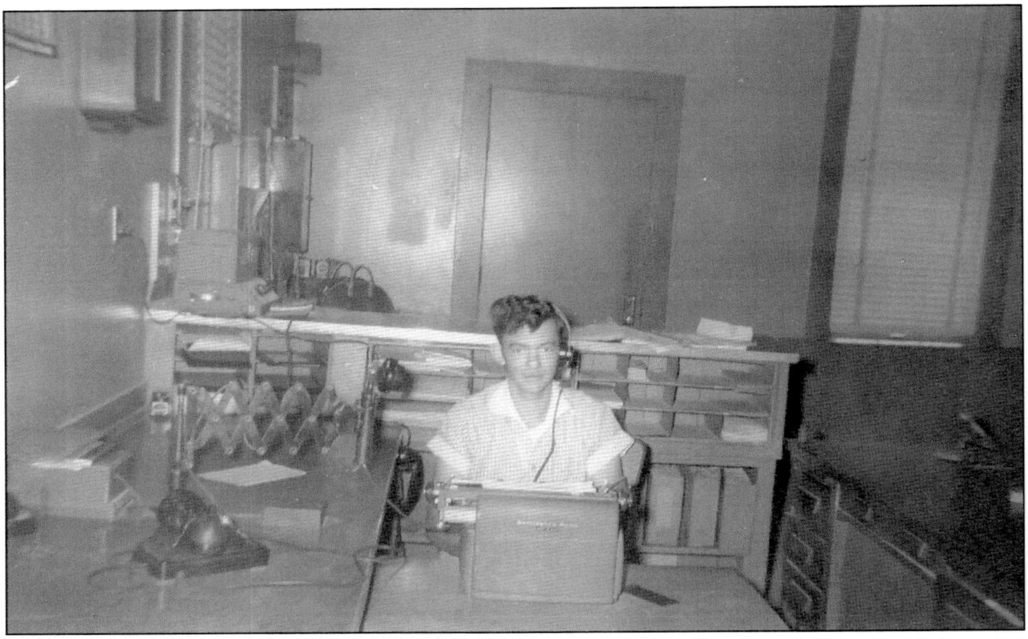

Weymon Lestage was a clerk with the railroad and came to Winnsboro in 1972 to schedule trains coming through town. Prior to that, he worked in Hope, Arkansas, starting there in 1957. Part of his job was to make sure that the switches all worked when more than one train came through town at a time. Weymon and his wife, Bea, were instrumental in starting the Catholic church in Winnsboro. (Courtesy of Bea Lestage.)

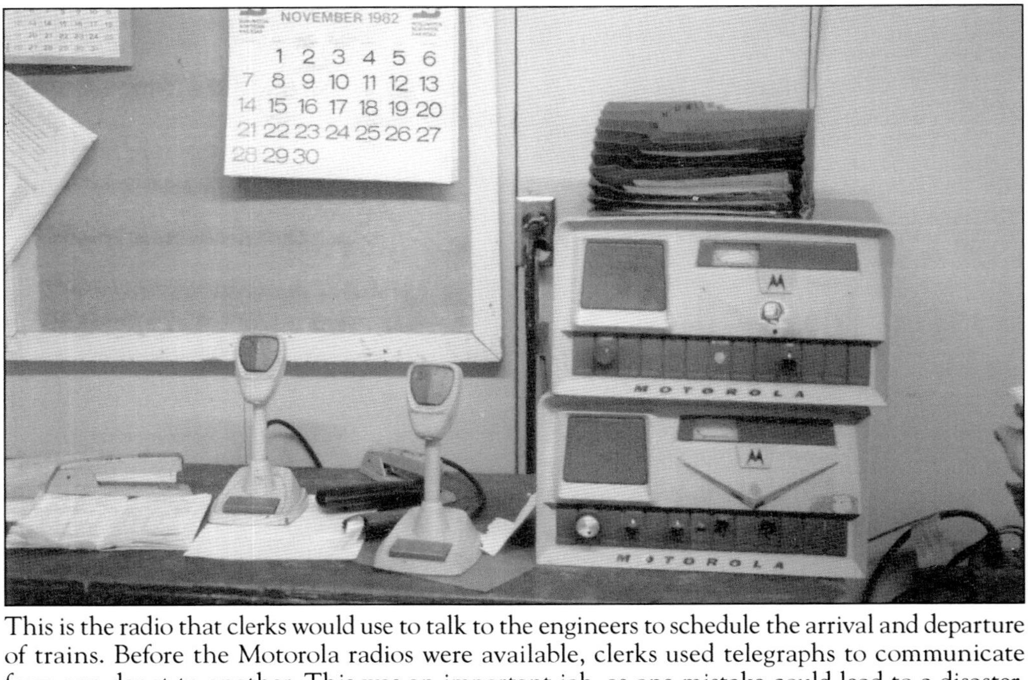

This is the radio that clerks would use to talk to the engineers to schedule the arrival and departure of trains. Before the Motorola radios were available, clerks used telegraphs to communicate from one depot to another. This was an important job, as one mistake could lead to a disaster. (Courtesy of Bea Lestage.)

It is rumored that Joe Stivers, a Winnsboro lumber baron, built the Henry Grady School in 1896 so his son, who had a clubfoot, would not have to walk all the way to the Texas Collegiate Institute. The school term lasted three months out of the year, and some families paid tuition in the form of syrups and other canned goods. This photograph of Joe and his wife, Genevieve, was taken at the turn of the century at the T.J. Bruce Studio, which was on Main Street in Winnsboro in the 1890s. (Courtesy of Bill Jones.)

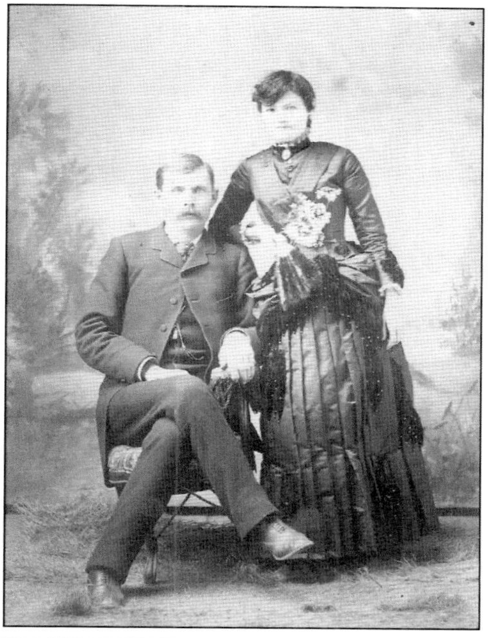

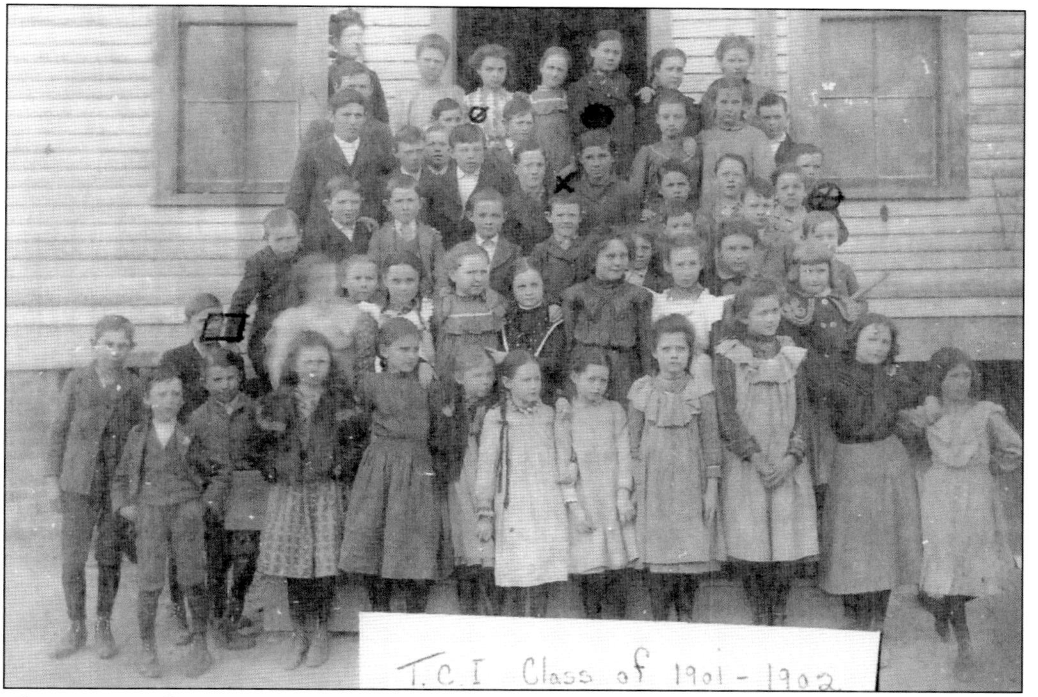

The Texas Collegiate Institute (TCI) was Winnsboro's first school. It was built in 1888 and operated until 1905 under the auspices of the City of Winnsboro School District. This is the class of 1901–1902. In 1909, the Winnsboro Independent School District was formed, consolidating the surrounding country schools with those in the city. TCI had four classrooms on the first floor, a study hall on the second floor, and an auditorium that converted to a basketball court on the third floor. (Courtesy of the *Winnsboro News.*)

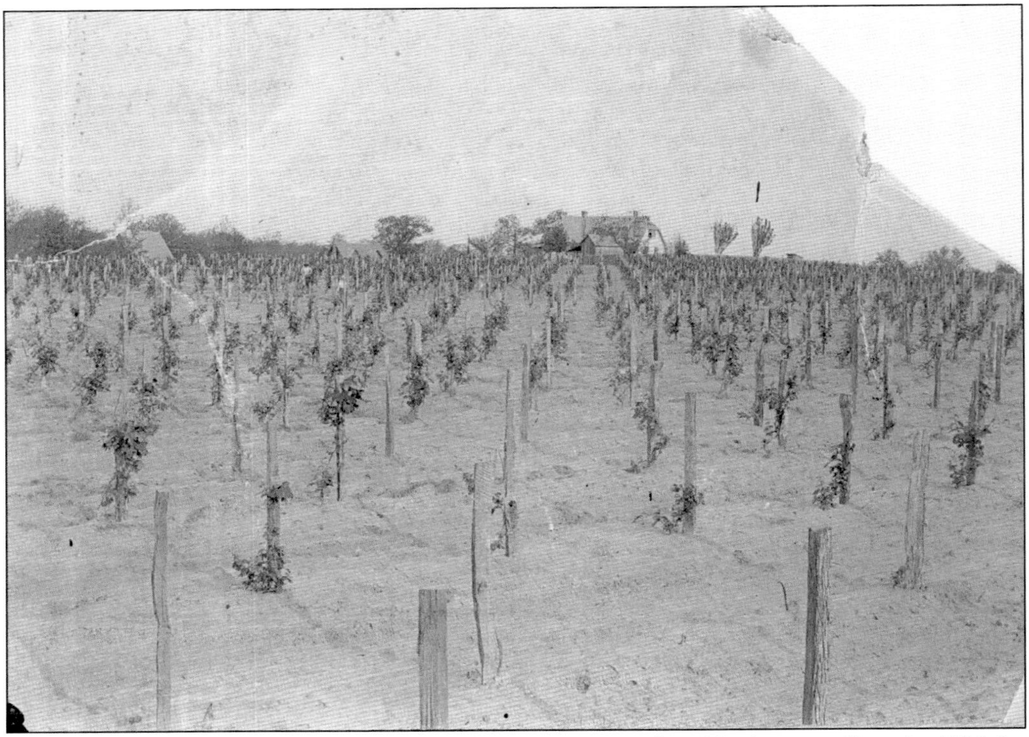

In the late 1800s, Charles W. Moore owned a grape vineyard and had wine cellars. In 1890, he won first prize at the Old Tyler Fruit Palace with his wine. The house was built about 1887 and had seven gables. (Courtesy of the *Winnsboro News*.)

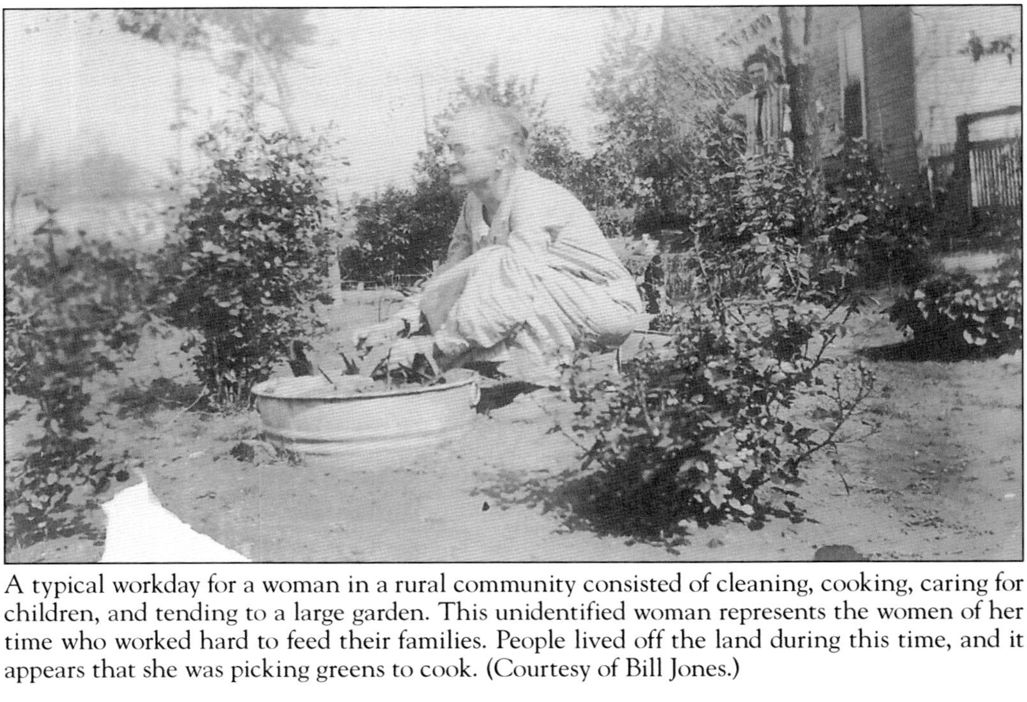

A typical workday for a woman in a rural community consisted of cleaning, cooking, caring for children, and tending to a large garden. This unidentified woman represents the women of her time who worked hard to feed their families. People lived off the land during this time, and it appears that she was picking greens to cook. (Courtesy of Bill Jones.)

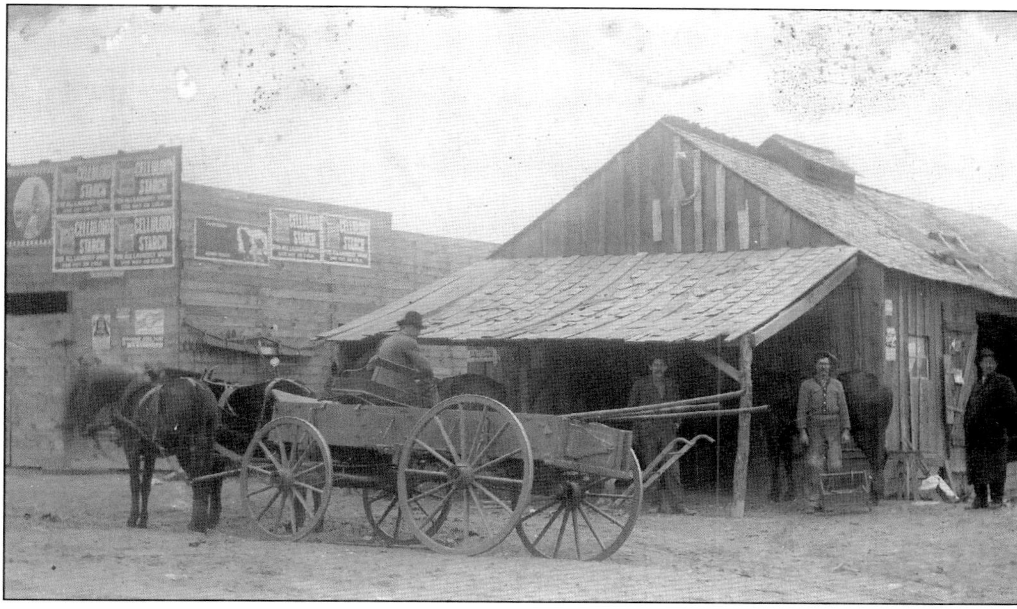

The Williams Blacksmith Shop was one of five or six on Franklin Street, called "Smoky Row" because of all the smoke from the blacksmith shops. They were all kept busy when farmers brought wagons to town to ship goods on the railroad. These unidentified men look like they know how to take care of business. (Both, courtesy of John Patrick.)

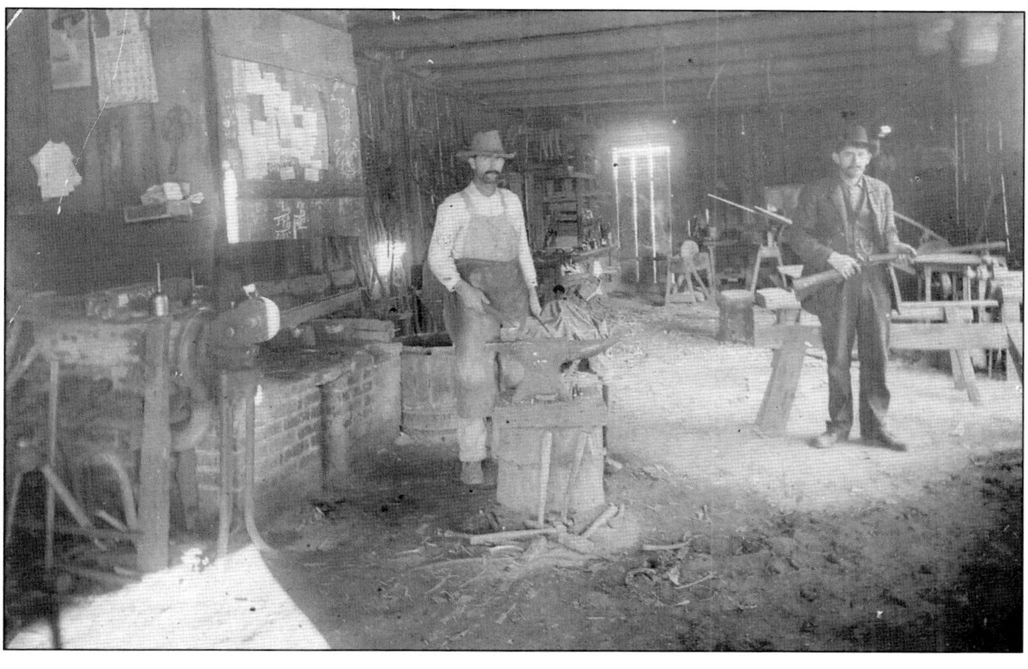

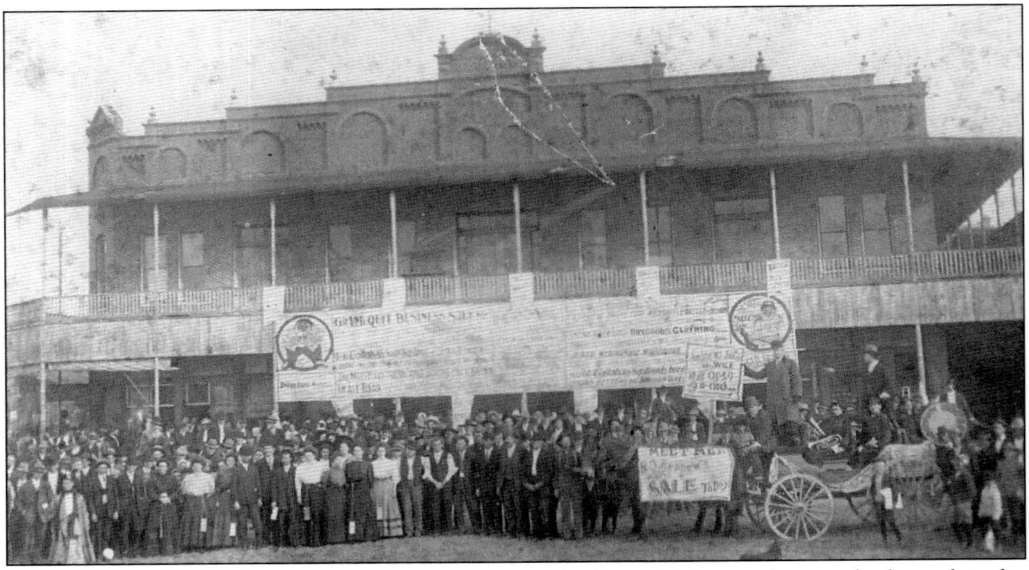

The R.G. (Roland Gwynne) Andrews Building was built in 1896, according to the legend in the center beneath the lightning rod. The building housed a hardware, a grocery, and a second-floor dry goods store. Andrews is standing in the carriage holding a sign announcing that "Andrews Store Will Open 9 O'clock." Andrews, who was the second mayor of Winnsboro, died in 1918 at the age of 49. The building covered the block at North Main and Broadway Streets. This first Andrews Building burned to the ground in the early morning hours of August 29, 1949. (Courtesy of the *Winnsboro News*.)

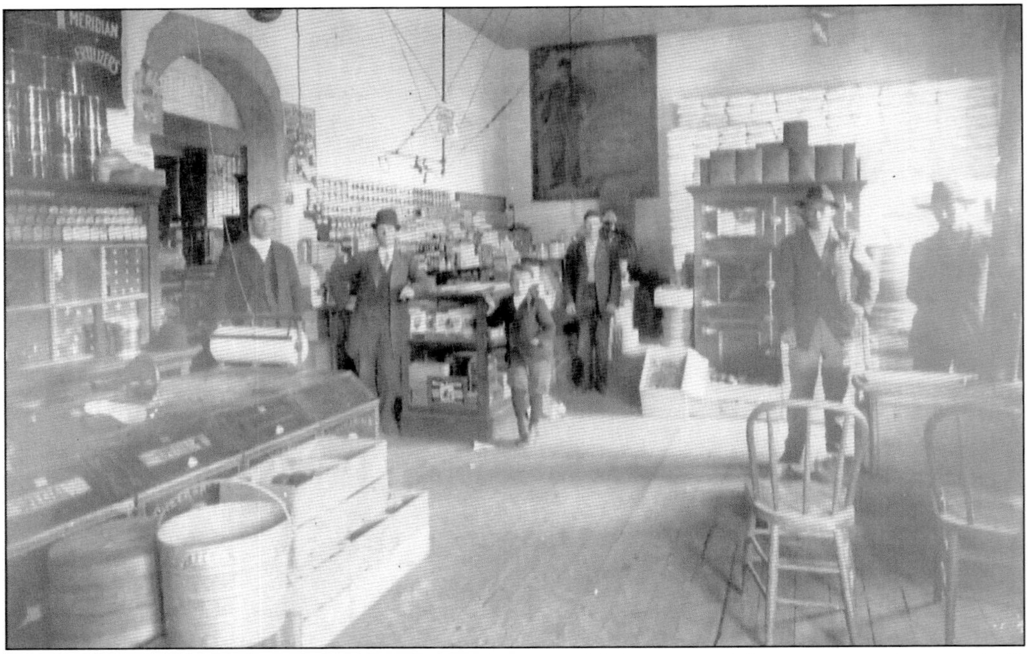

This is the interior of the R.G. Andrews store about 1901. Pictured, but not in order, are A.B. Ewing, Joe Key, Charles Sims, John Milford, W.W. Butler, R.L. Humphreys, Ms. Ray Goldberg, O. Marchman, and two unidentified people. (Courtesy of the *Winnsboro News*.)

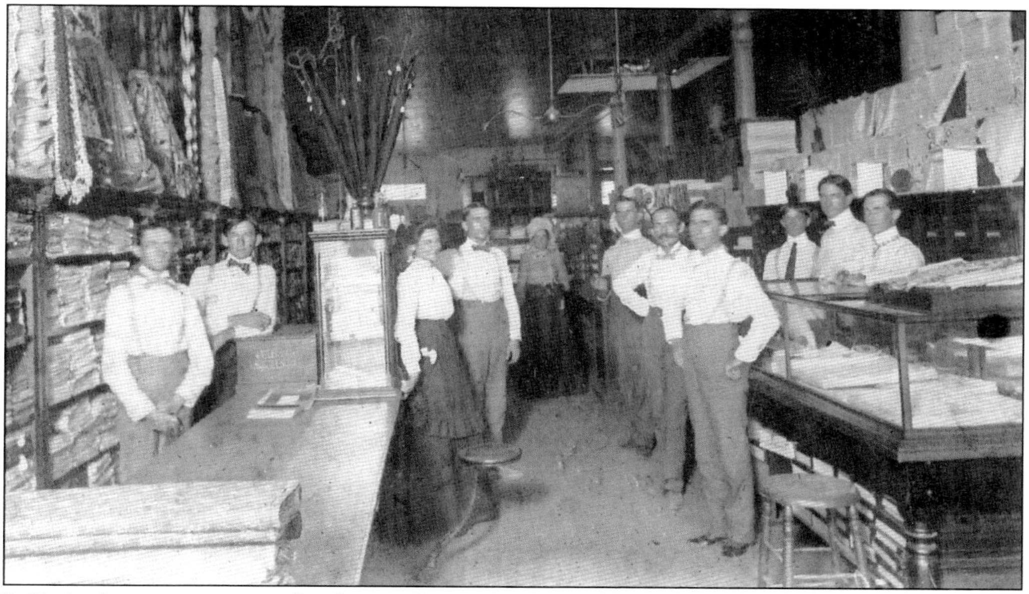

R.G. Andrews was quite a flamboyant businessman, and he had a running rivalry with Charlie Morris, the banker. One story told of the pair was that Morris refused to give Andrews a business loan, so Andrews went to St. Louis and secured a loan for $200,000. When he returned, he insisted that Charlie Morris personally handle the deposit of the check into Andrews's account. Andrews was a friend to US senators and served as Winnsboro's mayor from 1902 to 1903. He helped finance the first brick school in 1905 and was one of the founders of Southern Methodist University in Dallas. (Courtesy of the *Winnsboro News.*)

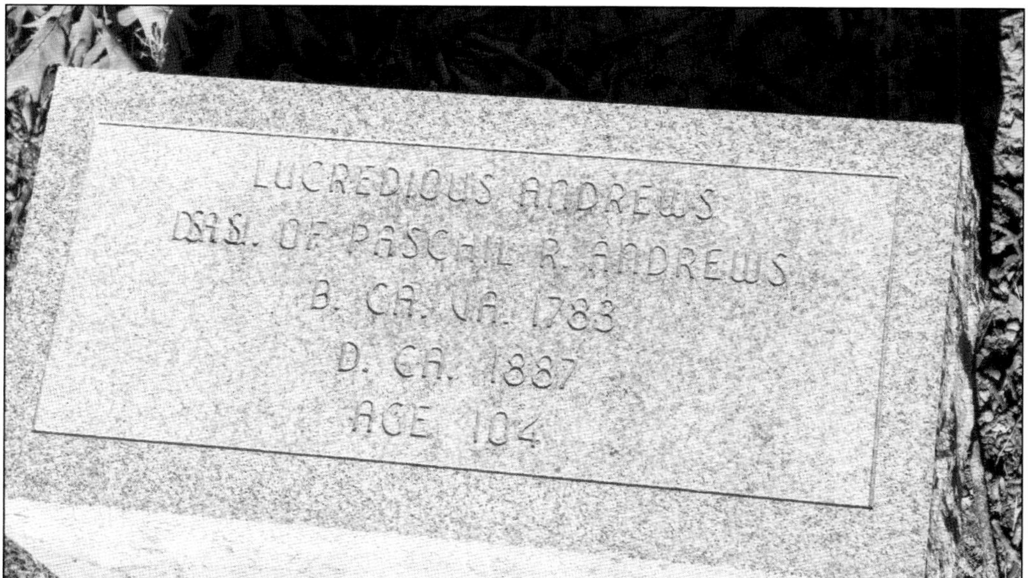

Lucredious Andrews was the son of Paschil Andrews and is the oldest man buried in City Cemetery. He died at age 104 in 1887. He was born in Virginia in 1783. One of his relatives, S.H. Andrews, father of R.D. and Joe Andrews, fought with General Custer in a number of battles. It is not clear if, or how, he is related to R.G. Andrews. (Courtesy of Bob Williams.)

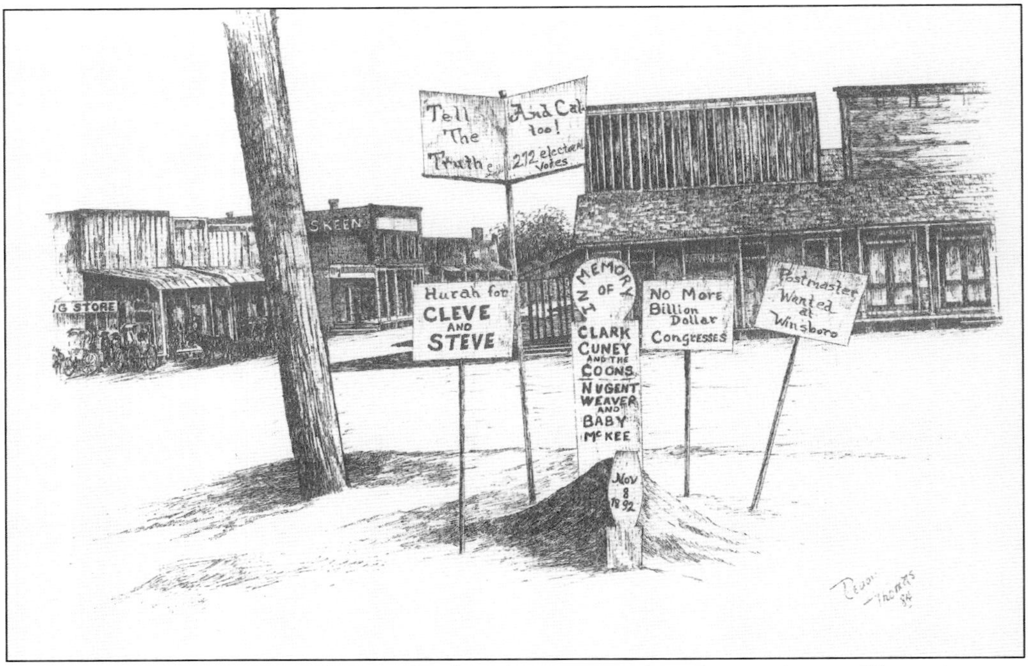

Even as far back as 1892, people posted political signs in yards and around town. These signs are from the presidential campaign in which Grover Cleveland was elected. The mock grave was in memory of James B. Weaver and other members of the Populist Party who were defeated in the election. The old Dr. Skeen Building on Main Street can be seen in the background. (Courtesy of the *Winnsboro News*.)

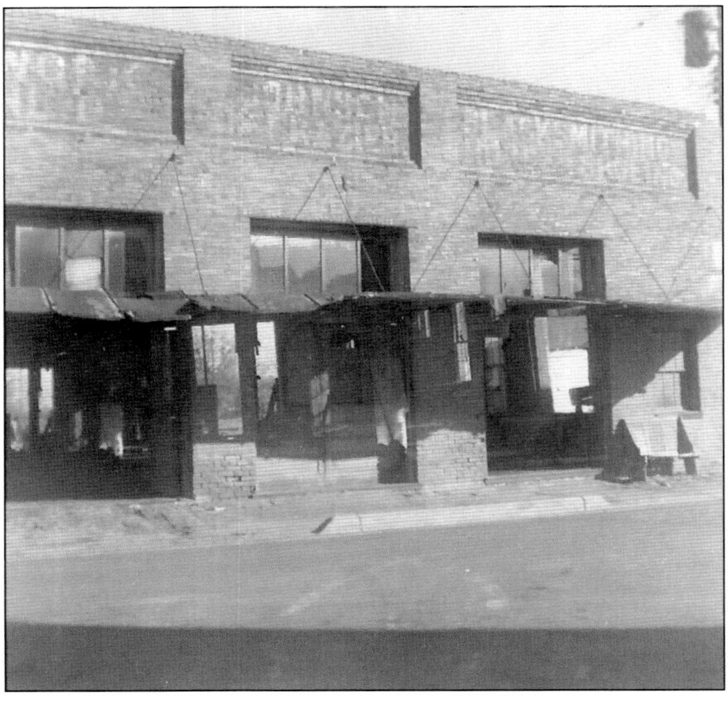

The original John Johnson Blacksmith Shop was another of the several that operated on Franklin Street, known as "Smoky Row," from 1899 to 1914. This became one of the biggest businesses in town, employing 18 men, who did blacksmithing, woodwork, building plow stocks, and repairing wagons and buggies. By 1911, the blacksmith shop expanded into one of the biggest in the United States, later serving as the town's first auto garage. (Courtesy of the *Winnsboro News*.)

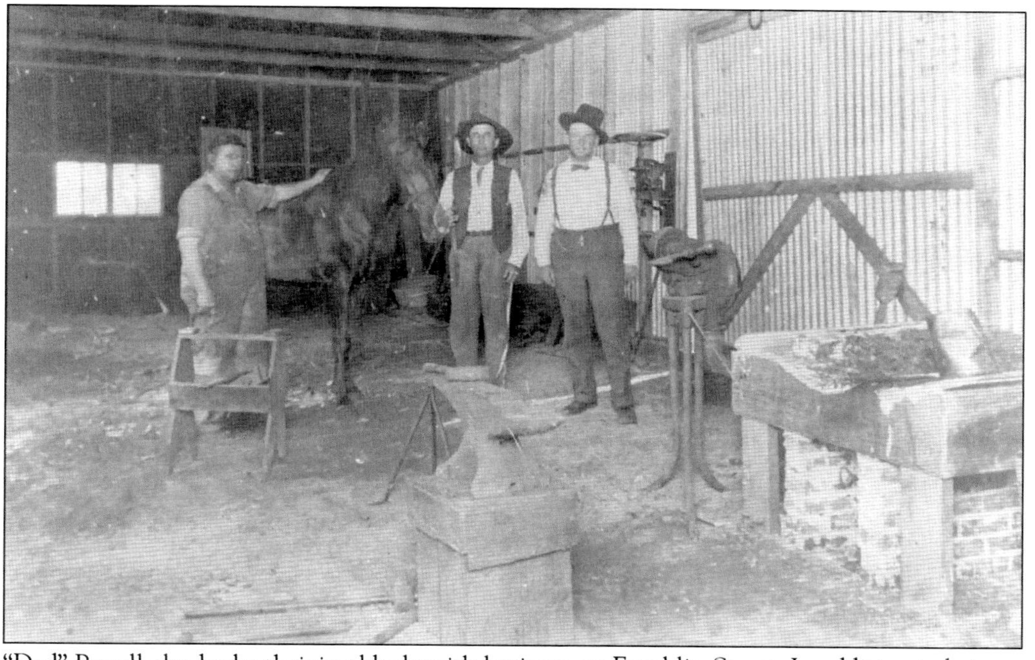

"Dad" Powell also had a thriving blacksmith business on Franklin Street. In addition to being a blacksmith, "Dad" Powell was also a horse trader. The man on the left is unidentified. The man in the middle is Doc Hollingsworth, who was a Winnsboro veterinarian, and "Dad" Powell is standing at right. (Courtesy of the *Winnsboro News*.)

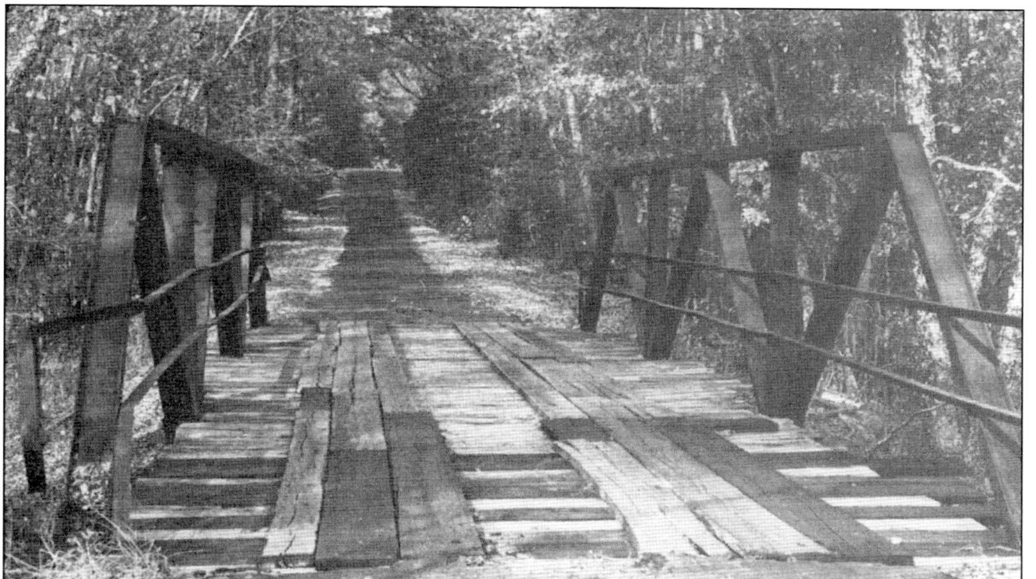

Many of the bridges in East Texas were constructed like this old iron bridge. Those that were built over gullies along the railroad lines would sometimes break under the load of a train. A similar type of bridge broke and led to the accident that was instrumental in the demise of the Marshall & East Texas Railroad. (Courtesy of the *Winnsboro News*.)

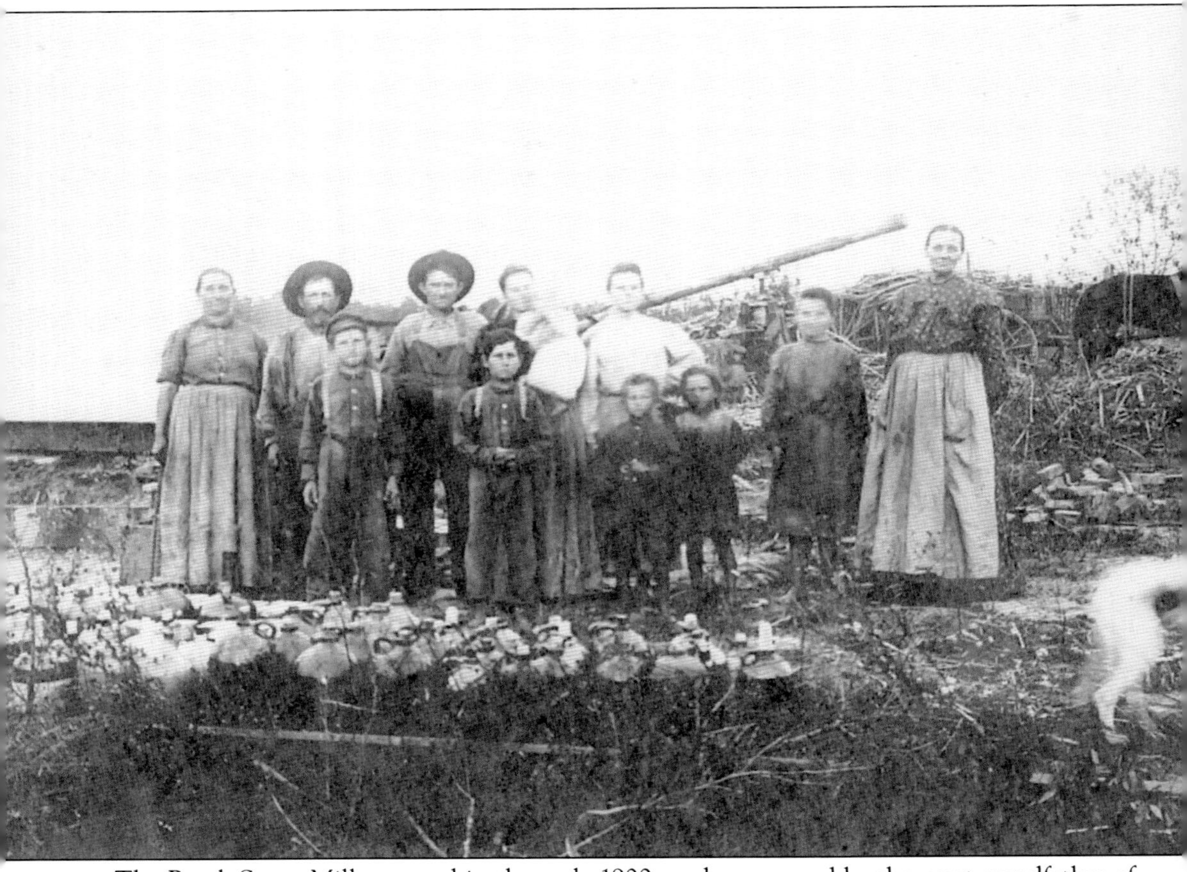

The Brock Syrup Mill operated in the early 1900s and was owned by the great-grandfather of Winnsboro's current librarian Vickie Friday Martin. The family members, from left to right, are Corilla Josephine Embry Brock; John Issac Brock; Thomas Ealice Brock, son of John and Corilla; Joe Campbell, son-in-law of John Isaac Brock; Bessie Bueloha Brock Campbell, holding Nehmiah Campbell, Joe and Bessie's oldest child; William Isaac Brock, son of John and Corilla; Raymond Van Brock, another son; Florence Victoria Brock (behind Raymond); Effie Viola Brock; Maudine Josephine Brock; and Nancy E. Moody Brock. (Courtesty of Vickie Friday Martin.)

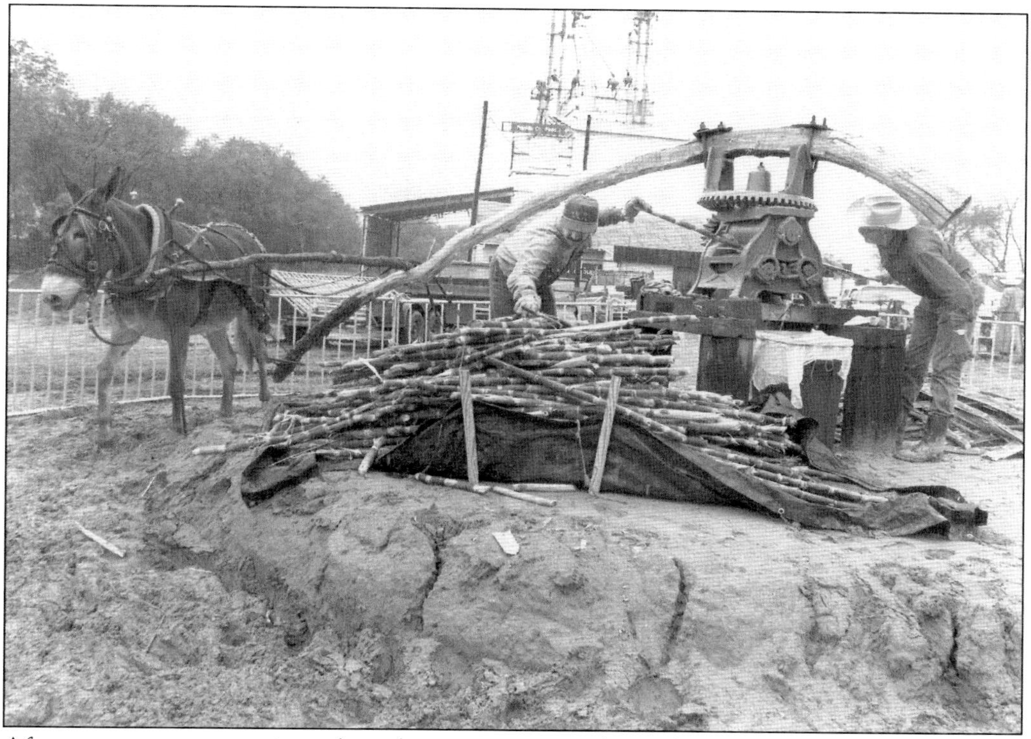

After sugar cane was cut, it was brought to a processing plant, where the juice was extracted. The pieces of cane were fed into the top of a syrup run and were either milled and the juice extracted with water or the sugar was extracted by diffusion. The juice was then clarified with lime and heated to kill enzymes. The resulting thin syrup had more water extracted through a process of evaporation. Eventually, the sugar would crystallize out. Sugar is still processed in much the same way, although on more modern machines. Molasses is a byproduct of the process, and the stems from the sugar cane are burned to provide energy for the sugar extraction process. (Both, courtesy of Bill Jones.)

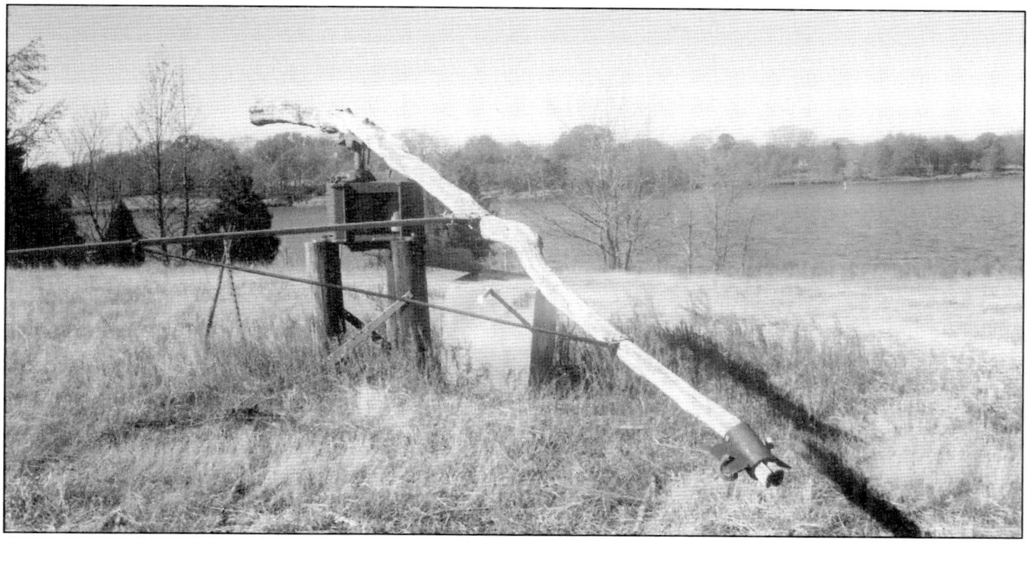

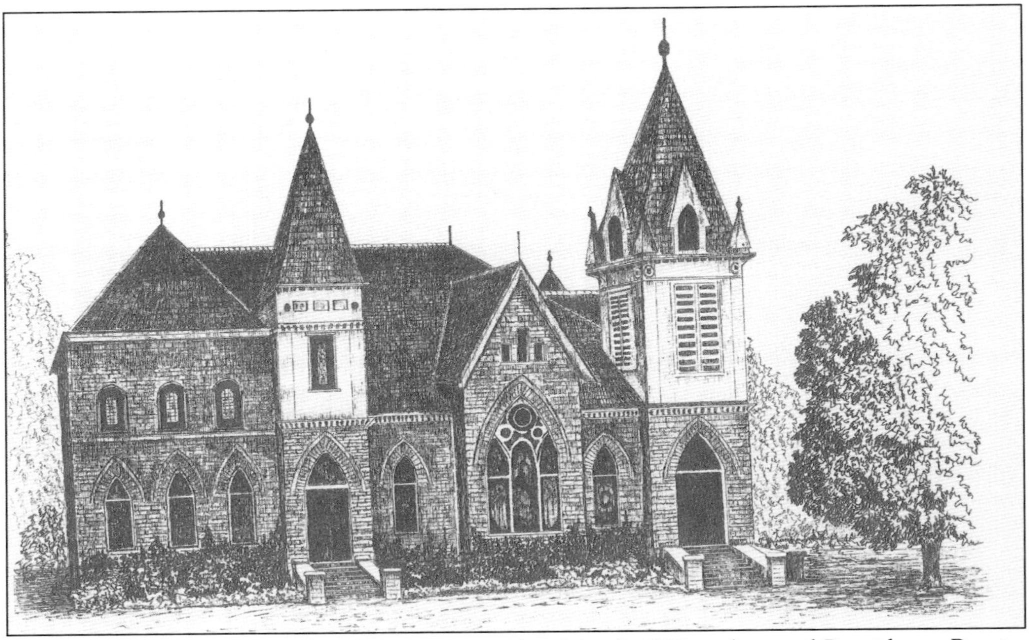

The original First Baptist Church was organized in March 1872 and named Providence Baptist Church of Christ, a name that held until 1880. This old sanctuary was built in 1904 of brick and was torn down in 1959 to make way for a new sanctuary that opened in October 1960. (Courtesy of the *Winnsboro News*.)

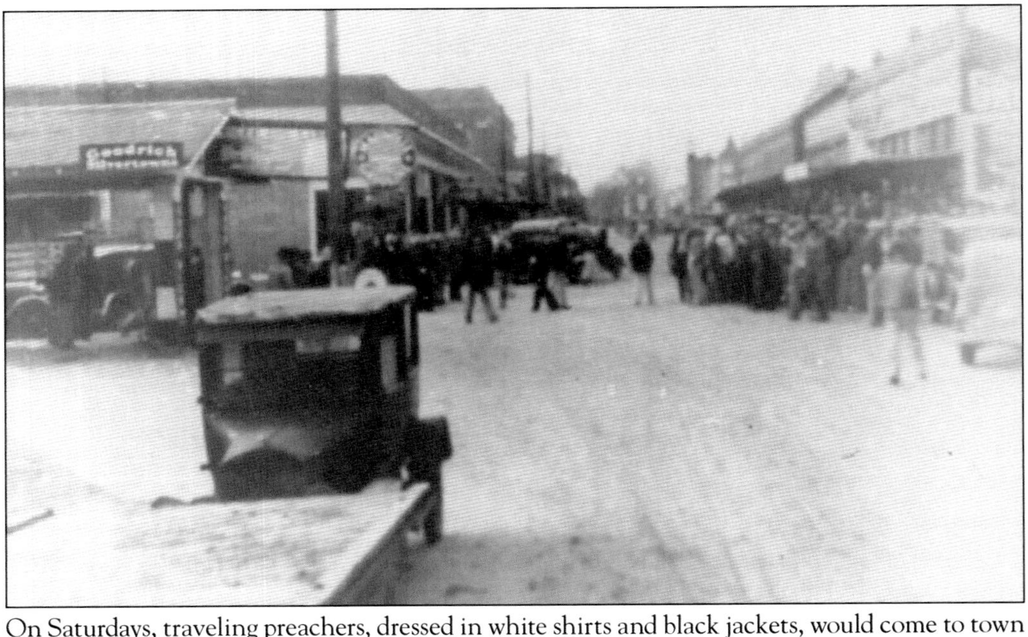

On Saturdays, traveling preachers, dressed in white shirts and black jackets, would come to town and stand preaching for hours on the corner of Elm and Franklin Streets. Sometimes a large crowd would gather, and other times, just a few people would meander by and pause to listen. The corner was called Nelson's Corner because of John Nelson's Grocery Store, and politicians often used the corner to "stump." (Courtesy of the *Winnsboro News*.)

Chalybeate Springs Hotel was east of Winnsboro, where there were natural springs known for their healing powers. Located on land owned by L.M. Musgrove, the springs were first known as Musgrove Springs and gave rise to a thriving resort community A school was built on land given by William and Susan Bolding in 1881, and the village included churches, stores, and a post office. Walker Fore bought the property in the 1880s and built a two-story hotel and spa. The hotel closed in 1895, and the building was razed in 1935. (Right, courtesy of Bill Jones; below, courtesy of the *Winnsboro News*.)

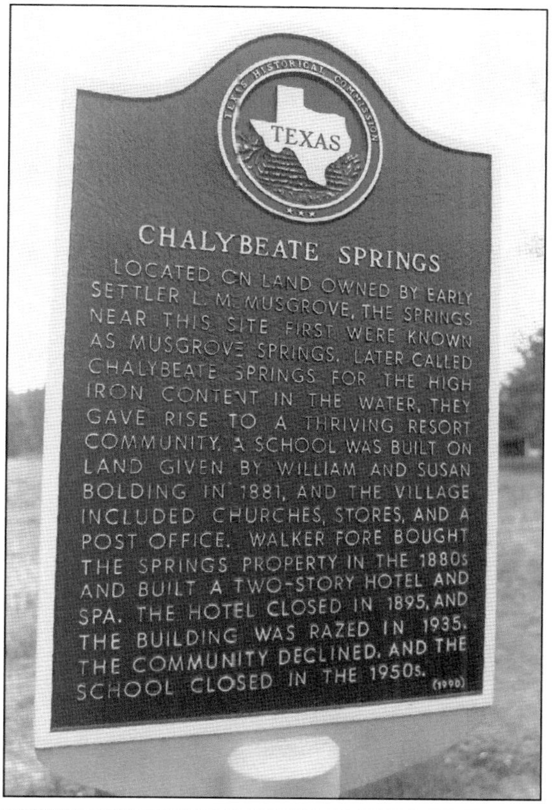

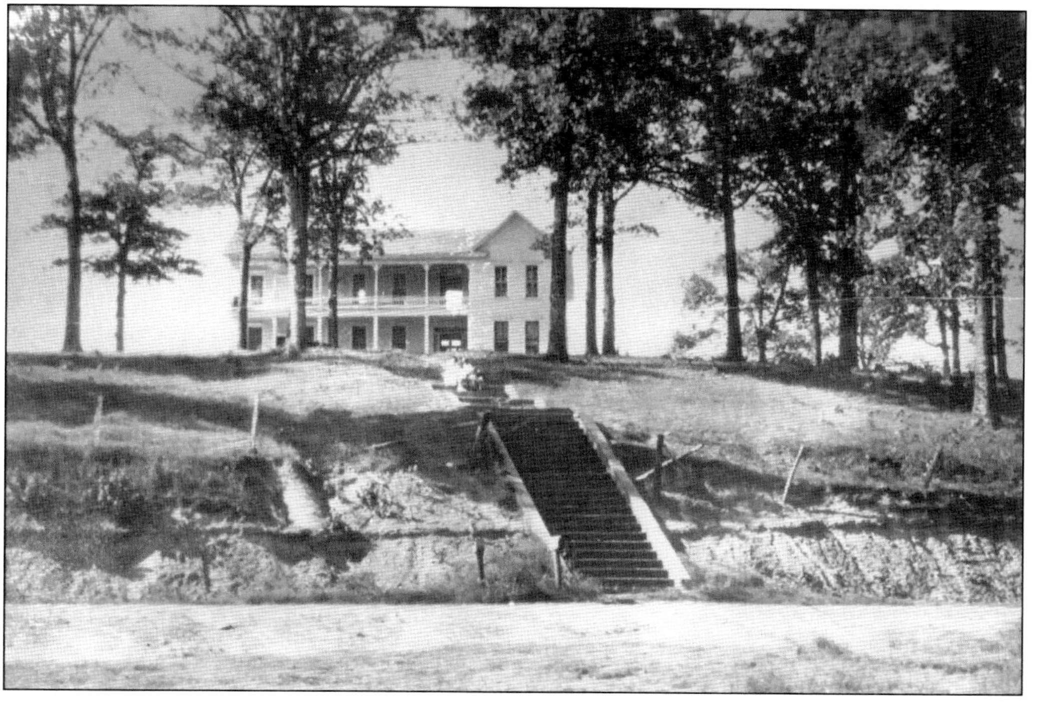

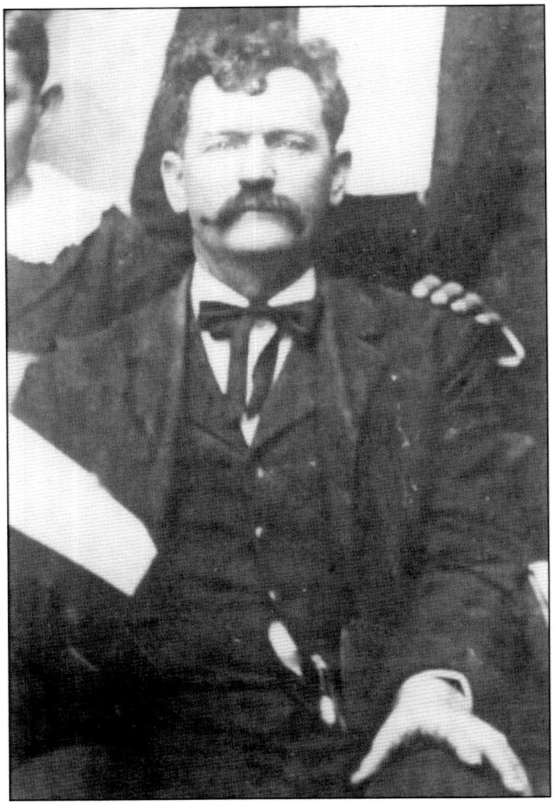

G.W. Folmar, the great-grandfather of James "Doc" Davis, came to Winnsboro in 1881 from Alabama and lived here until he died in 1911. Doc's mother, Ruby Louise Wright, was born in Winnsboro and then moved to California, making trips to Texas to visit family. Doc and his mother and father, Claude, made one such visit in the early 1950s, when Doc was about three years old. Doc lived in California until 1961 before moving to Winnsboro. He left for job reasons in 1985 and, in 2008, left Arizona and returned to Winnsboro. A reenactor like his father, Doc is a board officer of the Winnsboro Heritage Society, Inc., the Texas Rangers Law Enforcement Association, True West Historical Society, and the National Registry of Living Historians. (Both, courtesy of Doc Davis.)

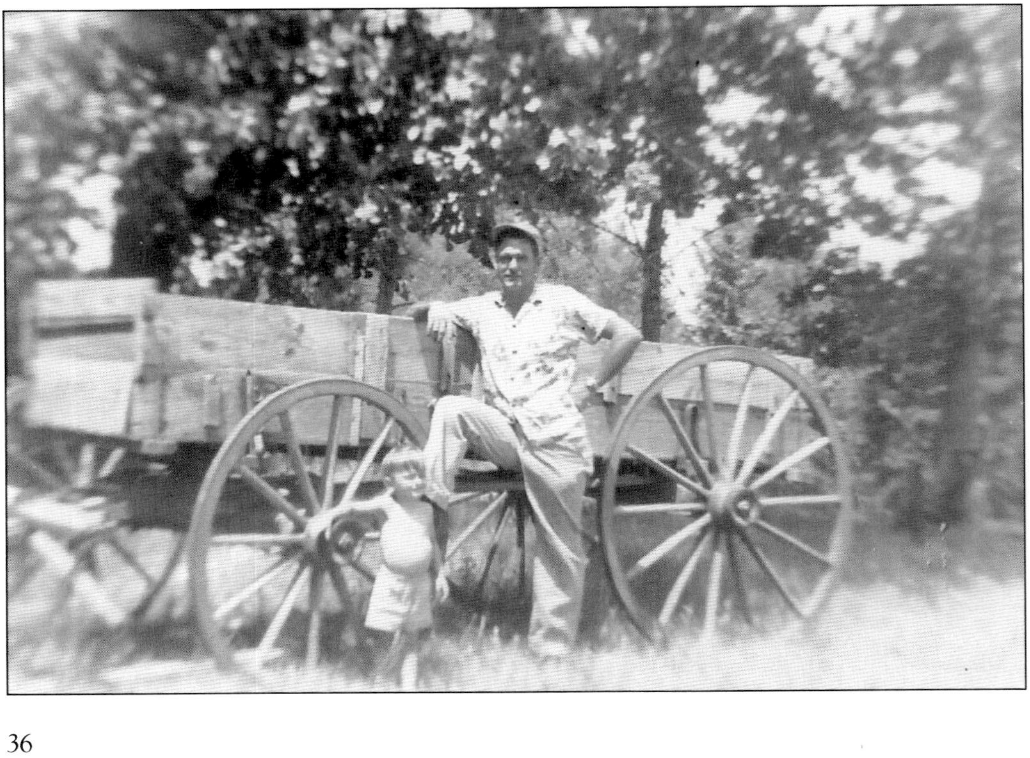

Three

The Saloon Era

From about 1893 to 1910, folks who wandered down Market Street, which was then referred to as "the Bowery," were usually armed with a pistol, especially after dark. One local resident said there were saloons on every corner with their cohorts of evil influences that included mysterious characters, drinking, and shooting. The better-known watering holes were the Massel, Harris, McElroy, Wright, Corley, and Milam saloons.

During that time period, there were 20 or more lumber camps operating around Winnsboro, employing several hundred men. Many were transients from all parts of the United States, as well as foreign countries. They came to town on Saturday afternoon looking for a good time, mostly to drink and to gamble, and may have visited every saloon in town.

By 1910, most of the virgin timber had been cut and the large lumber producers moved their operations south. About the same time, all the saloons in Winnsboro had closed as a result of a local option election. The unruly element either cleaned up its act or moved on to the next Texas boomtown.

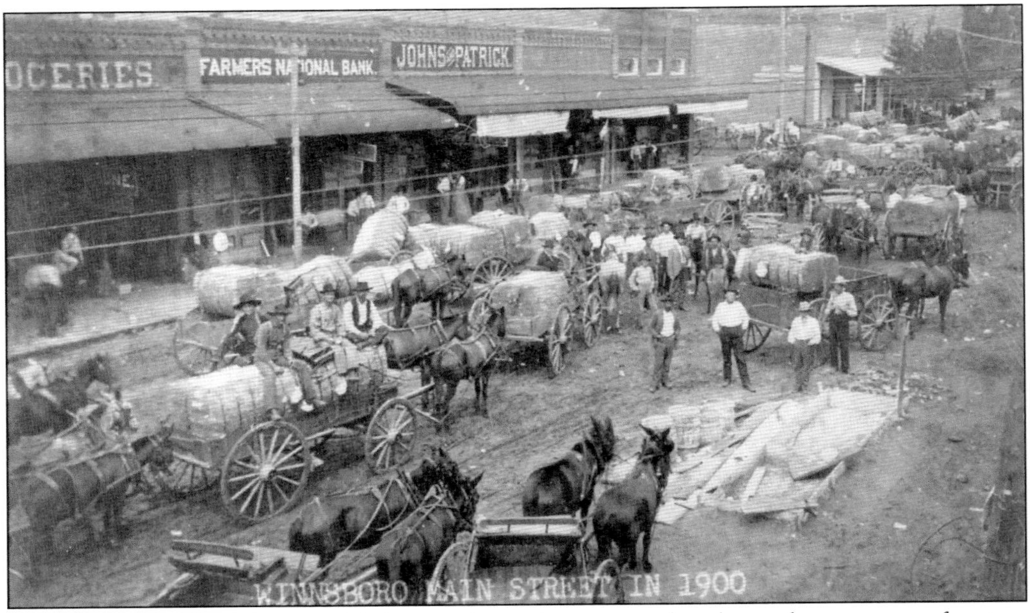

Main Street in Winnsboro in 1900 was a busy place on market days, when wagons of cotton would be brought to town. There were a number of cotton gins in and around Winnsboro where the cotton would be processed. While in town, some farmers visited saloons. (Courtesy of the *Winnsboro News*.)

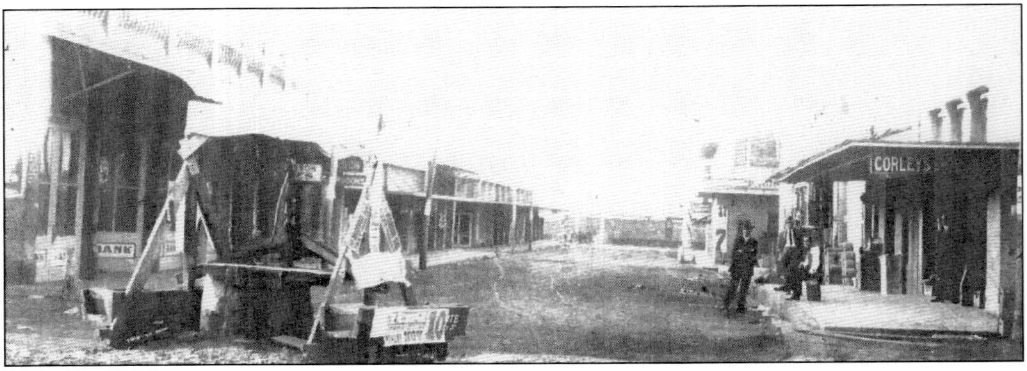

This picture of Market Street, "the Bowery," was taken in 1906, looking south from the intersection of East Elm and Market Streets; the railroad depot is at the far end, just as it is today. The streets were not paved, and the sidewalks were of wood construction. This is where the saloons were primarily located, although there were a few on Franklin Street, as well. (Courtesy of the *Winnsboro News*.)

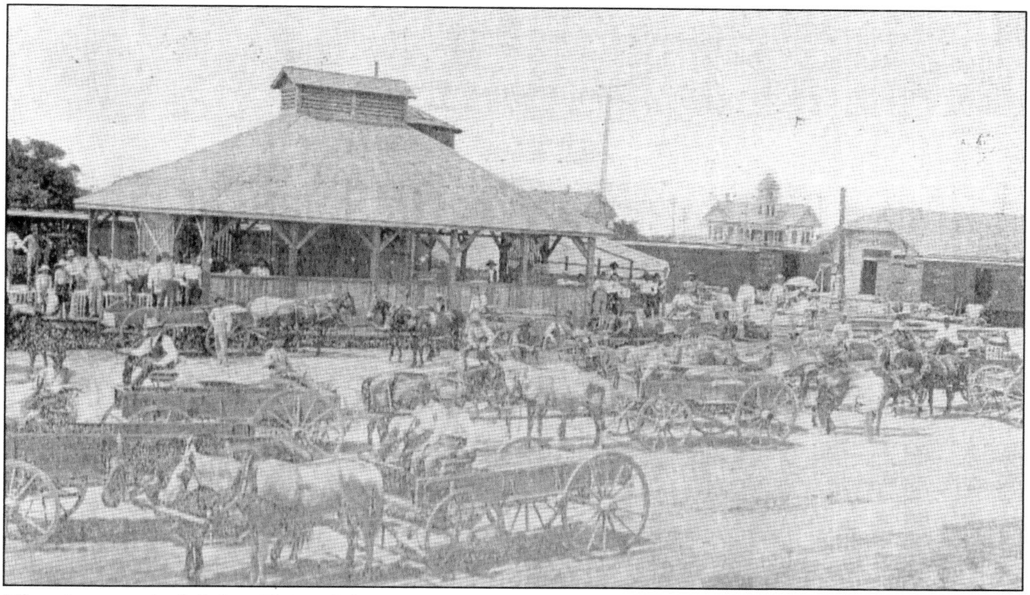

The city marshal, John Cain, did not bother the revelers as long as they stayed on Market Street and did not bother the citizens on Main Street. Those that did venture where the "refined" citizens went were put in jail, and the jail was often filled by 10:00 p.m. When the first city hall was built in 1924, it had a new jail with a door facing Broadway, and people could stop and see the prisoners through bars that used to be in the window of the jail door. This original jail door opened from another side of the building to the cells. (Above, courtesy of the *Winnsboro News*; right, courtesy of Bob Williams.)

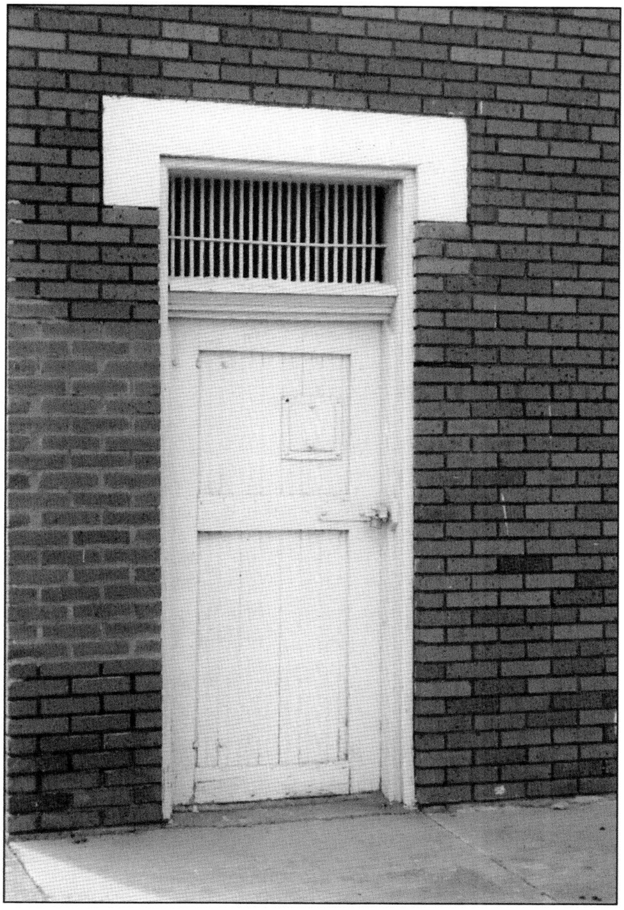

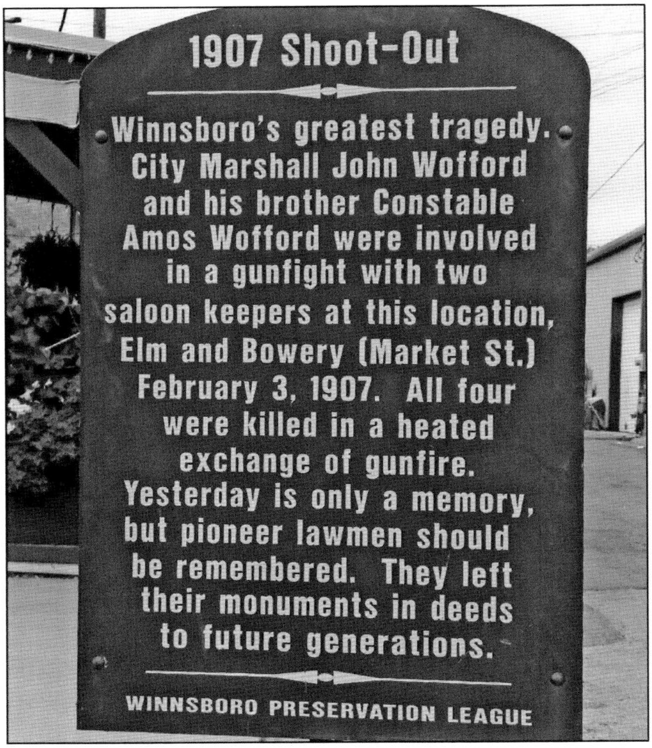

In 1907, there was a shoot-out at the intersection Market and Elm Streets, and city marshal Amos Wofford and his brother John Wofford, a Wood County deputy, were killed. An ongoing dispute between saloon owner Dick Milam and his son Bud came to an end when they confronted the two lawmen on the street. Gunfire rattled the windows, and in the ensuing shootout, the two lawmen were killed. Dick Milam was also killed on the spot, and Bud died nine days later because of his wounds. The Wofford brothers are buried near Sulphur Springs. In 1910, by local option election, Winnsboro was voted dry, but until then, unruly revelers were locked up in the local jail. (Left, courtesy of Maryann Miller; below, courtesy of Bob Williams.)

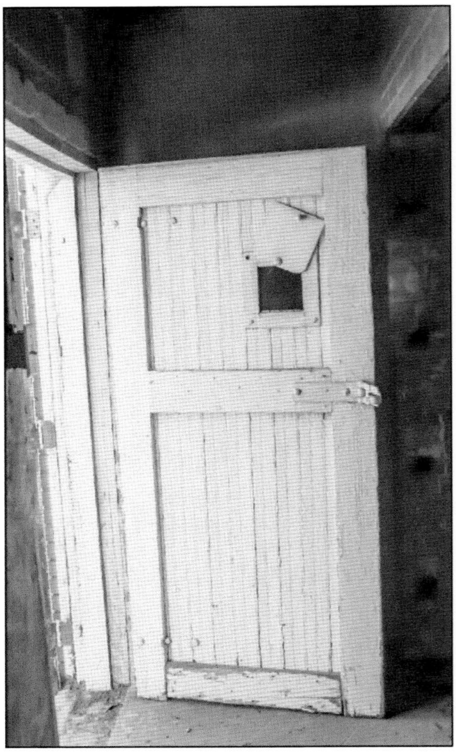

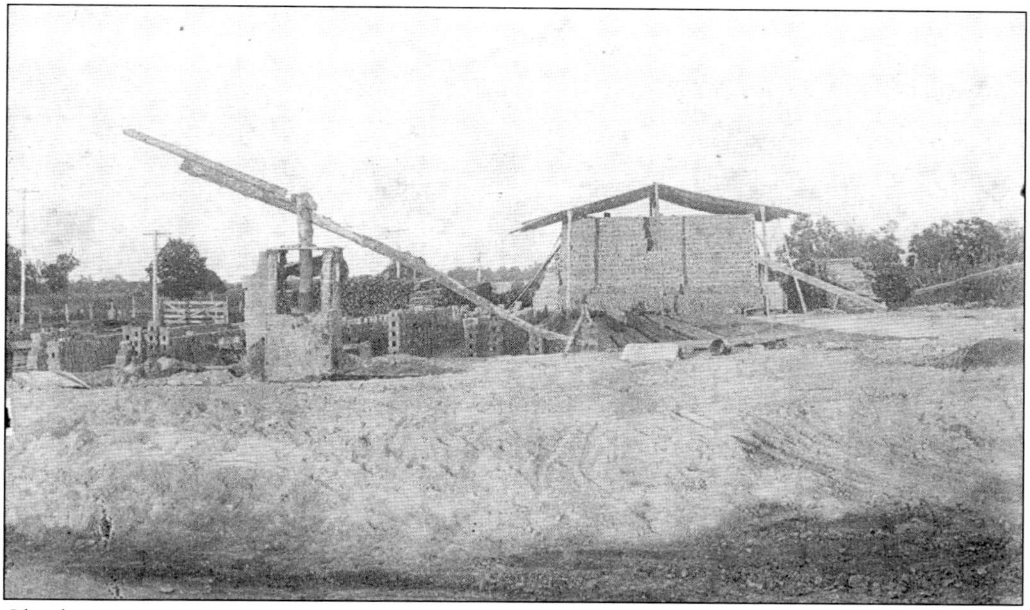

Charles W. Moore owned one of the earliest brick plants in Winnsboro. Mud and clay were placed in large vats and mixed by mule power. The bricks were then formed and set in the sun to dry. After they were dry, they were placed in a kiln to be fired. Because of the rich veins of clay around Winnsboro, bricks could be produced here at a reasonable price, so exporting bricks to neighboring towns became a big business around 1900. (Courtesy of the *Winnsboro News*.)

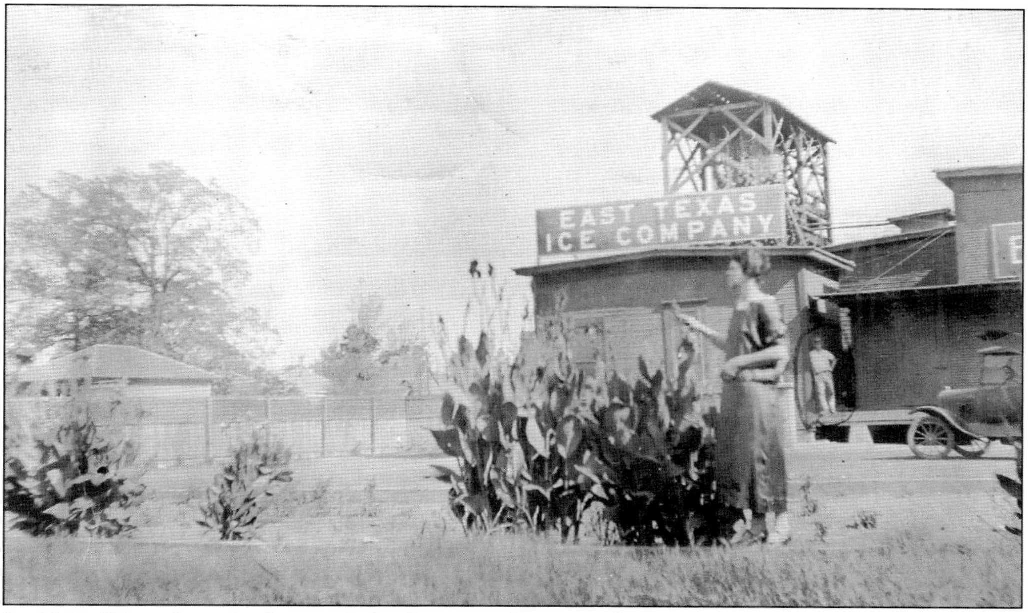

In 1901, Winnsboro had one of the first ice plants in the area. The plant was built by R.C. Campbell and was located on East Elm Street. The water came from Freeze Springs, and it was around the same time that the first electricity was brought to Winnsboro. Water for city buildings and residences north of town was provided by a storage tank located on the north side of the railroad tracks. (Courtesy of the *Winnsboro News*.)

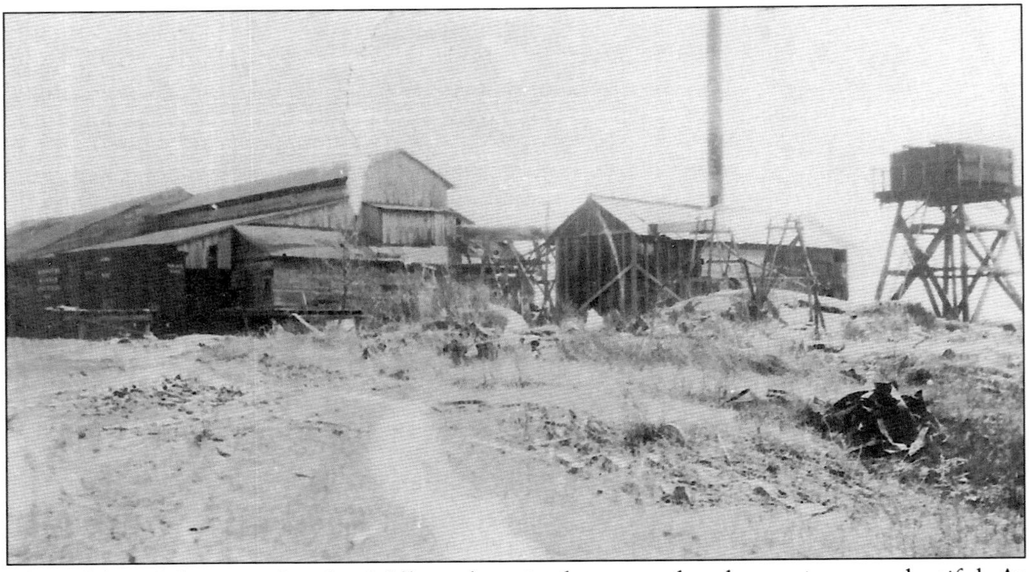

The Schluter-Whiteman Lumber Mill was busy in the years when heart pine was plentiful. At one time, this mill was one of the largest in the United States. The lumbermen left the area in 1909, when all the yellow longleaf pine was gone. The businessmen built the tram down to Peach and then sold the railroad to Texas Southern, which built a line to Marshall. (Courtesy of the *Winnsboro News.*)

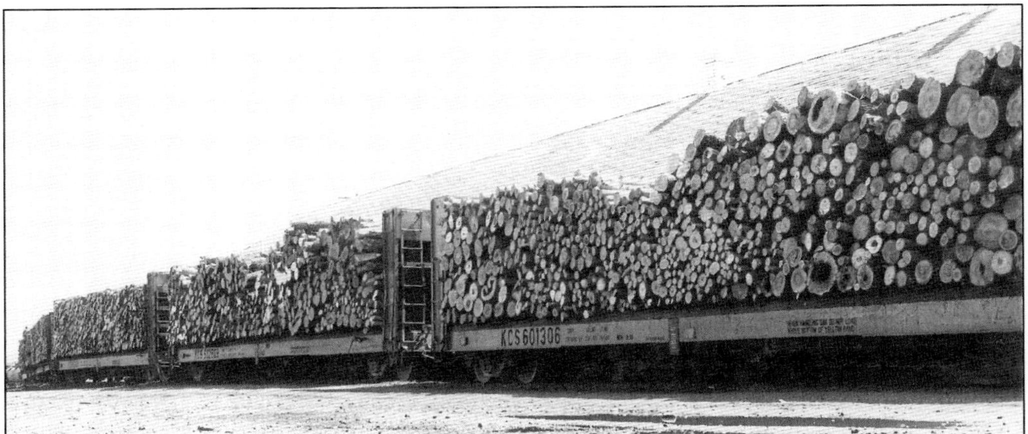

During the prime logging days, raw timber would be shipped from Winnsboro to points west for construction in Dallas and Fort Worth. In addition to the Schluter-Whiteman mill, there was a number of other mills surrounding Winnsboro that fed millions of feet of lumber products to the fast-growing markets of Dallas and Fort Worth. (Courtesy of the *Winnsboro News.*)

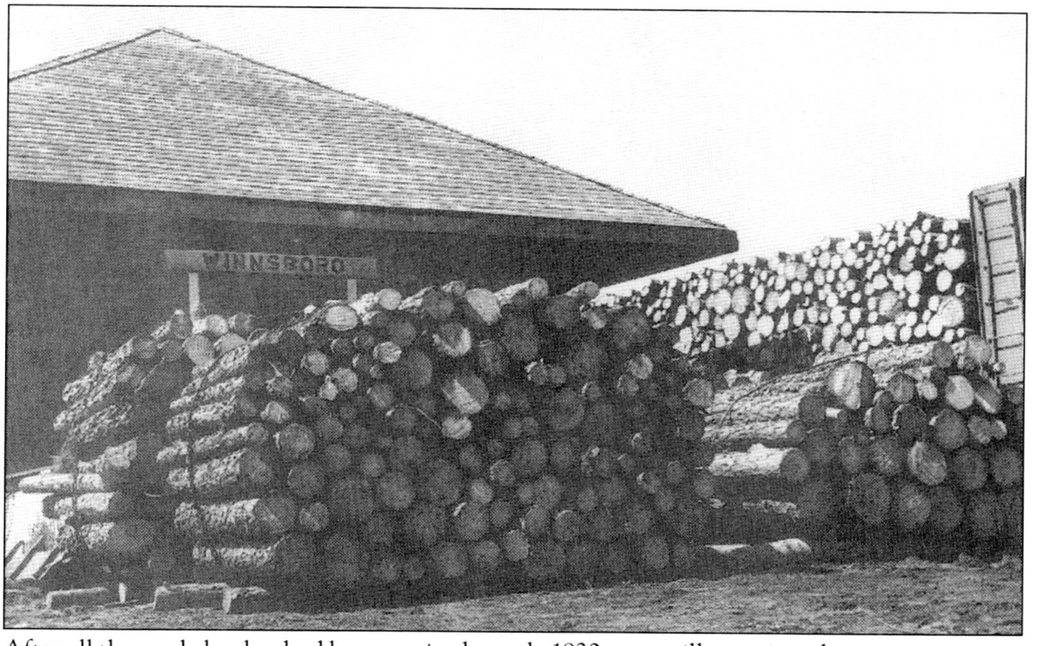

After all the grade lumber had been cut in the early 1930s, sawmills continued operating, cutting smaller trees for pulpwood. Pulpwood became big business, and load after load of small pine cut in six-to-eight-foot lengths was shipped by rail from Winnsboro from the 1930s until the 1970s. (Courtesy of the *Winnsboro News*.)

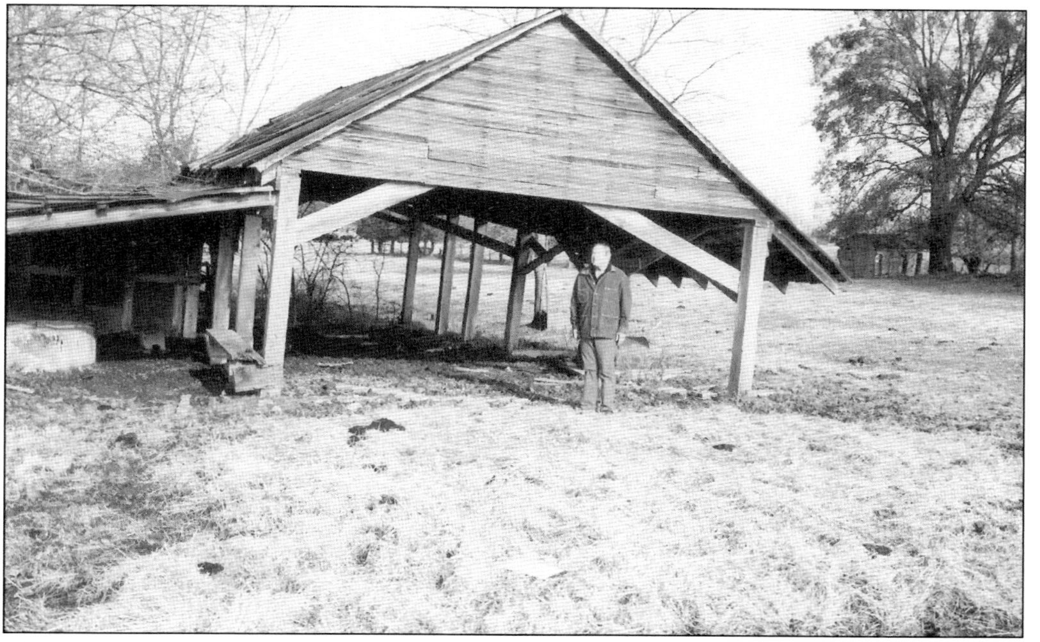

The Snodgrass Planer Mill is still standing on West Pine Street. Weldon Snodgrass, now deceased, stands in front of his father's mill, which was one of Winnsboro's largest sawmills. The Snodgrass Lumber Company operated in Winnsboro from the early 1920s to the 1970s, primarily cutting large timber. (Courtesy of Bill Jones.)

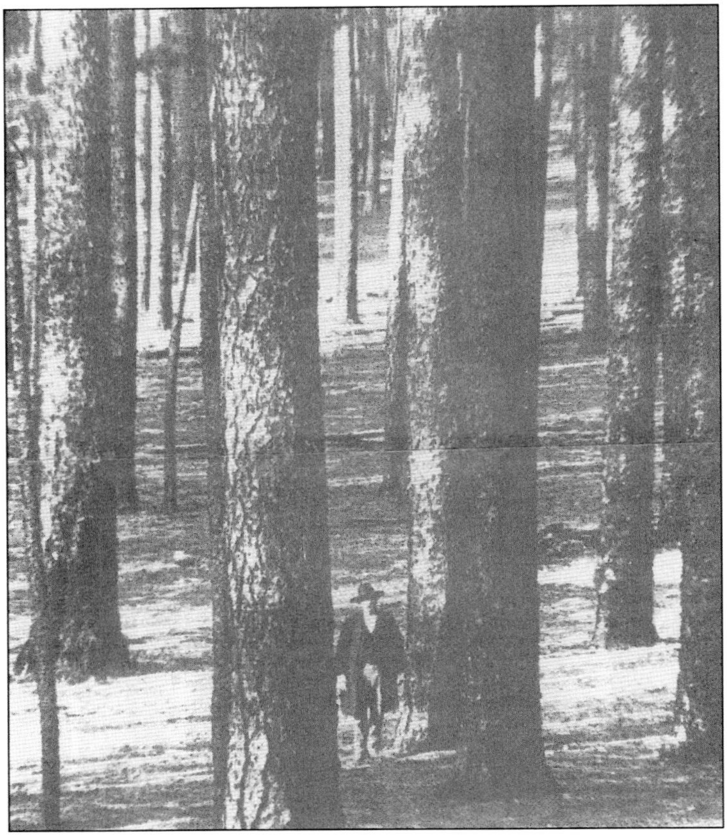

At the height of the logging era, the yellow longleaf pine trees grew over 100 feet tall and could have a trunk diameter of up to four feet. The wood from these trees, often called heart pine, was extremely strong, durable, and highly prized. (Courtesy of the *Winnsboro News*.)

Carved from curly heart pine, this staircase in the Oaklea Mansion, once the Carlock Mansion, is a work of art. It is believed to be the only representation of the beauty of curly pine in the area. (Courtesy of Bob Williams.)

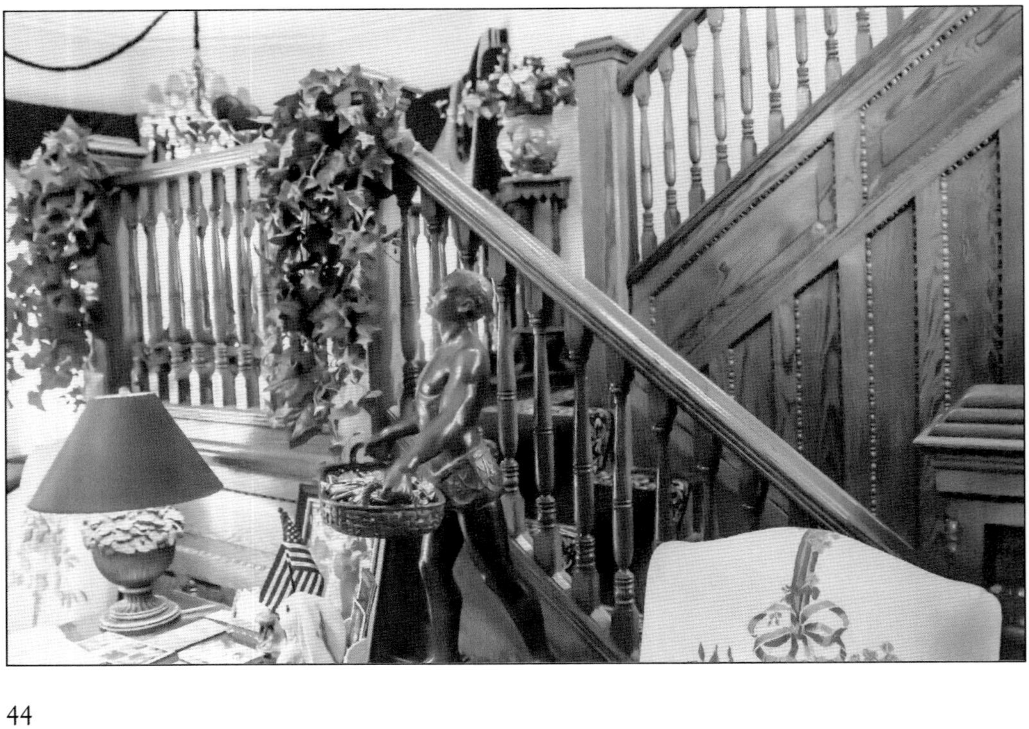

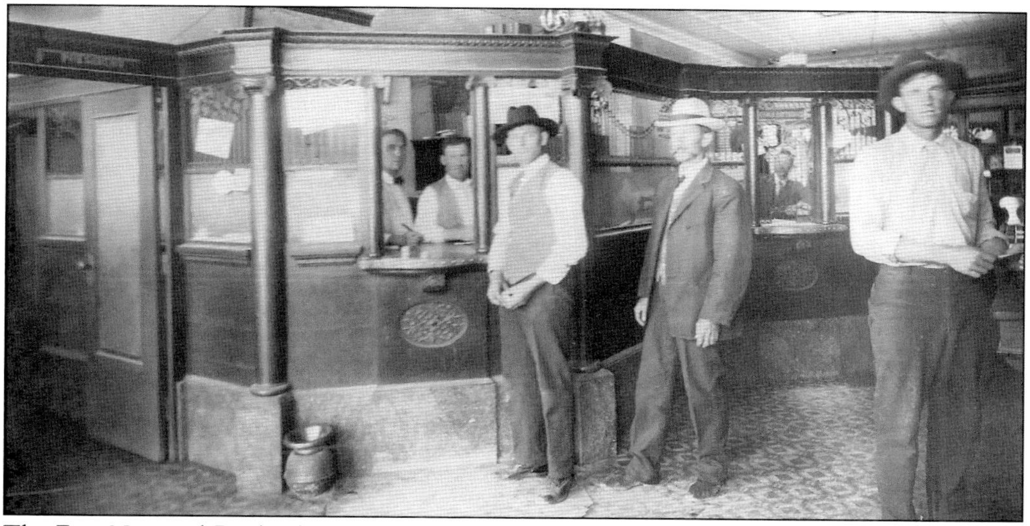

The First National Bank of Winnsboro was originally located at the southeast corner of Main and Elm Streets. This picture was taken in 1913 or 1914, but the bank first started business as a private bank in 1893. It was nationalized on January 15, 1901, starting with individual deposits of $28,309.04, and by January 1904, the bank reported deposits of $154,343.68. In a 1904 shareholders report, the First National Bank described Winnsboro as a town "that has a bright future." The men pictured here are unidentified. (Courtesy of the *Winnsboro News*.)

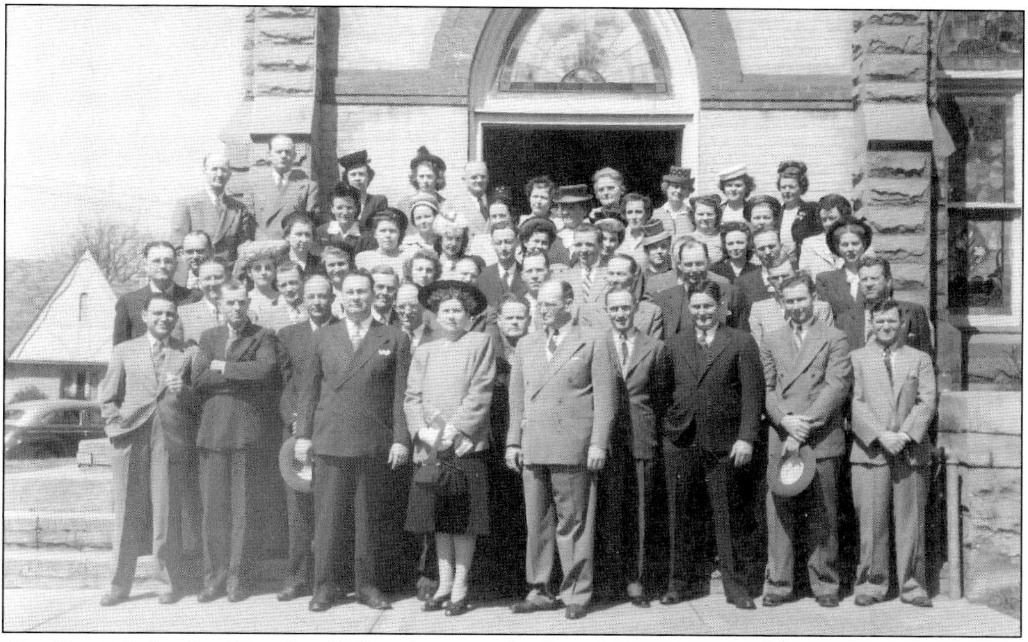

The First Methodist Church of Winnsboro was built in 1903 at a cost of $1,200 and was paid for in about four months. Before having a sanctuary, the congregation met in the opera house at South Broadway, now Carnegie Street at Chestnut Street. The Presbyterians used a little white building on Church Street for services. Other denominations were invited to use the facilities, and the little church was also used as a community center. Central Christian organized in 1893 and built its church around the turn of the century. (Courtesy of the *Winnsboro News*.)

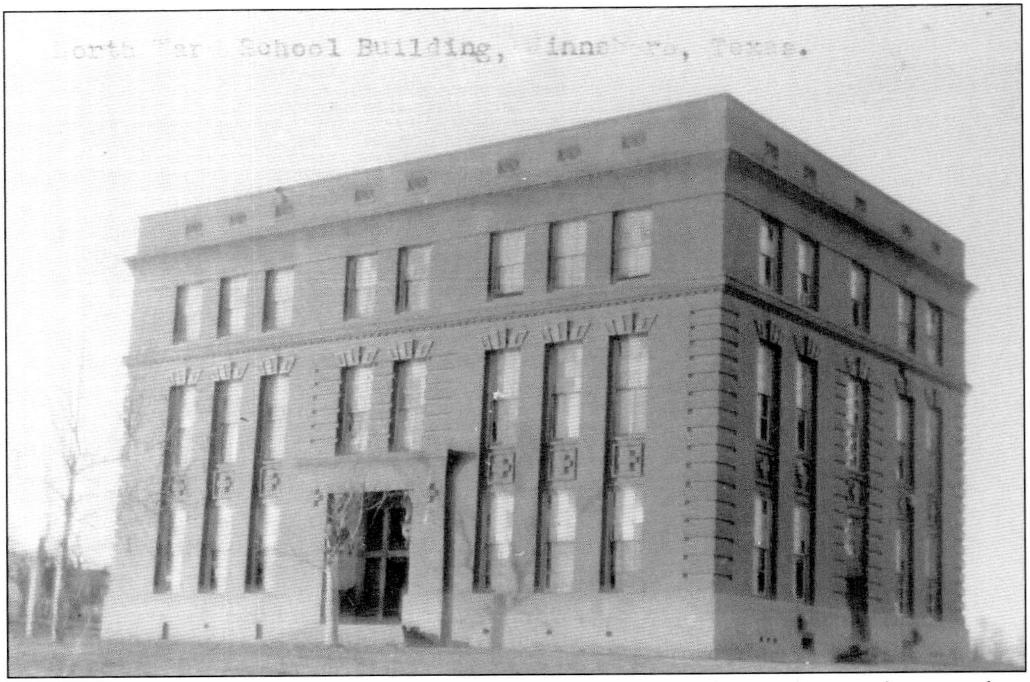

The North Ward School was built in 1905 to serve the students of Winnsboro and surrounding communities. It was later torn down, and in 1952, the Westbrook Elementary School was constructed. The Westbrook Building, named for S.A. "Dad" Westbook, who was a physics teacher in Winnsboro for 31 years, still stands and houses the school administration offices. (Courtesy of the *Winnsboro News*.)

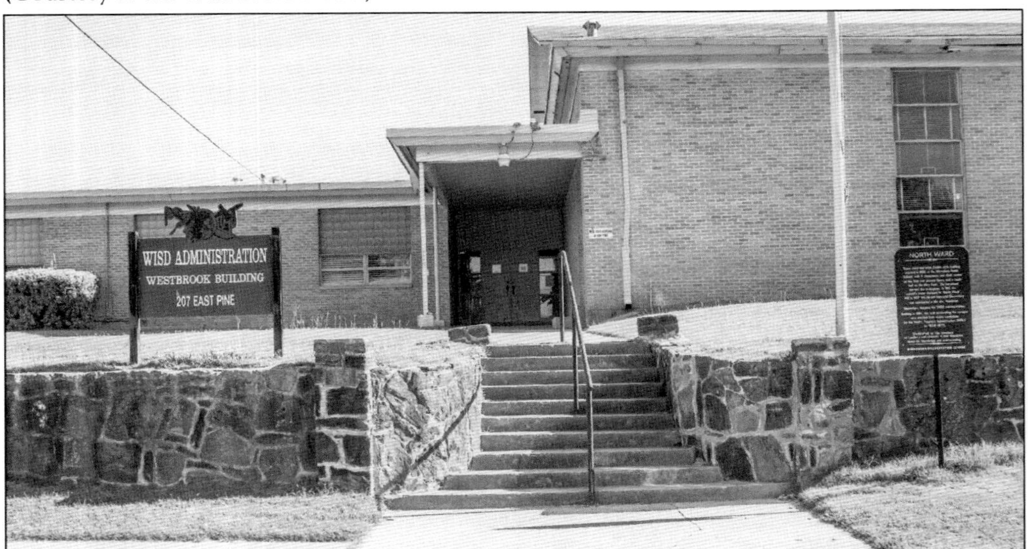

Built by the Works Progress Administration (WPA), this staircase and retaining wall in front of the Westbrook Building is comprised of stones from local quarries. This area of East Texas is rich in iron ore rock, and there are a number of homes and buildings built using these rocks. (Courtesy of Bob Williams.)

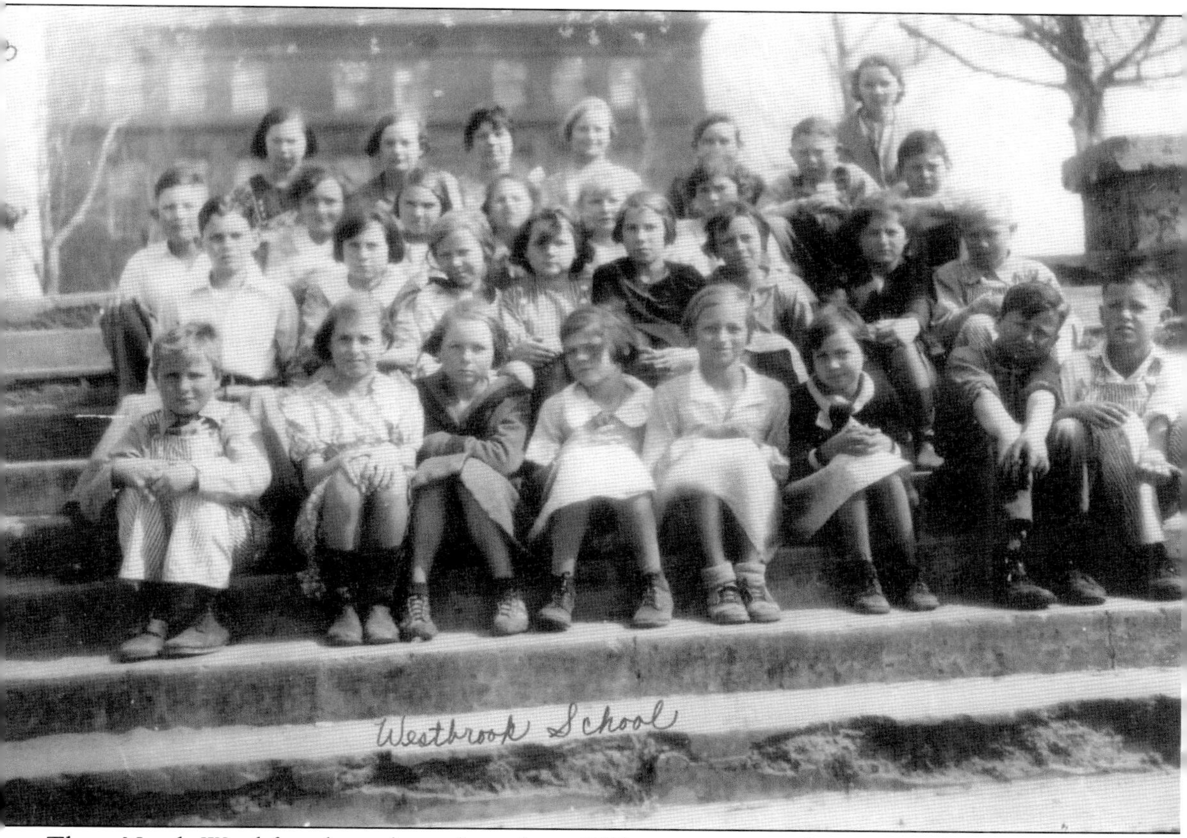

These North Ward fourth-grade students from 1933 are sitting on the steps in front of the school. Pictured are, from left to right, (first row) James Fridan, Dorothy Fox, three unidentified, Evelyn Reynolds, Avis Poe, and Bob Harrison; (second row) Bobby Ray Arrington, Louise Ayers, unidentified, Vonceil Wetzel, Laconia Harris, Mildred Watkins, Ruth Johnson, and Boyd Smith; (third row) James Arrington, Frances Dickens, Melverta Woodley, Julia Ann Wright, Sybil Mullins, and Juanita Sullivan; (fourth row) unidentified, Bonita Bullock, Clyrene Largent, Tosa Bell Dale, Benny Anders, Lisle Cofer, Randall Ayers, and Jewell Tillery (teacher). (Courtesy of the *Winnsboro News*.)

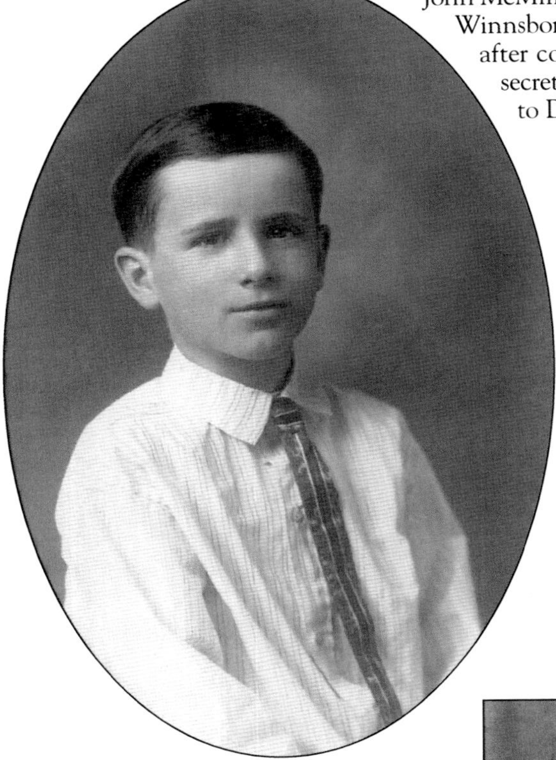

John McMillan, son of William McMillan, who founded Winnsboro, stayed in Winnsboro for a number of years after completing his education and worked as city secretary, recording the local history, before moving to Dallas in the 1920s. (Courtesy of Bill Jones.)

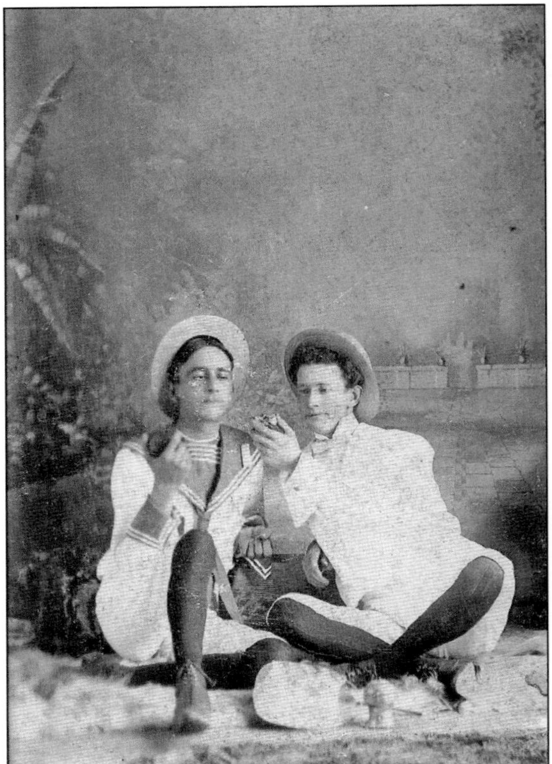

These unidentified men illustrate what a "man about town" in 1910 looked like. Men and women from prominent families had plenty of leisure time for parties, boating, and swimming. (Courtesy of Bill Jones.)

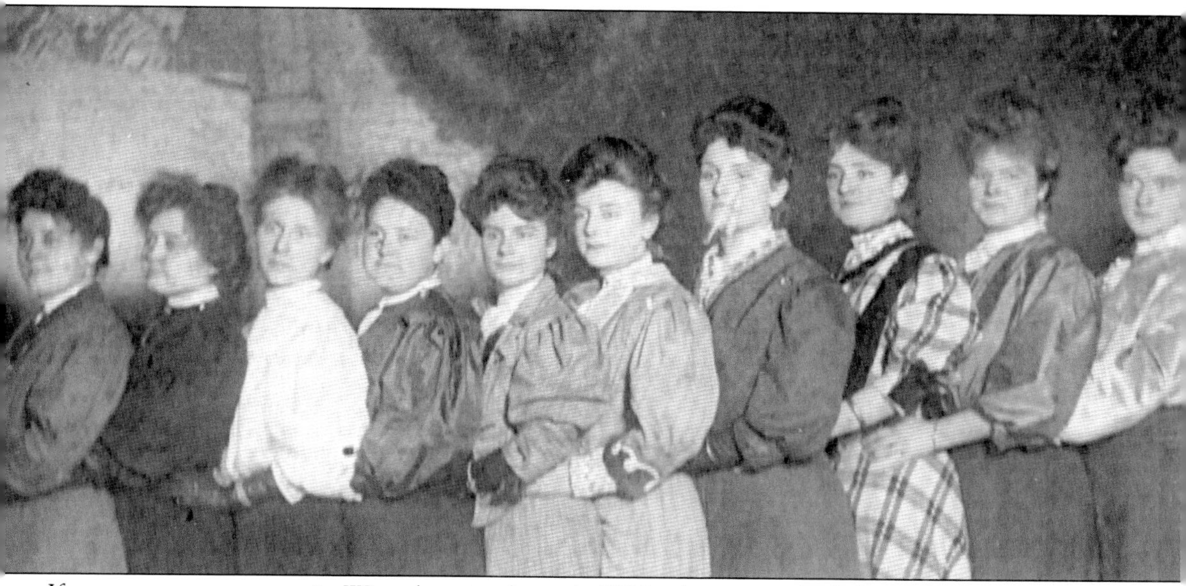

If one were a young man in Winnsboro in the early 1900s, these were the ladies to be seen with. They were the daughters of the most prominent and influential men in town. Pictured are, from left to right, Clara Moore Reeder, Sallie Craddock, Mary Langford, Alma Gibson Moore, Mamie Hopkins, Minnie Stevens, Craigie Wallace, Berry Daingerfield, Clara Hall, and Willa Rhone. (Courtesy of Bill Jones.)

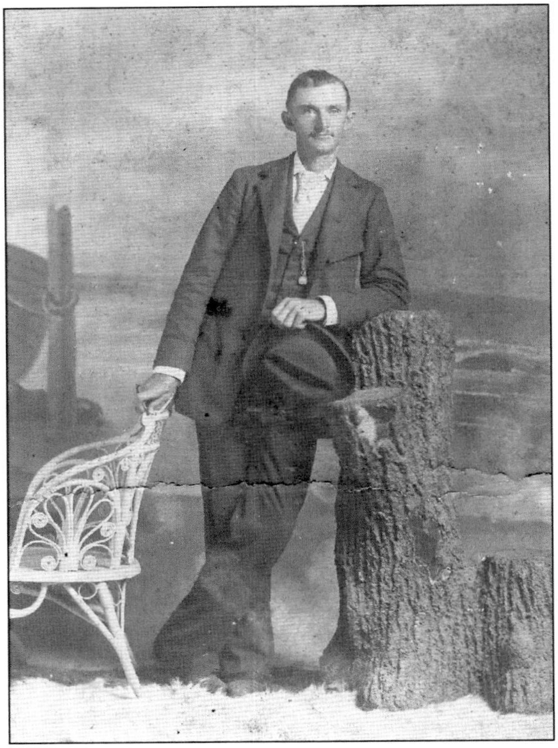

In the early 1900s, it was common for traveling photographers to come through town and offer to take pictures. People often posed in their Sunday best clothes, and the photographer would use props to make the pictures more interesting. Cook & Allbright, traveling photographers, took these pictures, but the subjects were not identified. The Camera Car Company out of Denver was another traveling photography company that came to Winnsboro and took pictures. (Both, courtesy of Bill Jones.)

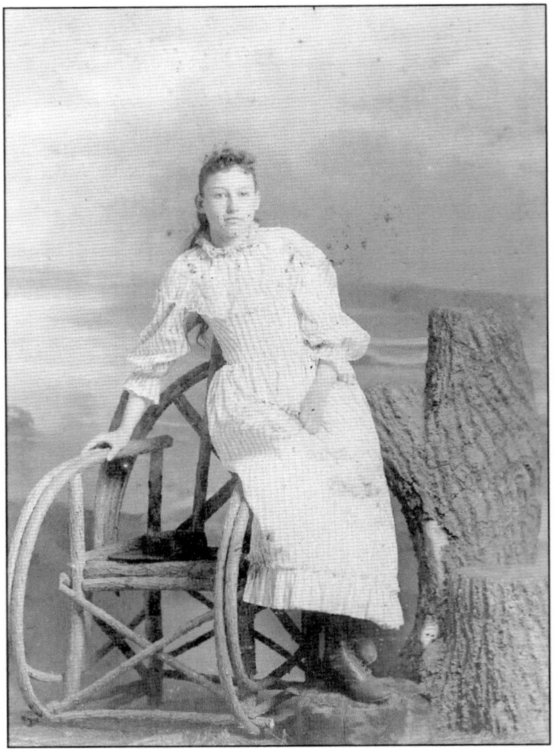

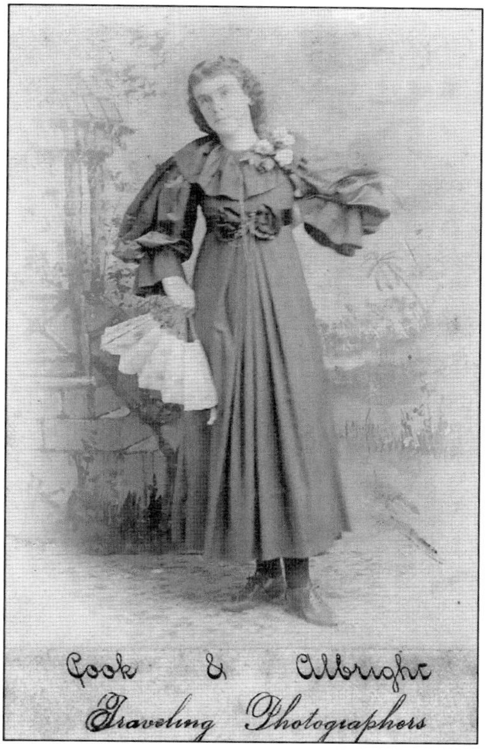

Cook & Allbright also took these pictures. Judging by their costumes, these unidentified folks are people of means. This was a time when ladies and gentlemen dressed to the nines when they were out in public. Ladies always wore gloves and often carried lovely fans. Men were always dressed in suits and ties. (Both, courtesy of Bill Jones.)

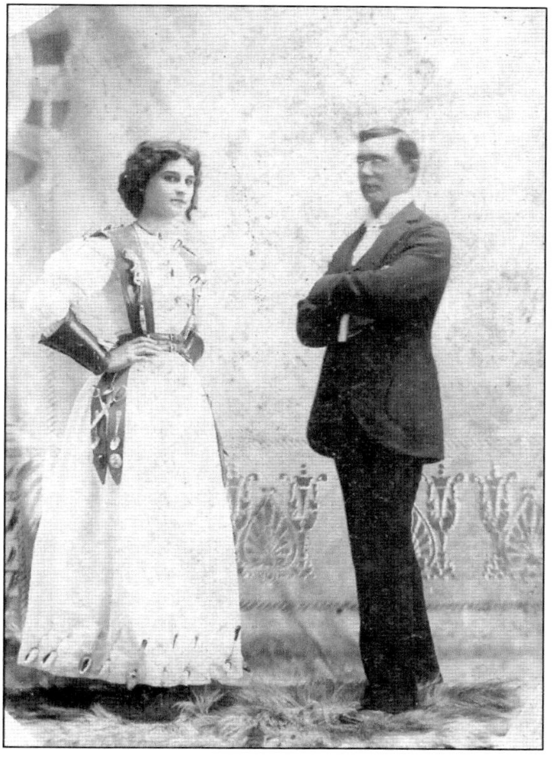

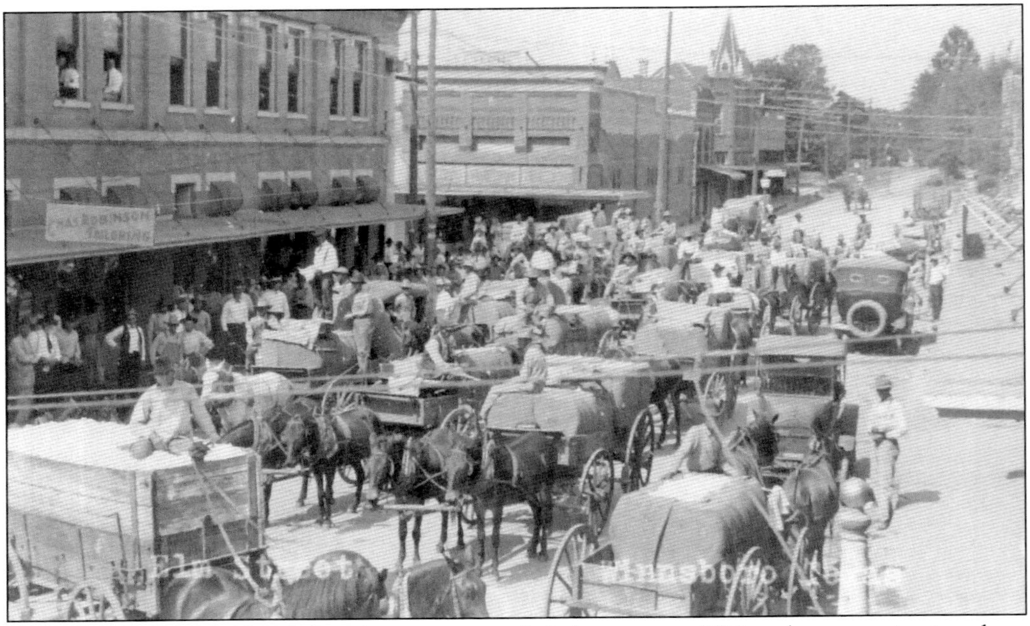

Farmers with wagons loaded with cotton crowded the streets of Winnsboro on ginning days, Monday, Wednesday, and Friday. Each large bale of cotton weighed 500 pounds or more. If the cotton was not selling for the amount the farmer thought it should, he carried it home and waited for a better price. This picture is from 1915, a time when the horse comfortably coexisted with the few automobiles in town and no one went outside without a hat. (Courtesy of the *Winnsboro News*.)

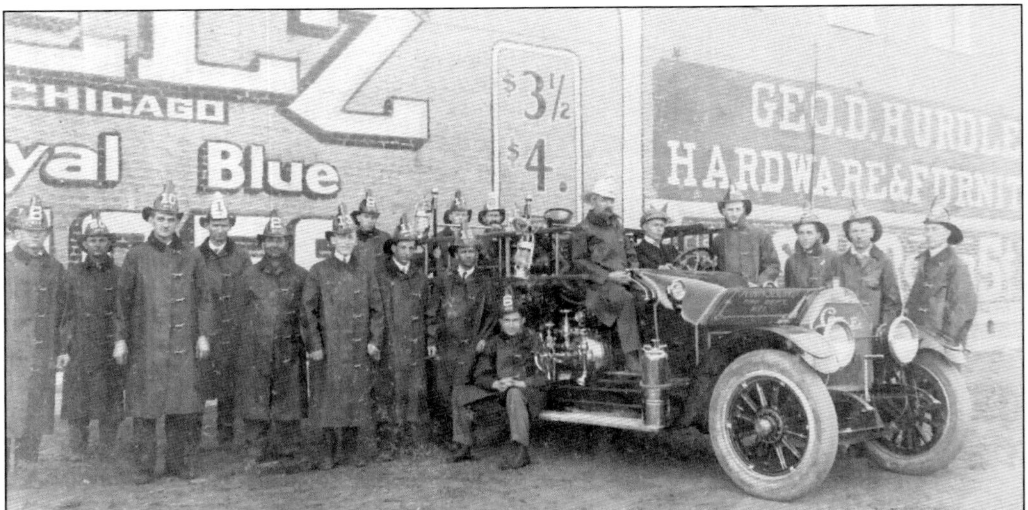

The first volunteer fire department formed in 1913. Prior to that time, there was no water supply in town to accommodate a fire department. The department had two carts with 500 feet of hose on them, and firefighters would pull the hose by hand to the fire location. By 1915, the department had a vehicle, but it would only run half the time. The firefighters would have to push it to the fire. Often, buildings and homes would burn to the ground because of the limitations the firefighters faced. (Courtesy of the *Winnsboro News*.)

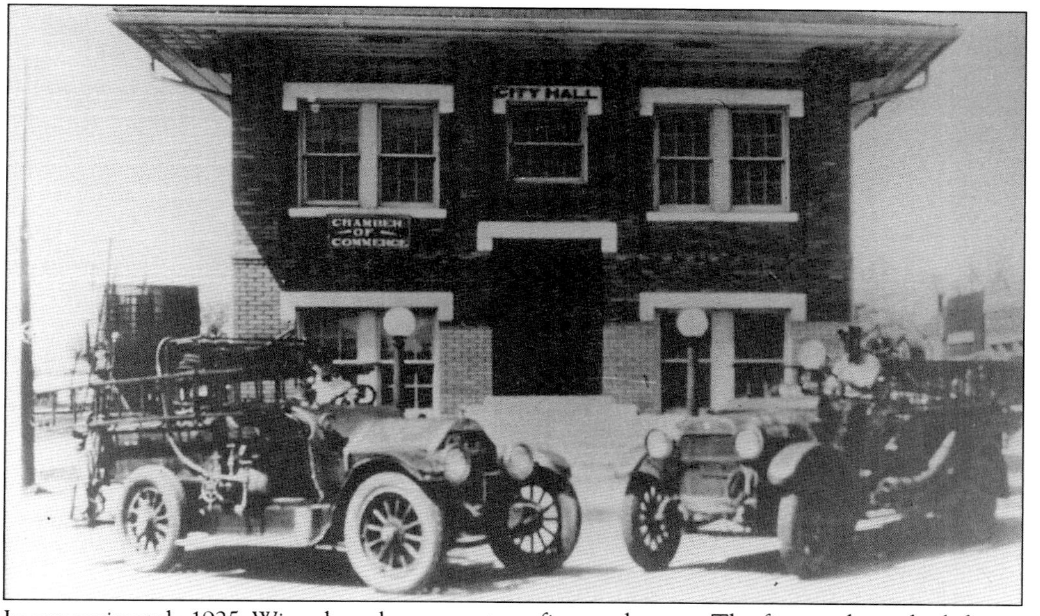

In approximately 1925, Winnsboro became a two–fire truck town. The fire truck on the left was a Cole, which Winnsboro purchased around 1920. Note that the two firemen are sporting white shirts and bow ties, much different from the attire of firefighters today. The trucks are parked in front of the old city hall. (Courtesy of the *Winnsboro News*.)

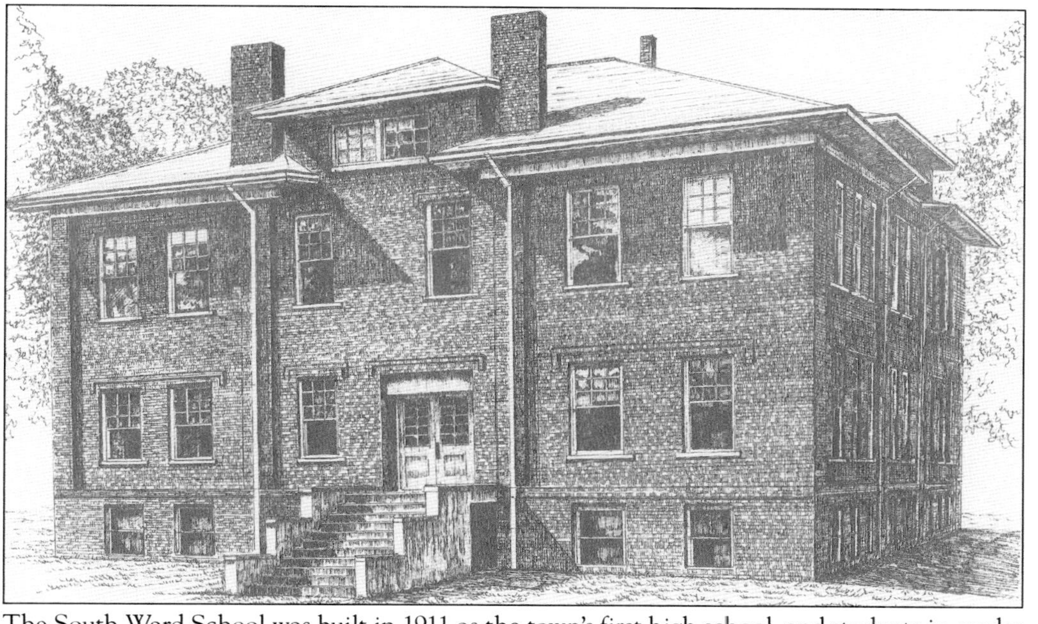

The South Ward School was built in 1911 as the town's first high school, and students in grades eight through 11 had classes there. According to locals, one Halloween night, some teen boys dismantled a wagon, carried it to the top floor of the school, and reassembled it on the stage. In later years, the top story was taken off, and the first floor and basement were used as a cafeteria, music room, and band hall for Memorial Middle School. It was torn down in 1973. (Rendering by Peggy Thomas, 1984.)

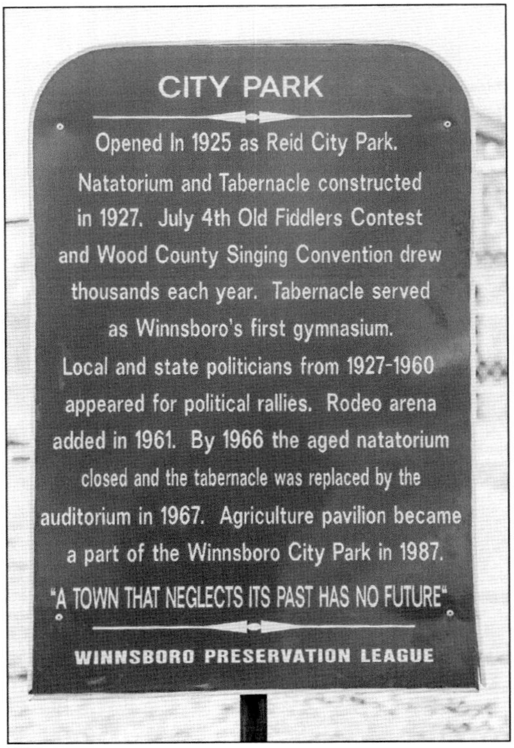

There was a time when City Park was the center for social and political events in Winnsboro. The area is thought to first have been a Caddo Indian campground, and early settlers described it as a beautiful grove of century oaks. Charles Moore purchased the park property in 1888 and then sold it to A.H. Schluter, a lumber merchant, in 1896. He built a beautiful Victorian home, which later burned down, and had a track around the property to train his Kentucky racehorses. He later sold the land, and it changed hands a few times before J.F. Reid acquired it in 1914. In 1925, the Reid holdings were conveyed to the City of Winnsboro, and Mayor R.B. Howell allocated the land for a city park, named the Reid City Park. An auditorium was built that served as a civic center, and an outdoor pool was built, where people could swim in the summer. It cost a dime to swim all day and a nickel for a soda pop. (Both, courtesy of the *Winnsboro News*.)

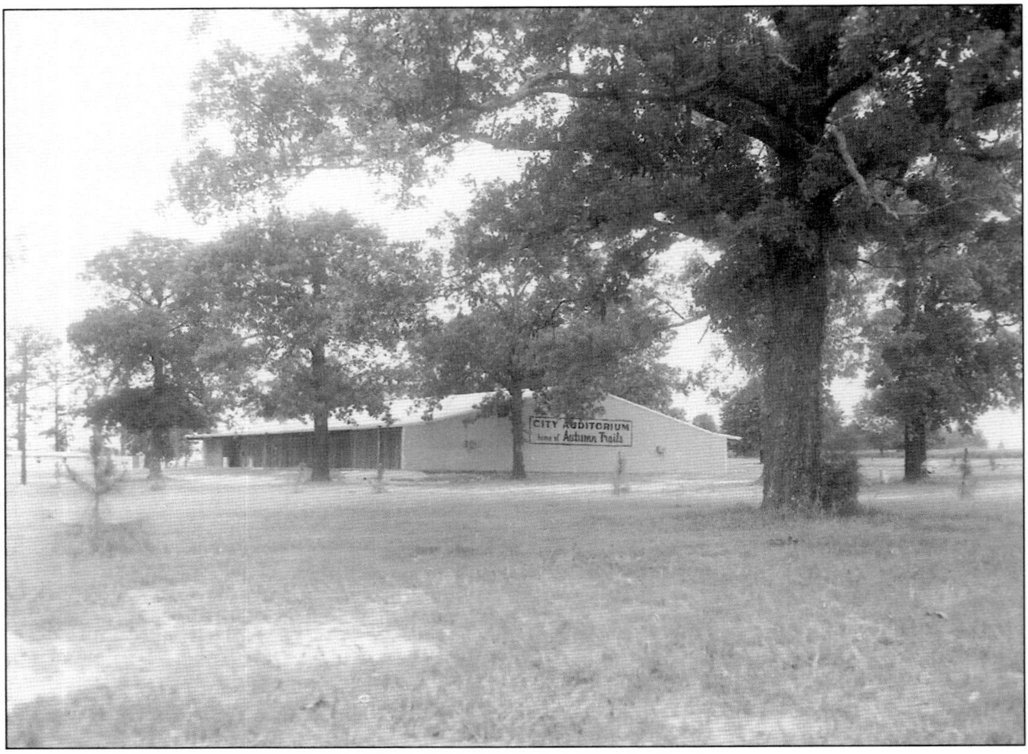

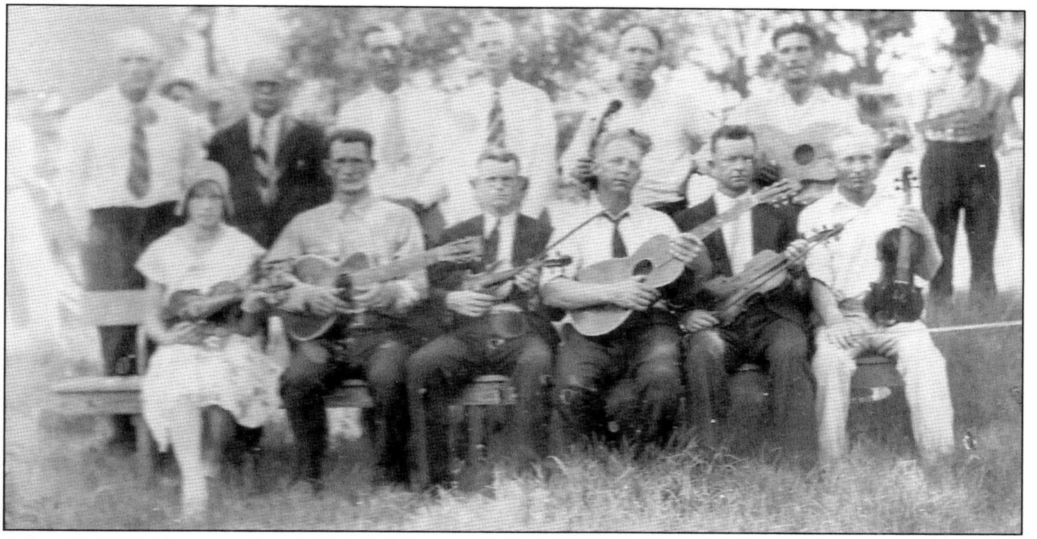

After Reid Park opened in 1926, fiddlers and the Tri-County Singing Convention gathered at the pavilion. In 1927, the musicians officially organized and named the event the Fourth of July Fiddlers' Convention. The first year, 4,000 people attended, and by the 1932 event, attendance had grown to 6,000. Times were tough and money was tight during the 1930s, and the music provided an outlet for folks struggling to survive during the Great Depression. During World War II, the event was canceled for the duration of the war. While the contests were cancelled, there were a number of bond drives held in Winnsboro, bringing such stars as Johnny Mack Brown, Chill Wills, Gayle Storm, Gabby Hayes, and Ann Jeffries. They performed at the State Theater on Main Street. (Both, courtesy of the *Winnsboro News*.)

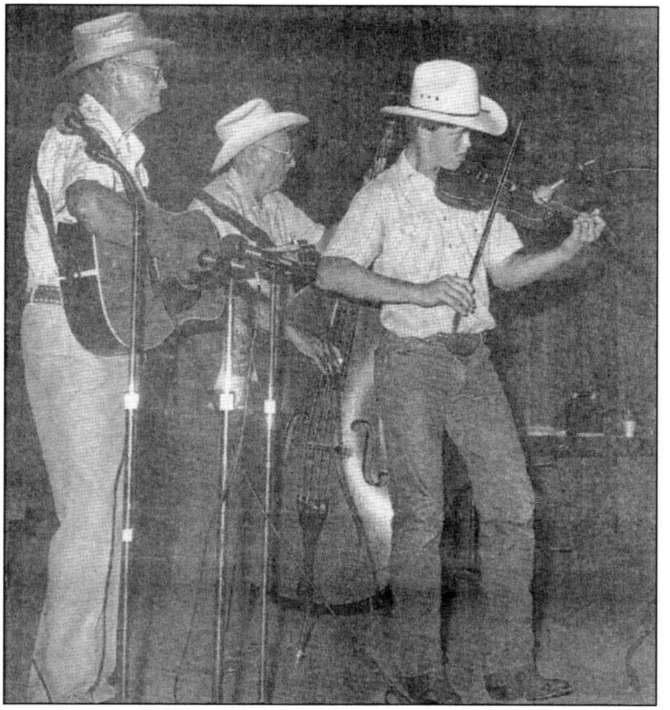

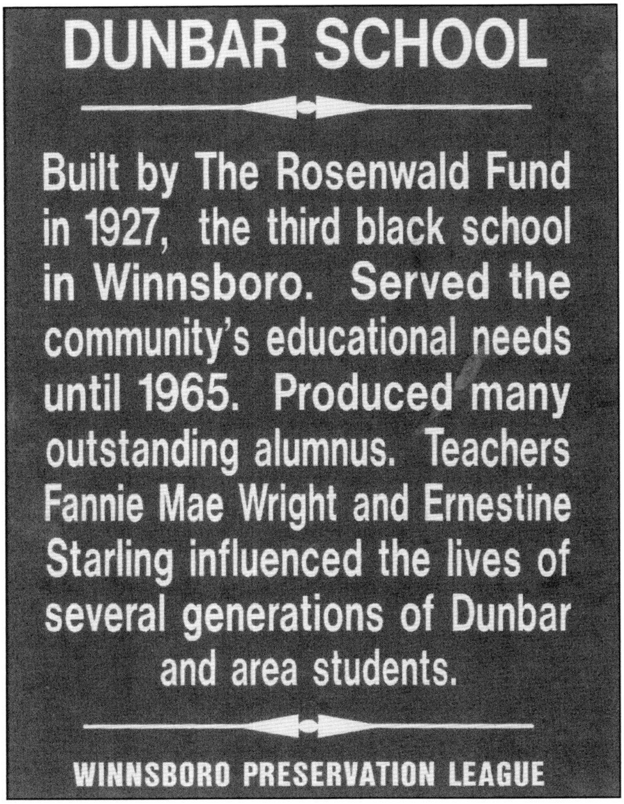

The old Dunbar School was built in the black community east of town in 1927 and consisted of one room with a porch on the north side. A water keg on the porch supplied drinking water, and a wood stove provided heat. The school was named for Paul Dunbar, a black 19th-to-early-20th-century poet and writer who gained national prominence for his work. The funding for the school came from the foundation established by Chicago millionaire Julius Rosenwald, president of Sears, Roebuck & Co. (Courtesy of Earnestine Starling.)

Some of the students from the Dunbar School are, from left to right, (first row) Robert Martin, Kenneth Robinson, and William ?; (second row) Gloria Dean Henson, Trenal Lynn Jones, Marla Smith, and Gloria Faye Henson. (Courtesy of Earnestine Starling.)

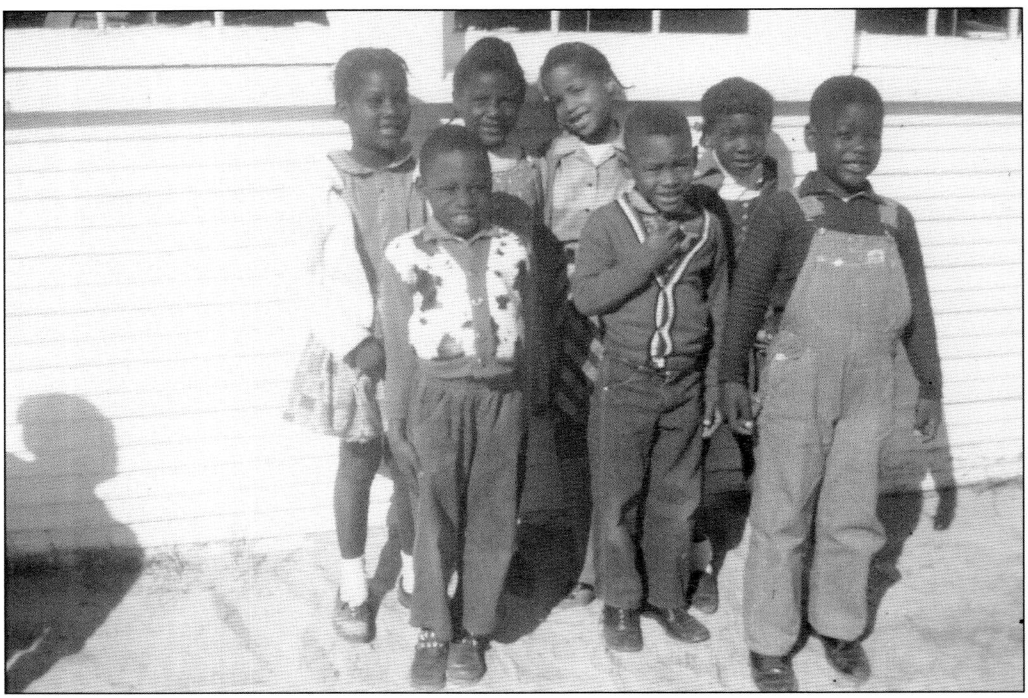

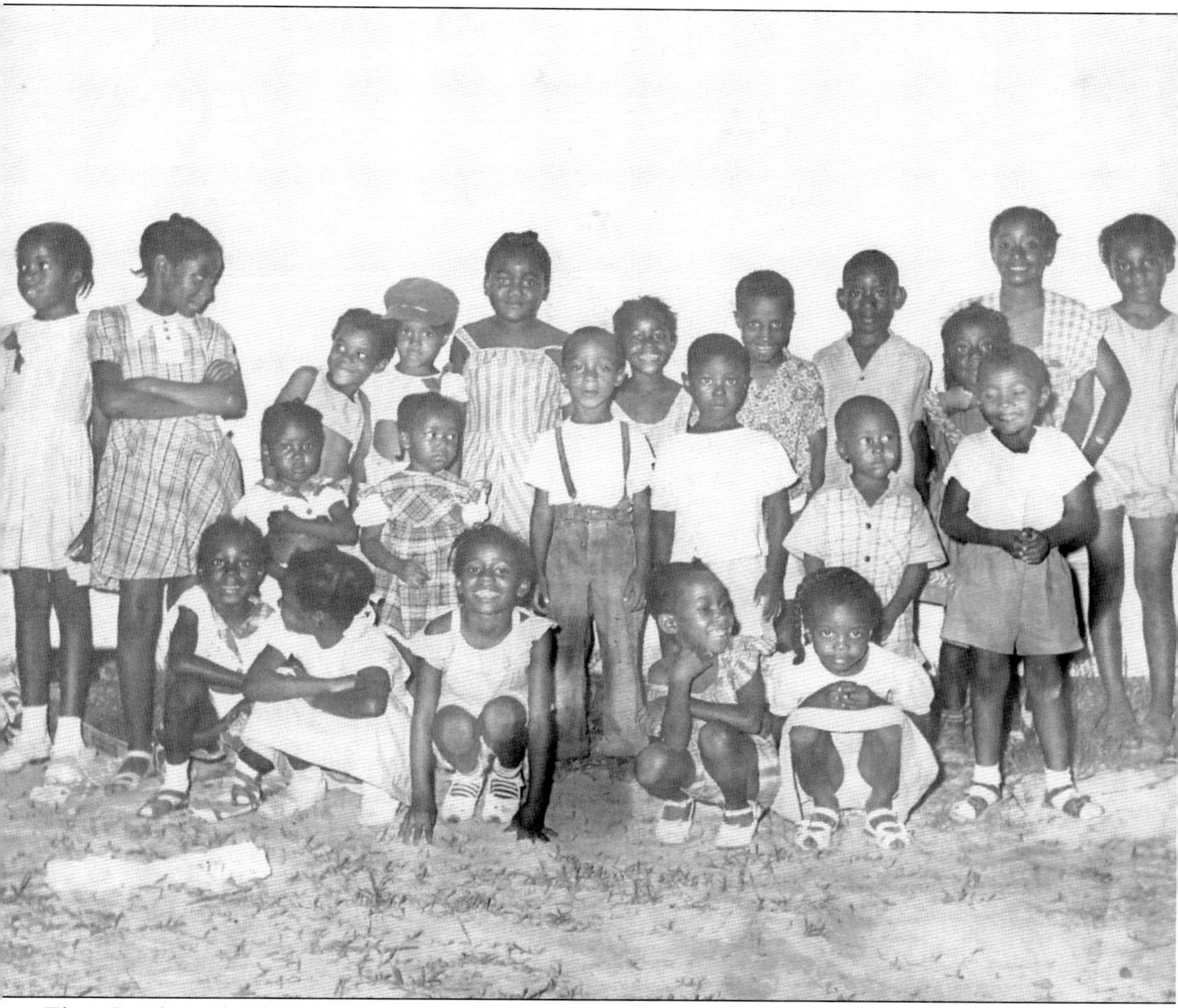

These Dunbar School students are, from left to right, (first row) Norma Jean Simmons, unidentified, Lavonne Starling, Georgie Clyde Austin, and Bobby Jean Blackwell; (second row) two unidentified, "Furry" Blackwell, Curtis Ray Henson, Robert Charles, and Harold Don Christian; (third row) Delaores Wade, Lela Ann Shaw, Vivian Phea, Glenda Jones, Eddie Ruth Ross, Brenda Henson, William Harvey "Bill" Kelly, James Lawrence Everett, two unidentified, and Johnny Mae Henson. Many of these students lived in homes constructed near the Dunbar School by Eli Lawson, a Winnsboro builder. (Courtesy of Earnestine Starling.)

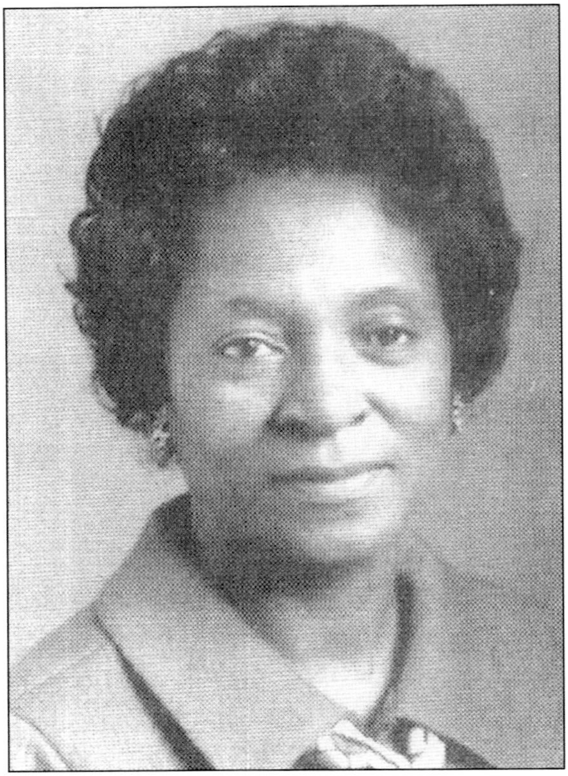

Earnestine Starling attended Dunbar school and, in 1942, began a long teaching career there. She continued teaching until desegregation 23 years later. Earnestine was a student of the beloved Fannie Mae Wright, a lady who personified black education in Winnsboro and East Texas. Later in her career, Earnestine taught at Westbrook Elementary School until she retired in 1984 after 41 years of teaching. (Courtesy of Earnestine Starling.)

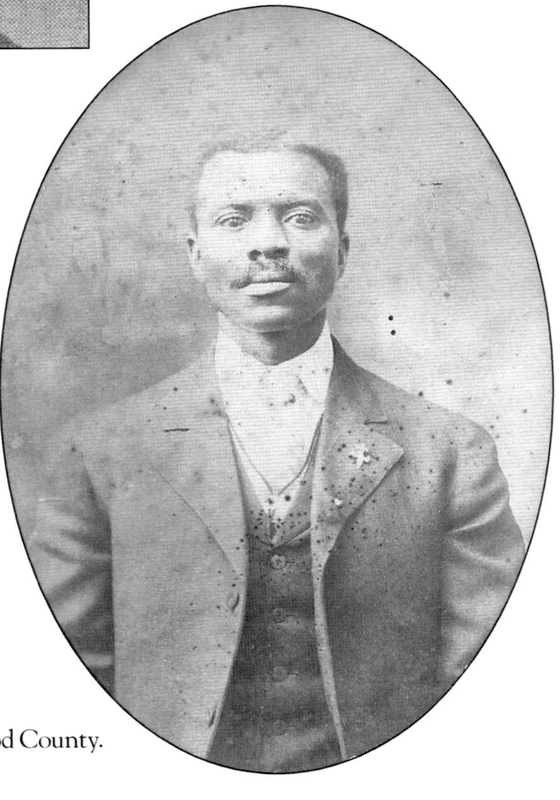

J.J. Grundy was the first black teacher in Wood County. (Courtesy of Earnestine Starling.)

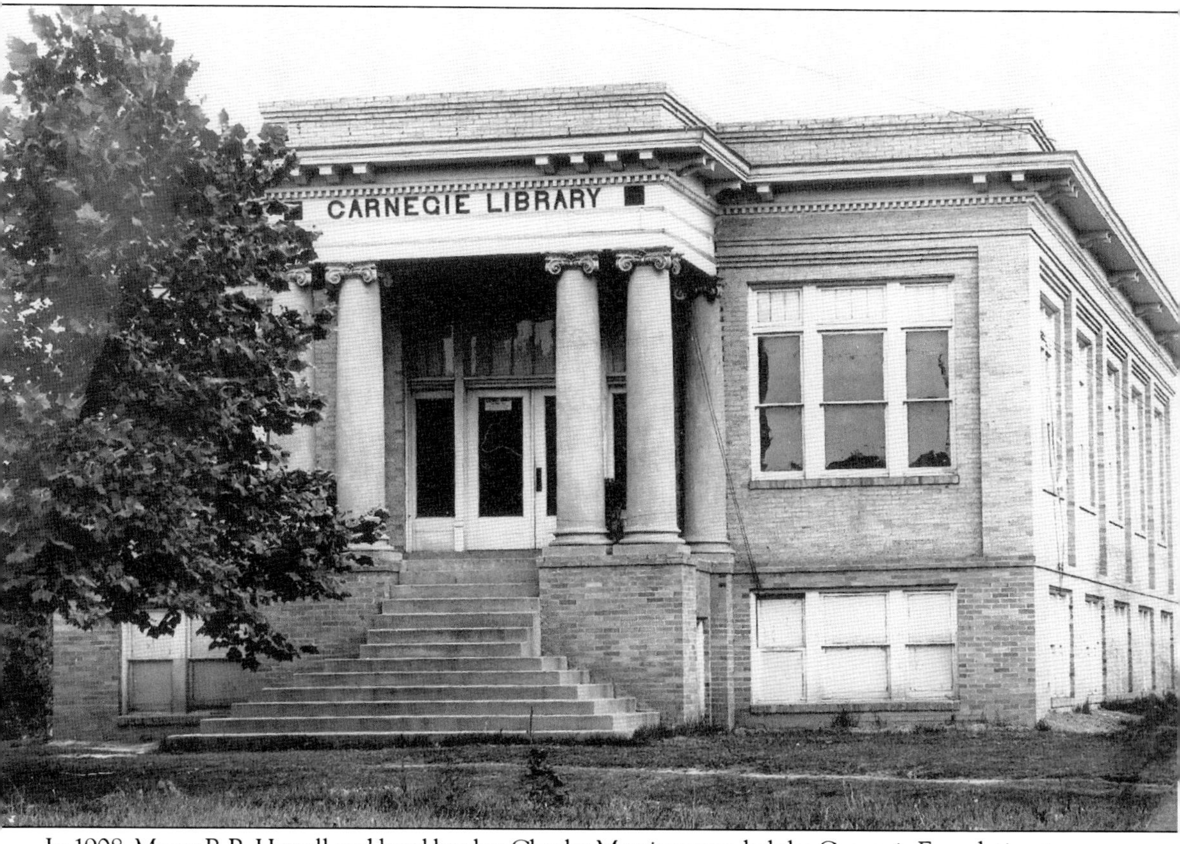

In 1908, Mayor R.B. Howell and local banker Charles Morris persuaded the Carnegie Foundation to donate $10,000 for a public library. The grant stipulated that the library must be wholly supported by the community. The city acquired a location at the southwest corner of South Main and Carnegie Streets. The library was completed in 1909, with the ground floor used as an auditorium or an opera house while the upper floor housed the library. In 1910, the Standard Club formed an alliance with the library to sponsor a book donation and opened the library to book lending. Virginia Bozeman, a member of the organization since 1904, became the first librarian, with a salary of $10 a month. She remained in that position for 40 years, and the Carnegie library and Virginia "Bunny" Bozeman were synonymous. The Carnegie library site was sold in 1967, and the historic building was razed. (Courtesy of the *Winnsboro News*.)

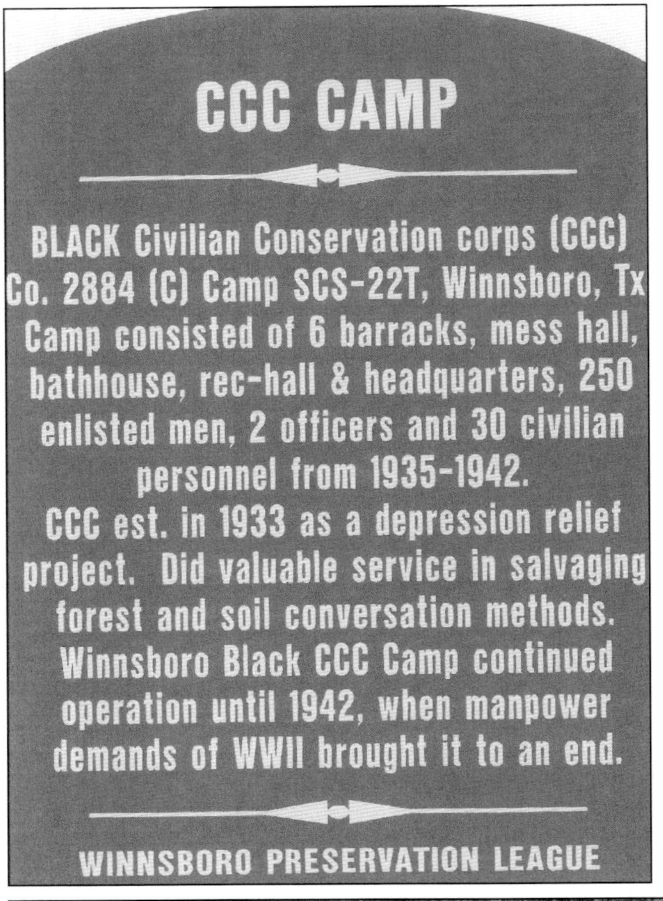

On March 9, 1933, the 73rd Congress authorized President Roosevelt's Civilian Conservation Corps (CCC) to be used in forestry work, soil erosion, flood control, and other similar projects. Through the efforts of Judge Will Suiter, Winnsboro was selected for a black CCC camp. J.J. Carroll leased 10 acres to the federal government for the campsite. CCC Camp SCS-22T, Company 2884 (C), was established in Winnsboro on August 20, 1935, and had six barracks that housed 250 enlisted men, two Army officers, a doctor, eight teachers, and six operations foremen. Winnsboro's black CCC camp continued operation until 1942, when manpower demands of World War II brought it to an end. While the men at the CCC camp were there primarily to work, they did find time for recreation. They formed a baseball team that played for fun after work. (Both, courtesy of the *Winnsboro News*.)

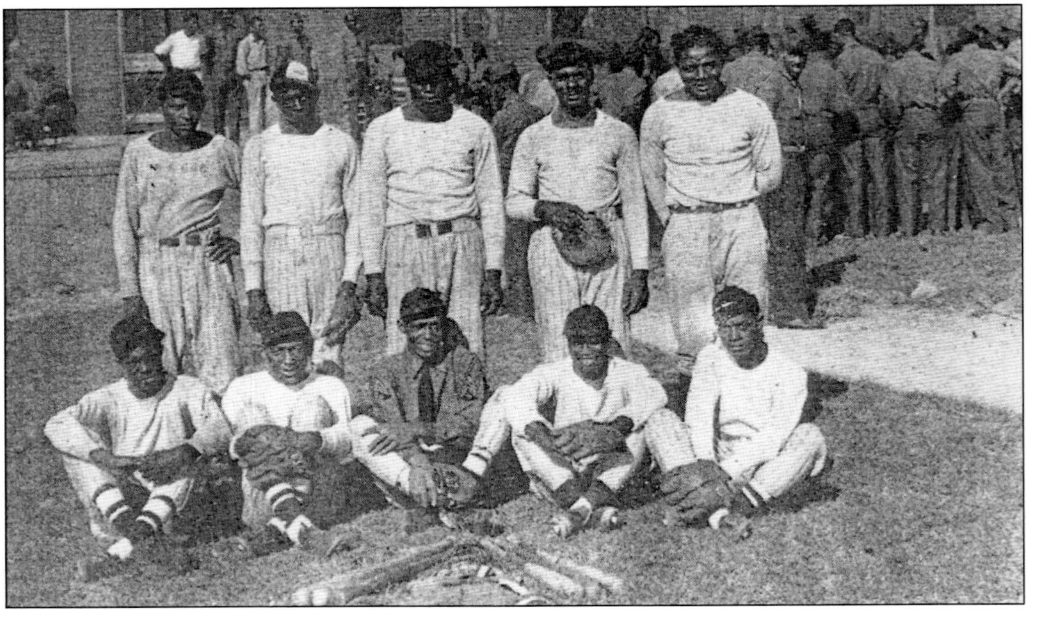

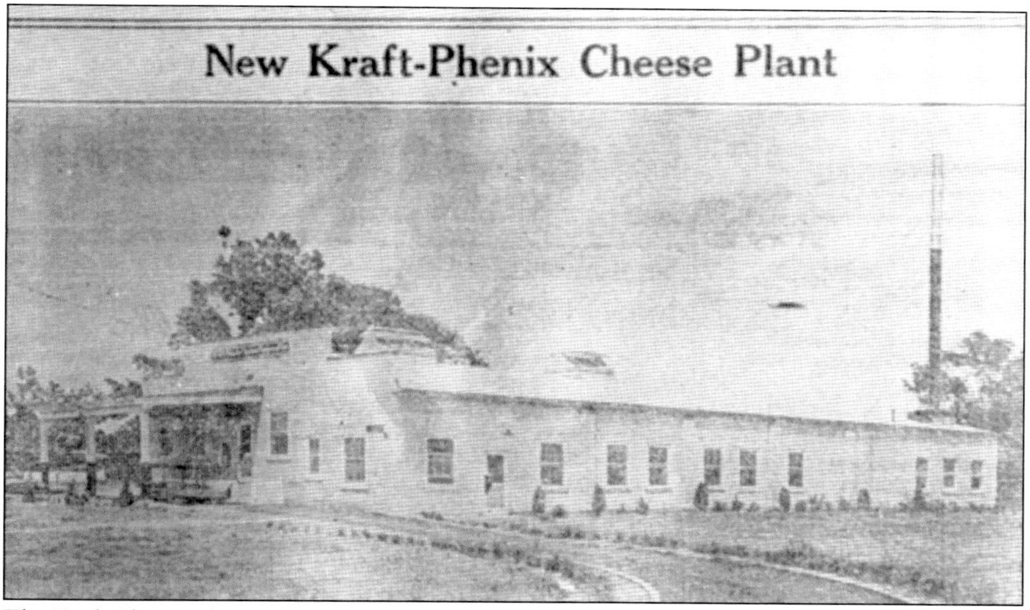

The Kraft Cheese Plant was opened in 1930, and local dairy farmers provided milk in five 10-gallon cans to the plant for processing. In the summer, the cans of milk were kept from spoiling by putting them in tubs of cool water until the route men from the Kraft plant could pick them up. Because of the Kraft plant, local farmers who had four to five milk cows were able to survive during the Depression. In 1935, the Kraft Phenix Corporation constructed a large, modern operation and boasted that the Winnsboro business represented one of the most advanced cheese-making operations in the world. It closed in the late 1940s. (Courtesy of the *Winnsboro News*.)

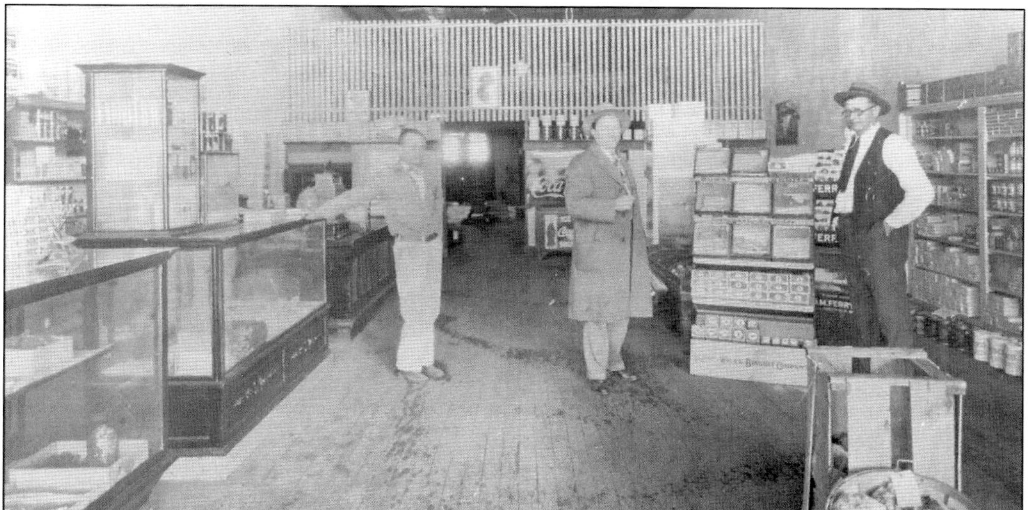

Luther Dodgen's General Store was just one of the many businesses owned by the Dodgen family through the years. Like many other Winnsboro settlers, the family moved to Winnsboro from Pleasant Grove. Other stores owned by the family included the W.C. Dodgen dry goods store, which was on the corner of Main and West Elm Streets for many years. That building later became the home of Bell's Pharmacy, owned by Sammy Bell, until 2011. Luther Dodgen went to California in 1920. (Courtesy of the *Winnsboro News*.)

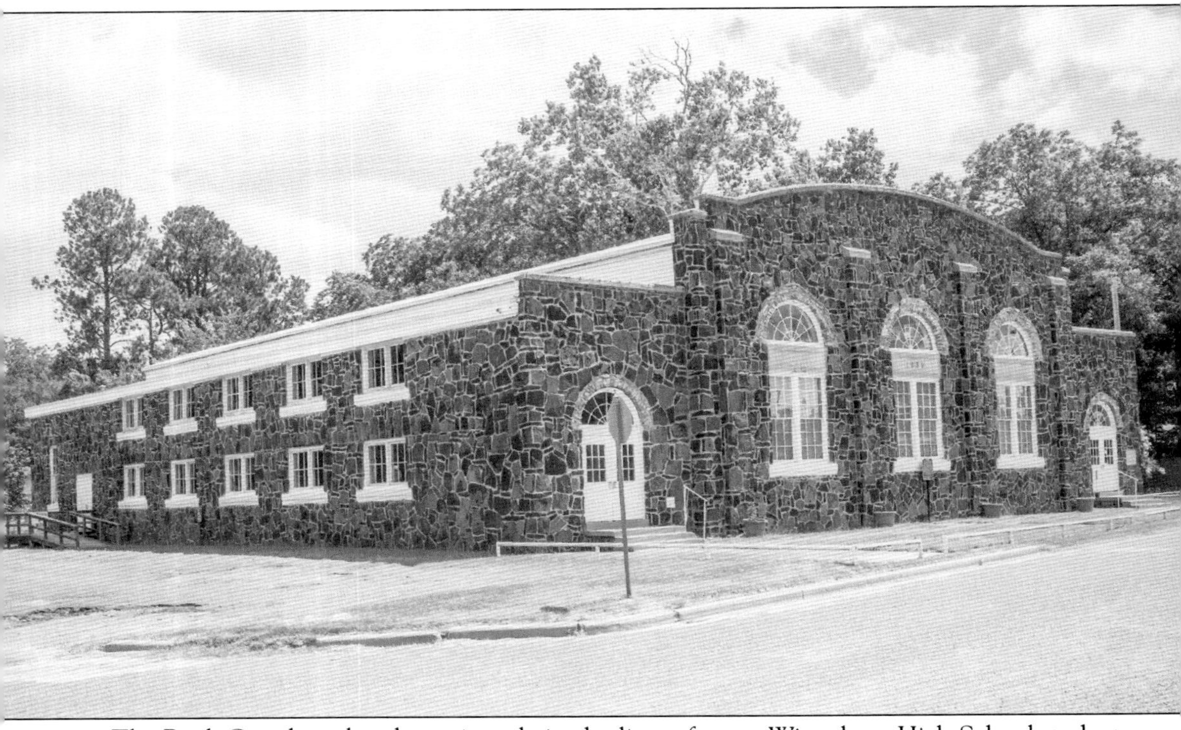

The Rock Gym has played a major role in the lives of many Winnsboro High School students and graduates from 1939 through the early 1970s. It was where basketball games were played, and it was also where many graduation ceremonies were held. Young people danced there for the junior-senior prom, as well as many sock hops, and the building also hosted band concerts, Halloween carnivals, and donkey ball games. In the 1980s, it almost fell to a wrecking ball when some members of the school board proposed razing the building for a school parking lot. The Winnsboro Preservation League contacted Jerry Hardy, then school superintendent, to ask for his assistance in forming a committee of citizens to save the building. Today, the Rock Gym is the site of the annual all-school reunion that is held in conjunction with Autumn Trails every October. (Courtesy of Bob Williams.)

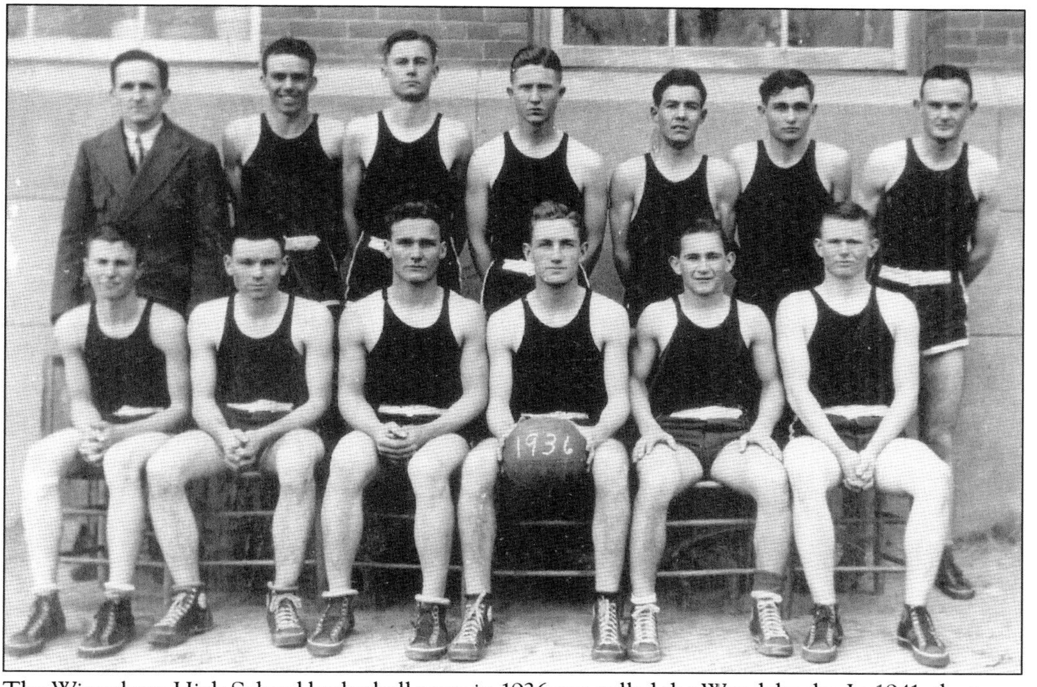

The Winnsboro High School basketball team in 1936 was called the Woodchucks. In 1941, the team was renamed the Red Raiders, a name that has continued to the present. When the Woodchucks played, there were only county leagues, and there would be a big county meet each year, with the winners advancing. The men pictured are unidentified. The 1934 girls' high school basketball team, called the Chuckettes, won all the tournaments in Texas and played for the national championship in Kansas City. The team traveled north in two cars, and one had an accident on the way, injuring a few of the girls. Some people thought the team would have won the national title had all the girls been able to play. Pictured below are, from left to right, (first row) Jackie Covington Thompson, Jackie Phillips, Clissie B. Wilson, Joyce Taylor, Nona Dell Walling, and Dorthea Irby; (second row) coach Joe Winkle, Opal Bailey, Maureen Sparks, Blanche Reid, Wanda Bellomy, Rachel Covington, and Mozelle Dacus. (Both, courtesy of the *Winnsboro News*.)

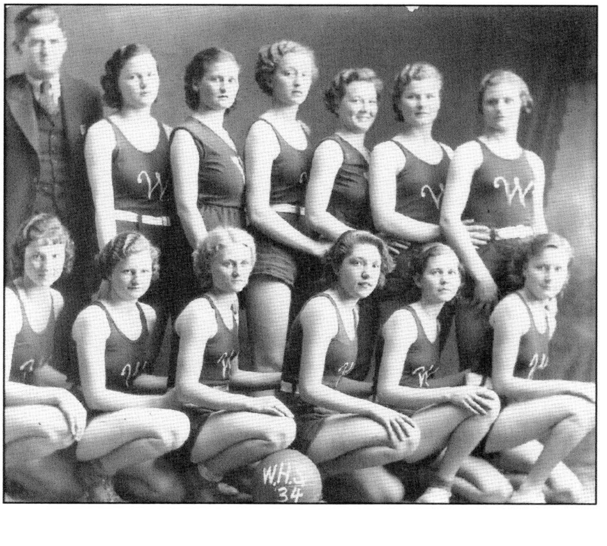

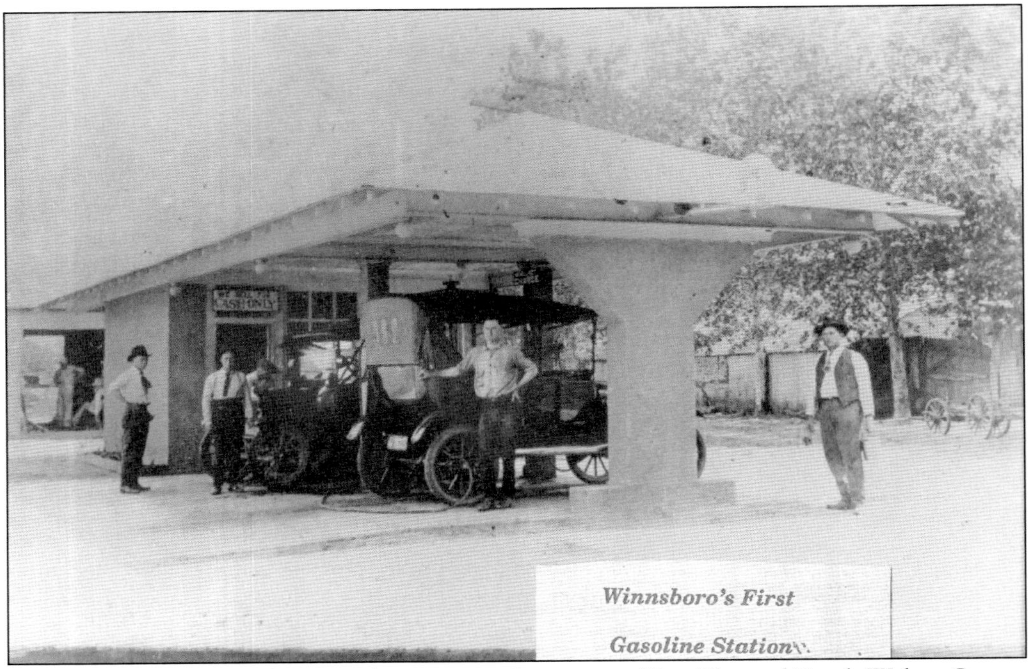

The first service station for Winnsboro was on the corner of East Elm and North Walnut Streets and opened in 1915. The station was owned by Clint and Claude Miller, who operated it with their uncle, J.C. "Buster" Davis. The men on the left are, from left to right, Claude, Clint, and Buster. On the far right is Jim Galt, who had a business behind the station. The men in the bottom picture are not identified. (Both, courtesy of the *Winnsboro News*.)

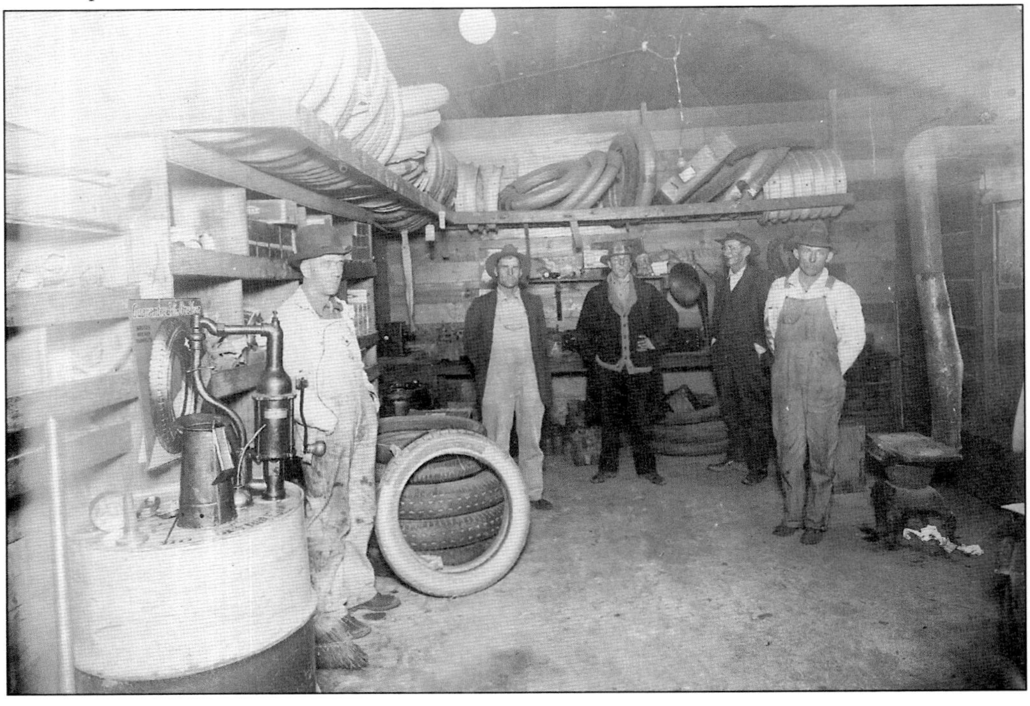

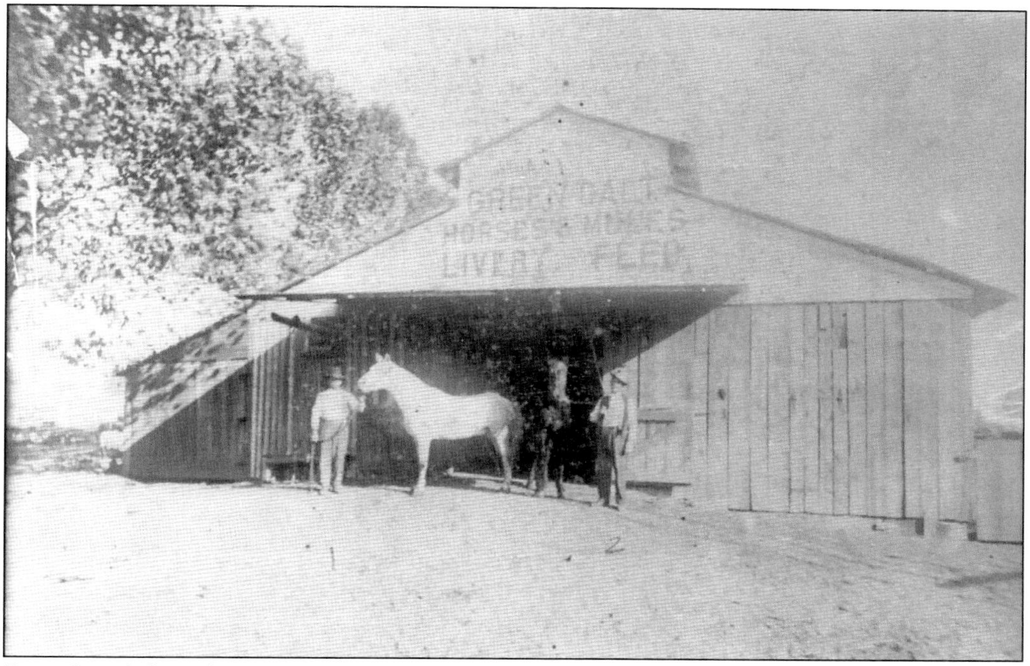

Even though horseless carriages were starting to be more popular in the 1900s, there were still plenty of people who relied on animals for transportation. Jim Galt had a stable on the northeast corner of East Elm and Walnut Streets, where riders could leave a horse while doing business. A sign on the Green Galt Barn read, "Horses, mules, milk cows and shingles for sale." (Both, courtesy of the *Winnsboro News*.)

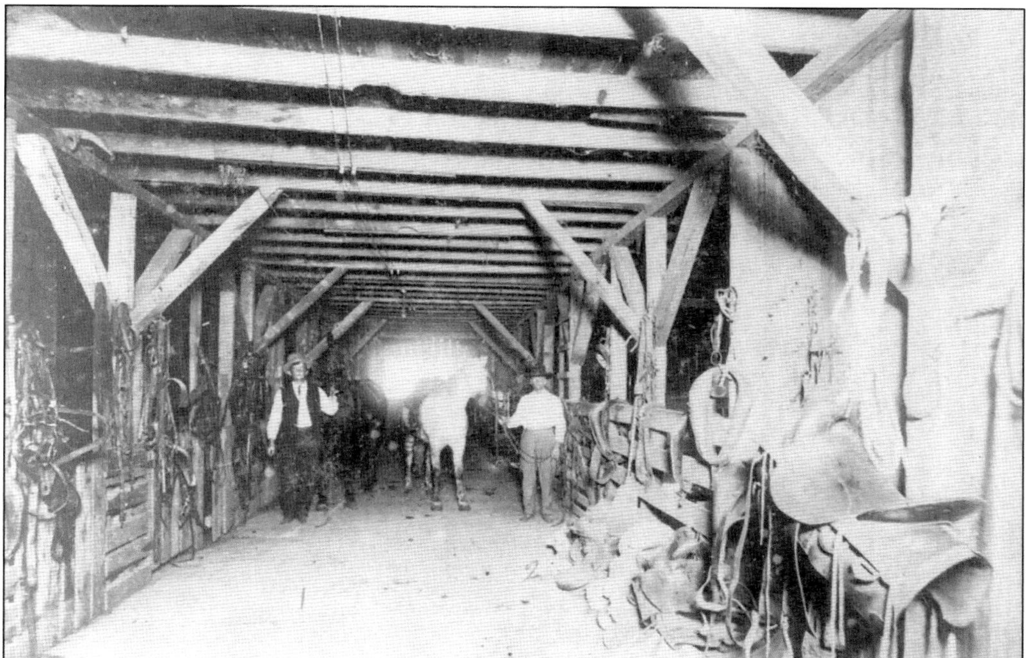

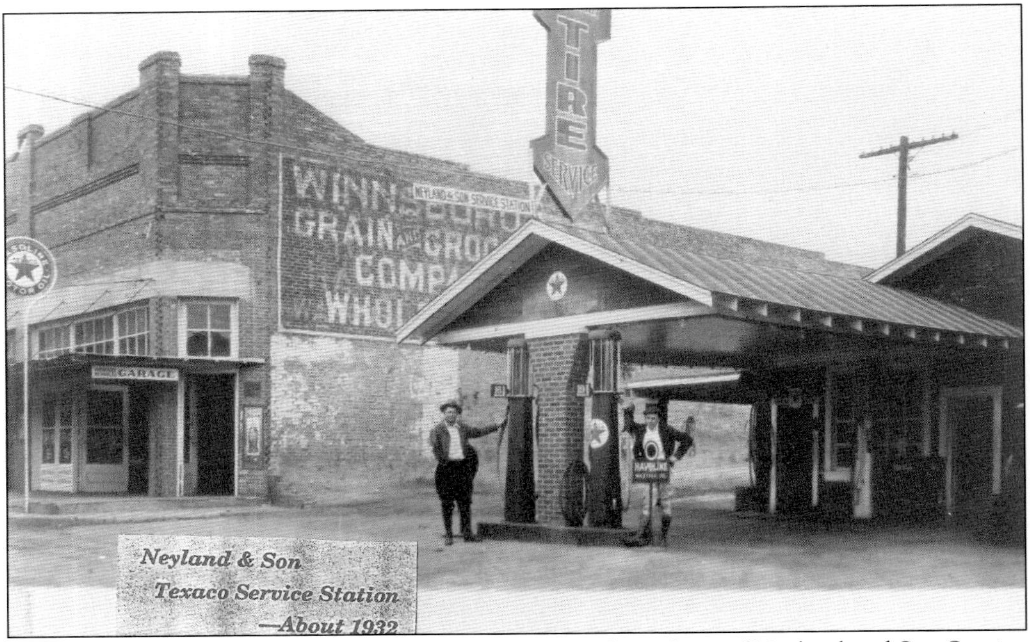

E.L. "Lefty" Neyland (left) and Morris Petty posed proudly in front of Neyland and Son Service Station on West Elm Street. The station sold National tires and Texaco gasoline—16¢ a gallon for regular and 19¢ for ethyl in the early 1930s. The building, minus the carport, is still there today. The Howard Reynolds Garage, in the building to the left, was replaced by a movie theater later in the 1930s. (Courtesy of the *Winnsboro News*.)

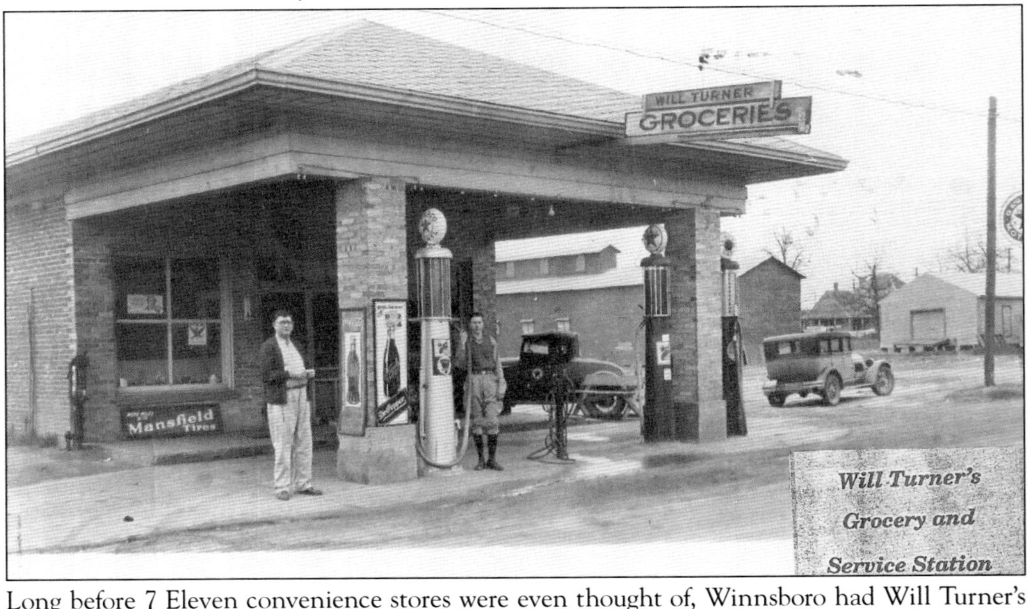

Long before 7 Eleven convenience stores were even thought of, Winnsboro had Will Turner's Grocery and Service Station. Will Turner (left) owned and operated the station on East Elm Street in the early 1930s. At right is Turner's assistant Robert Brewer, the husband of Bertha Brewer and father of Sara Pollard and Charles Brewer. Horace "Red" Martin was the Texaco consignee when this picture was taken. (Courtesy of the *Winnsboro News*.)

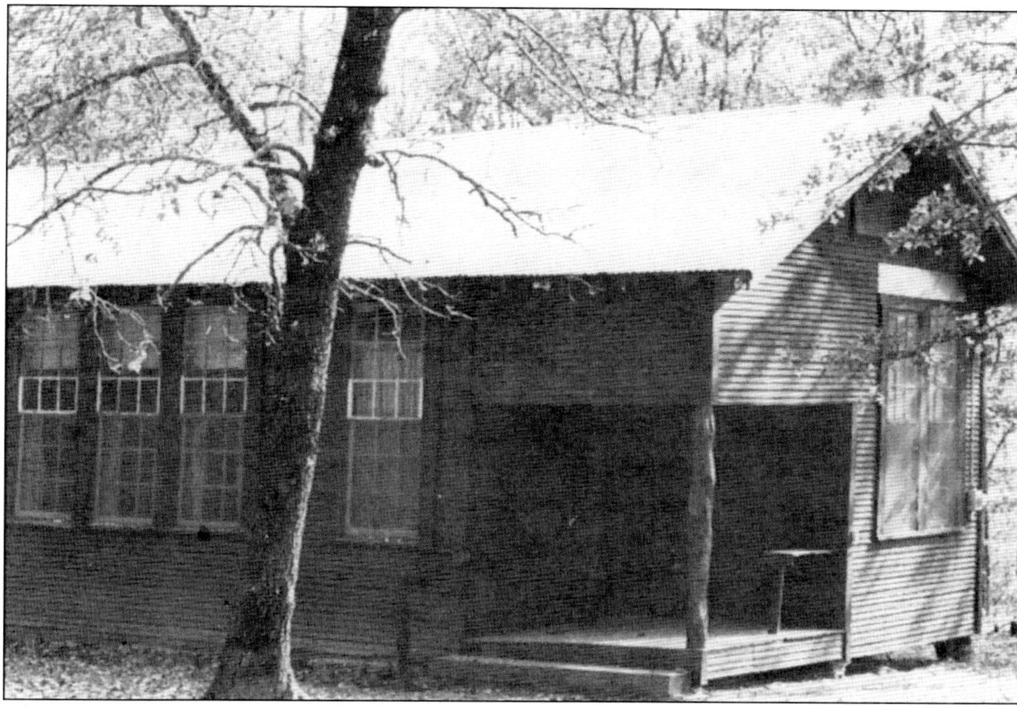

The McGee School House was known as the little red schoolhouse and was built around 1929 on an acre and a half donated by Billy McGee, father of May Bell Cunningham, Lena LaRue, and Velma Blackstone. Classes were held there until 1945, when the district consolidated with the Winnsboro Independent School District. (Courtesy of the *Winnsboro News.*)

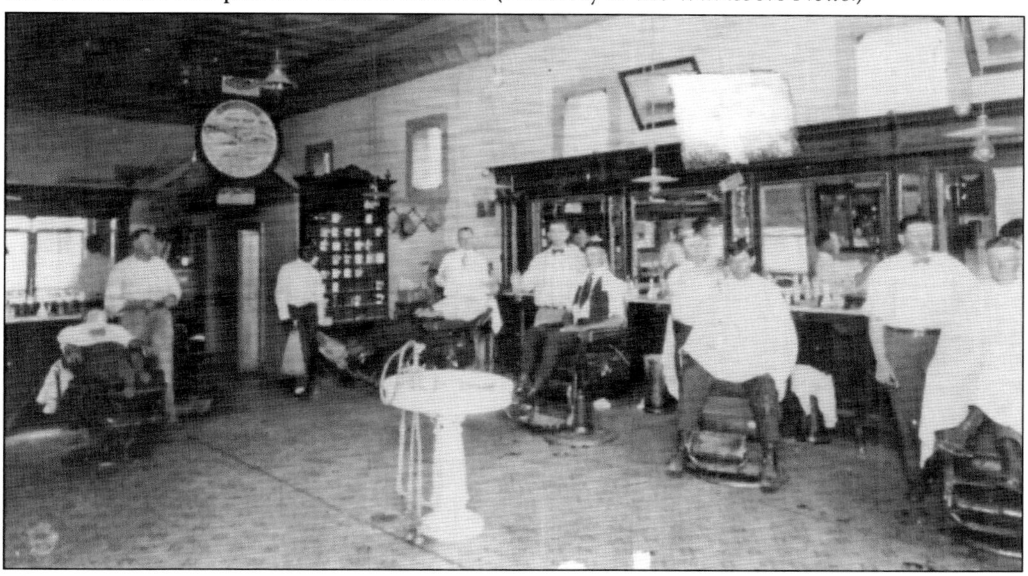

The Star Barbershop, owned by Bill Stokes, had five barbers, and they were all busy, especially on a Saturday. The shop also had a bathing area, and farmers would come to town on Saturday to take a bath in the 1920s. The business also offered a rudimentary cleaning service for dirty clothes, and it was the first cleaners in Wood County. (Courtesy of the *Winnsboro News.*)

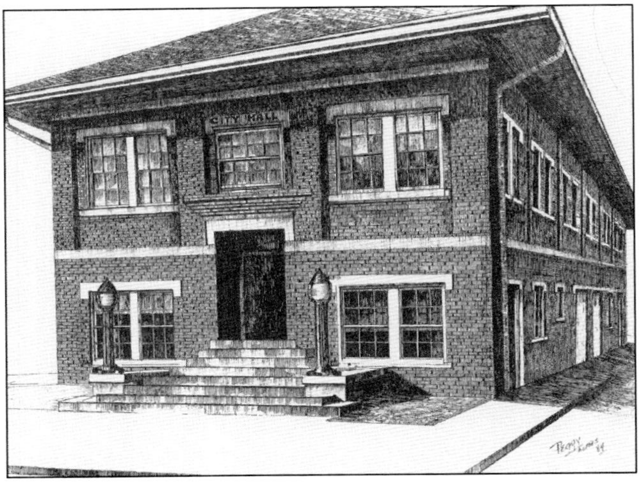

Completed in 1924, Winnsboro's first city hall had an apartment on the first floor for the town's only paid fireman, who also served as night watchman. It also had the only public restroom for women and children in town, a fire station, and a jail at the west end. The second floor had offices for the city secretary, the mayor, and the city marshal. A large area served as the council chamber, a courtroom, and election polling place and was used for official town meetings. (Courtesy of the *Winnsboro News*.)

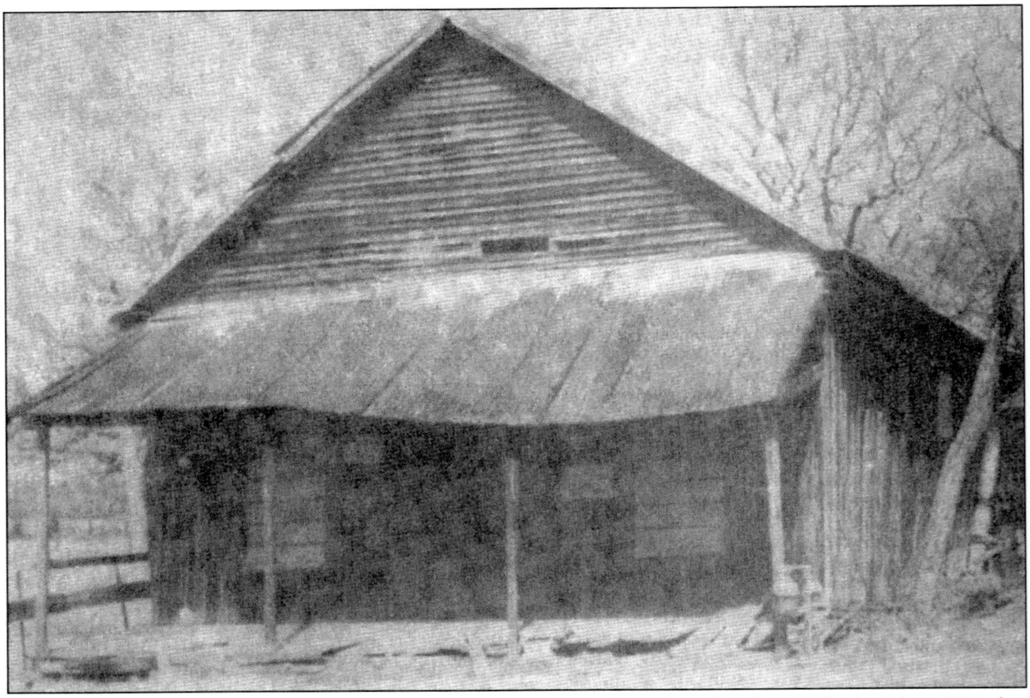

This store in the Cartwright community was first opened just after the Civil War by Elmo Wright, and in 1929, it became the U.B. Winkle's Grocery Store. The store contained everything from dry goods to groceries, and even a wagon wheel could be ordered there. Winkle ran the store until his death in 1981. Following his death, his wife kept the store in operation until 1984. When it closed, it held the distinction of being Wood County's oldest continual business. (Courtesy of the *Winnsboro News*.)

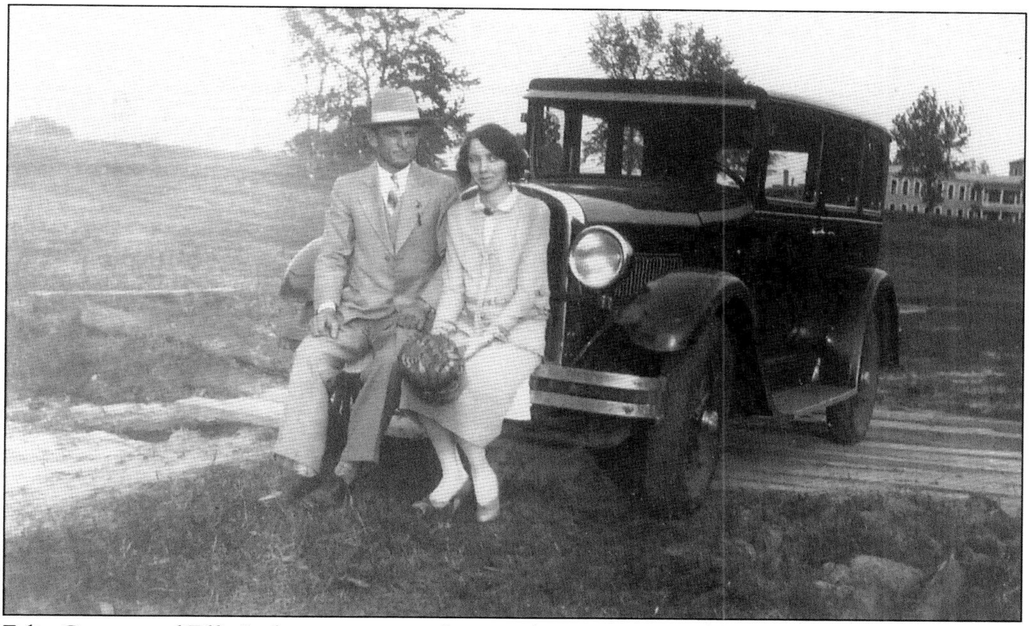

Felix Carnes and Effie Jackson were sweethearts who never married because they could not agree on a church in which to marry. One was Methodist, the other Baptist, and each wanted the ceremony in their home church. On Sundays, Felix would pick up Effie for a drive in the country. The couple is pictured in front of the Musgrove Springs Depot in the early 1930s. (Courtesy of the *Winnsboro News*.)

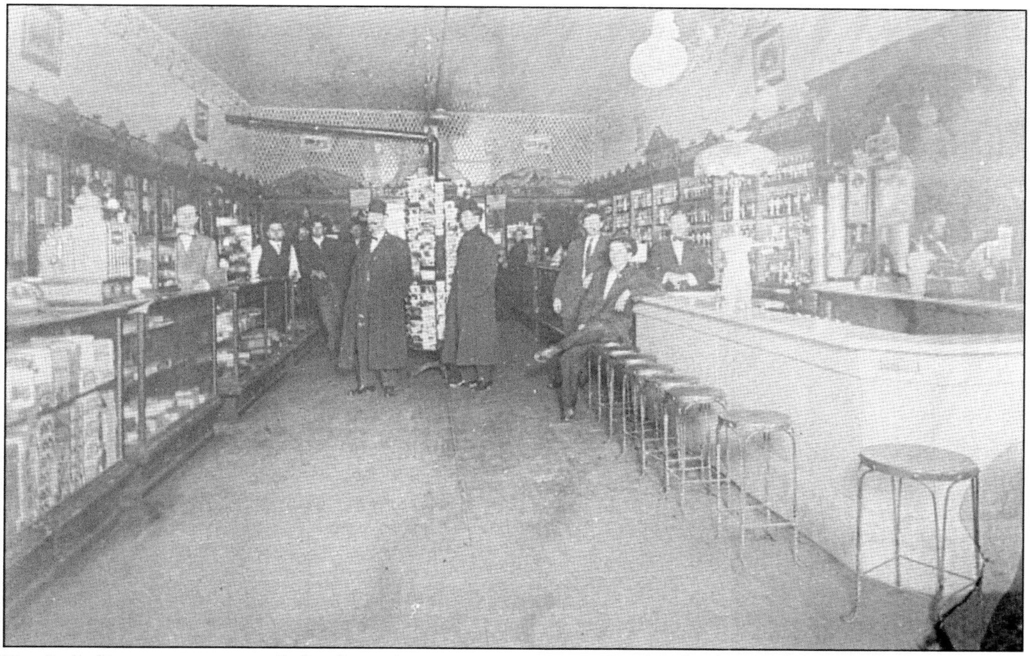

Fowler's Drugs was one of the first drugstores in town. It also had a soda fountain, and many young couples, including Felix and Effie, would go there for ice cream. (Courtesy of the *Winnsboro News*.)

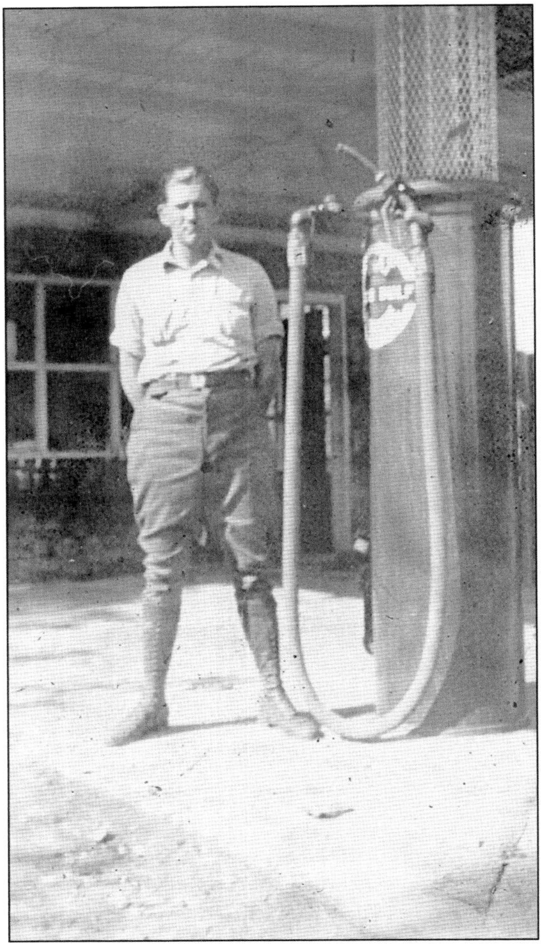

Percy Williams ran a gas station at Walnut and East Elm Streets in 1925. He operated the station for a few years before going into the plumbing business. He had a thriving business and was a well-respected man. (Both, courtesy of John Patrick.)

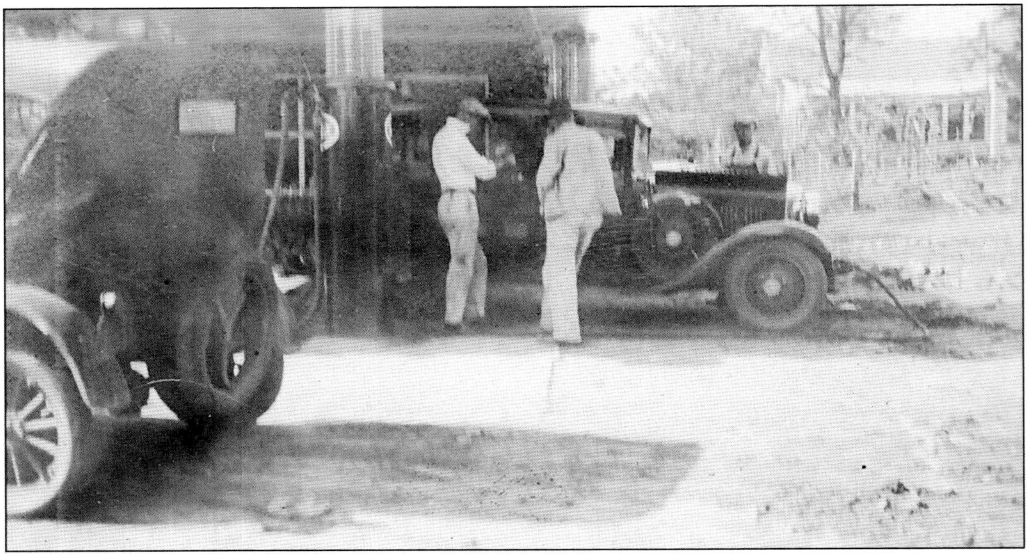

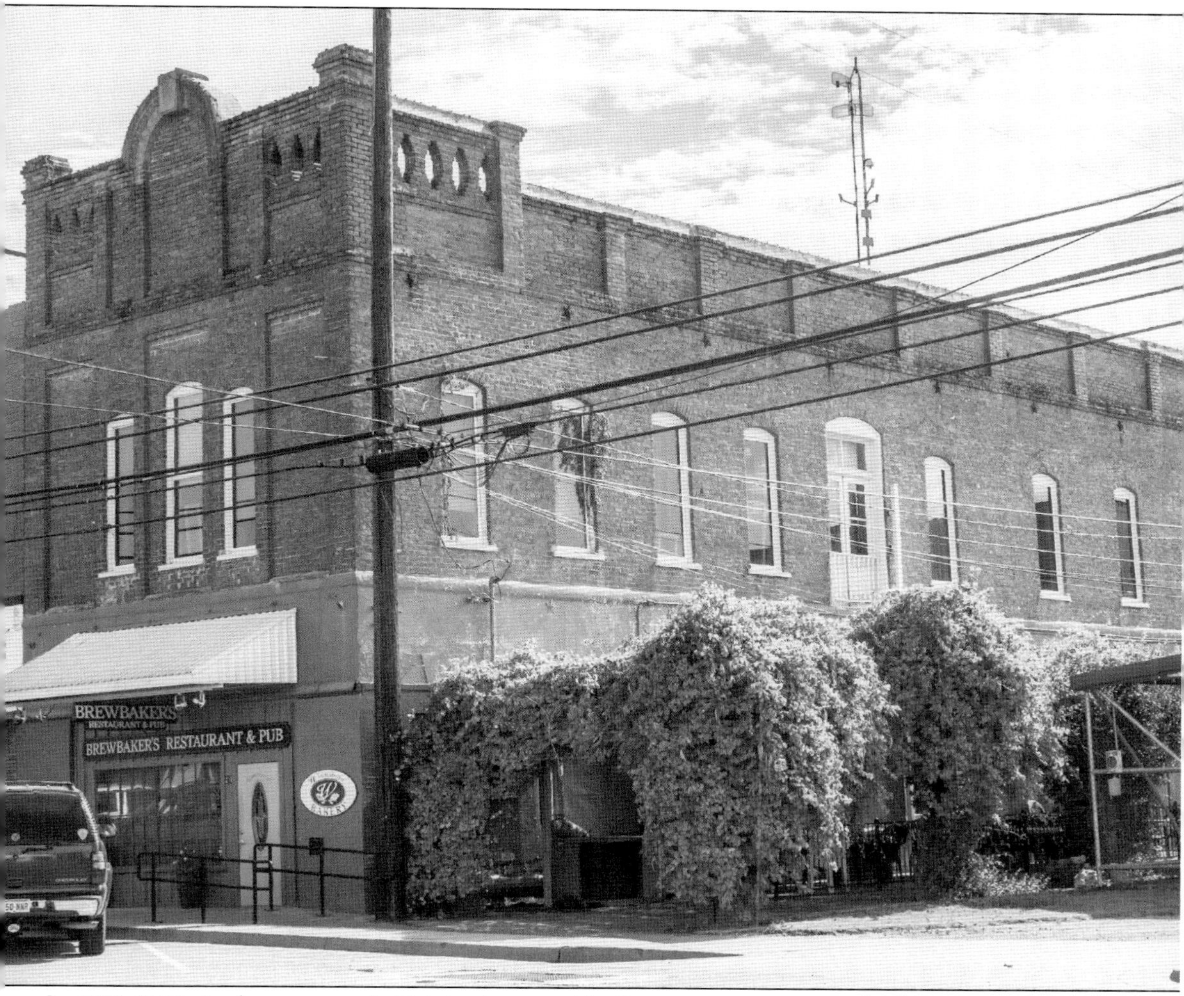

In 1901, R.G. Andrews expanded his business and built a spacious two-story building extending from Main to Market Streets. A crosswalk was built over the alley to connect this new building to the Andrews Building. The new building housed the Merchants and Planters State Bank (Ma & Pa Bank) until 1927. In 1928, it was the home of the Citizens State Bank for a few months, and then it became the site for the Cain Banking Company for 38 years, starting in 1929. In the early morning hours of August 29, 1949, the original Andrews Building burned to the ground, but this other building was spared. It fell into disrepair for a few years when the Cain Bank closed in 1977 but was later fully restored and became the Winnsboro Bakery. Now, it is the home of Brewbakers Pub. (Courtesy of the *Winnsboro News.*)

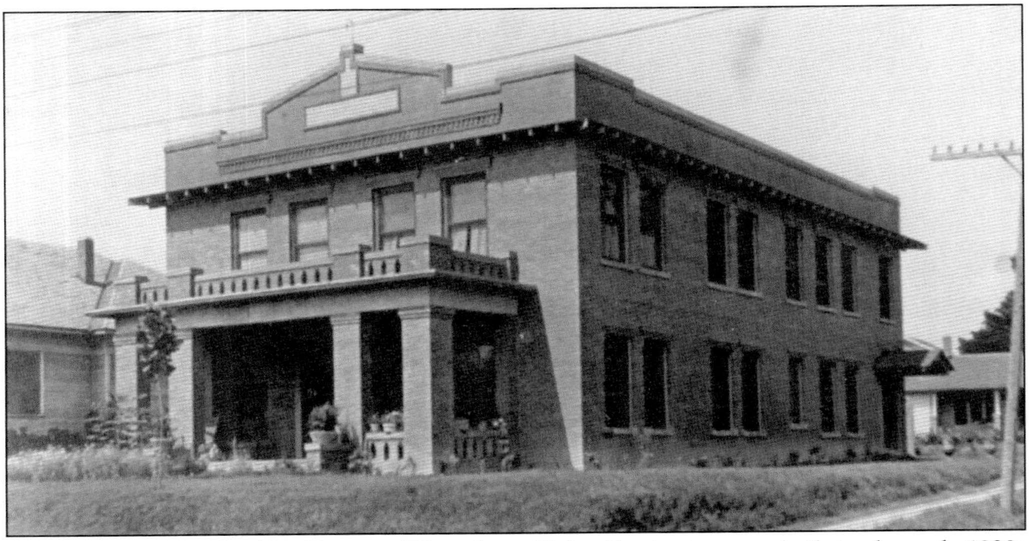

One of the first medical buildings in Winnsboro, Baber Sanitarium was built in the early 1930s and operated by Dr. George Baber. The building is now Main Place Apartments but was used as a hospital until the late 1950s or early 1960s. Dr. George Baber's brother Dr. Will Baber also had a hospital on West Myrtle Street. (Courtesy of the *Winnsboro News.*)

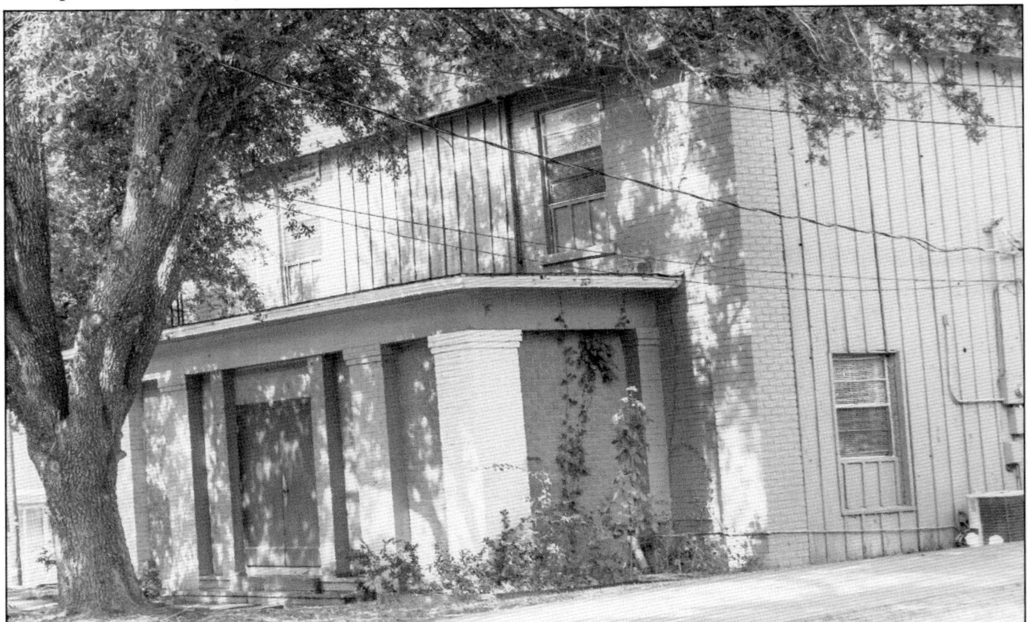

A house on South Main Street that was built by Hardee Russell around 1900 was sold to Dr. Will Baber about 1914. Will was a brother to George Baber, who had the Baber Sanitarium on North Main Street. Will Baber discovered the parasite that causes yellow fever. He did so much research they would call him from Johns Hopkins and the University of Chicago. The house served as clinic, and Dr. Baber did his surgery on the screened-in front porch. The light was best around nine in the morning. He was one of most well-known medical doctors to come from Winnsboro. (Courtesy of the *Winnsboro News.*)

Dr. Robert T. Dickey was a well-respected doctor in Winnsboro, and the community was devastated when he was killed in car accident in 1936. His father was a doctor in Quitman. (Courtesy of the *Winnsboro News*.)

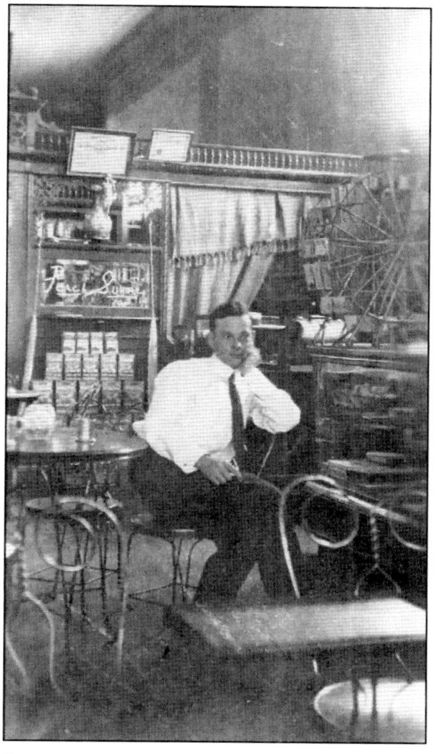

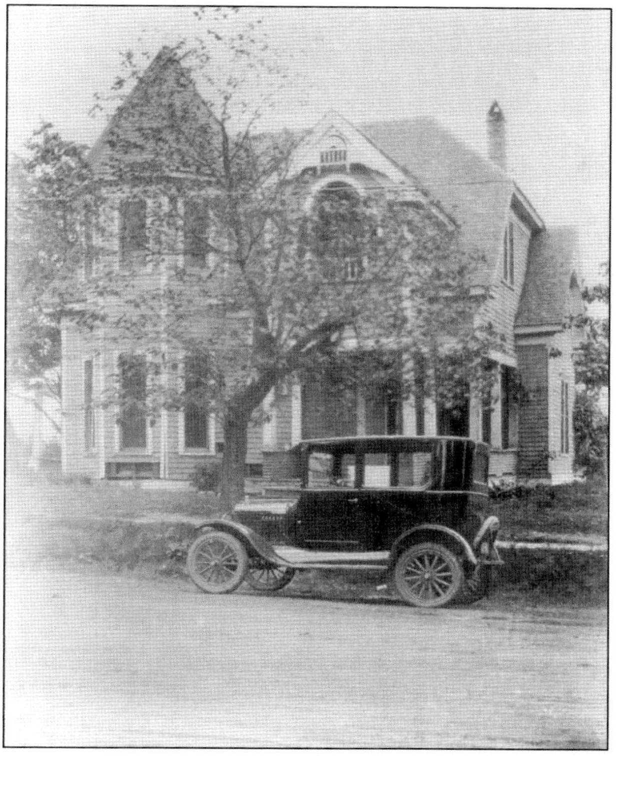

Dr. C.E. Eskridge had a home on North Main Street where he practiced medicine. He was the first doctor in Winnsboro to perform abdominal surgery. After Dr. Eskridge died, his wife, Anna, married M.D. Carlock Sr., and she was the mother of M.D Carlock Jr. Dr. Eskridge was born in 1863 and died in 1905 at the age of 42. (Courtesy of the *Winnsboro News*.)

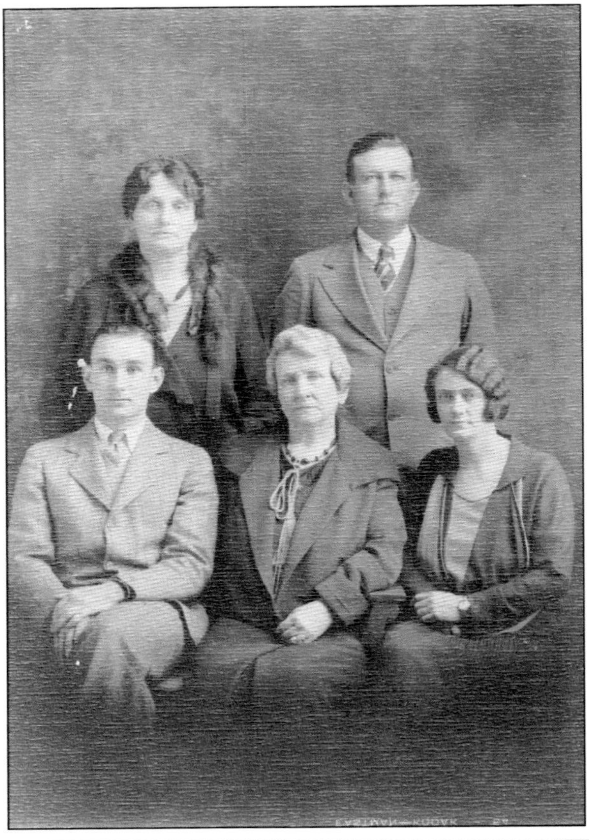

The man seated is M.D. Carlock Sr., and the woman to the right of his is Dr. Dickey's wife, Lucy. The woman beside her is unidentified. Standing are Mrs. Alf Morris (Craigie) and Dr. Eskridge. They were very prominent Winnsboro residents in the early 1900s, active in civic and community affairs. (Courtesy of Bill Jones.)

Dr. Titus Skeen came here from Georgia after the Civil War and practiced medicine in his home. A well-respected man in town, Dr. Skeen constructed the town's first medical clinic. All of his children except one died in infancy, but he adopted two girls. Anita Thompson's great-grandfather, Dr. Skeen was born in 1843 and died in 1919. (Courtesy of Anita Thompson.)

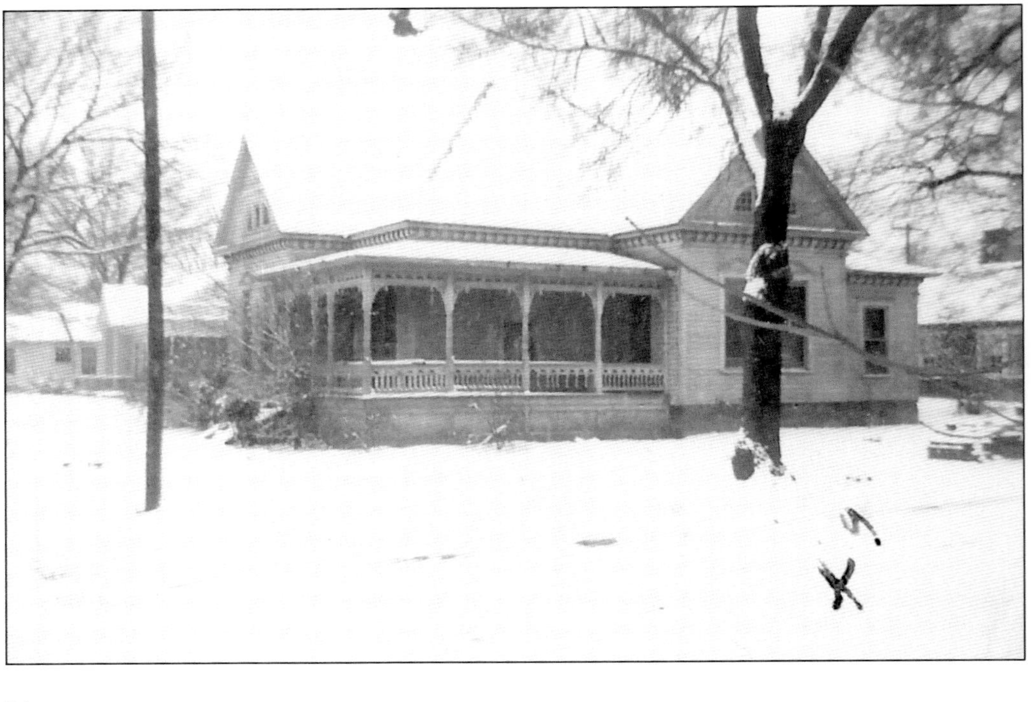

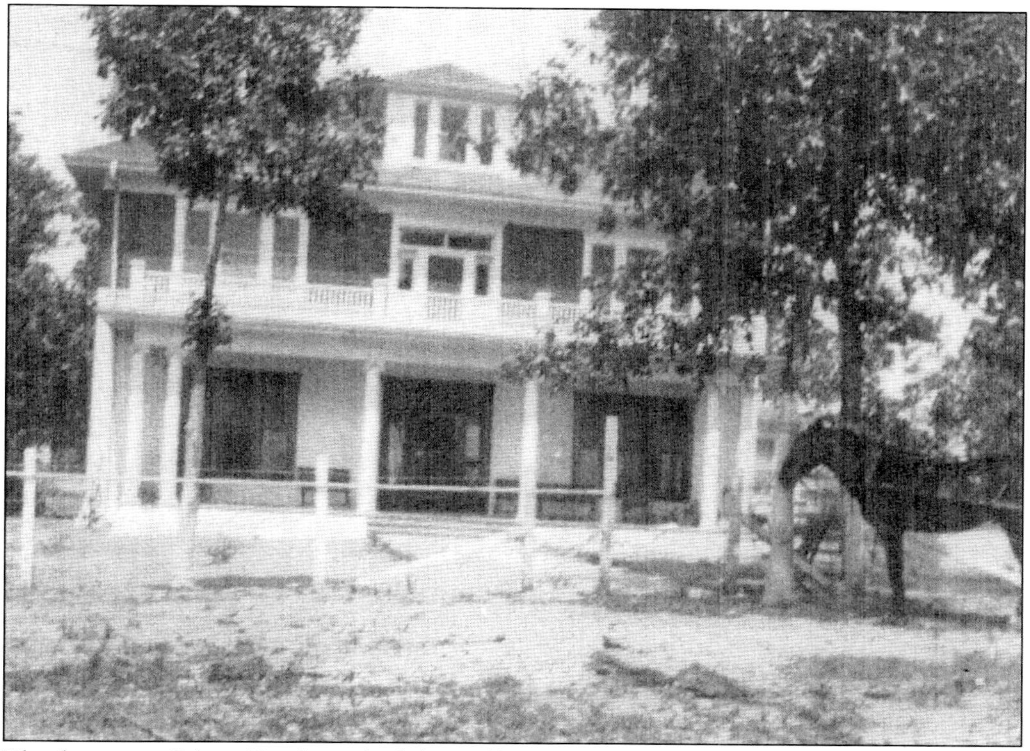

This home on Gilmer Road was built by Will Gorman, one of the early well-known property owners in Winnsboro. He had one of the brickyards in town and was also in the gin business. Like Charlie Moore, who owned the other brickyard, Will Gorman had a large family and owned considerable property around town. He was born in 1860 and died in 1939. His wife, Mattie, died in 1922. (Courtesy of the *Winnsboro News*.)

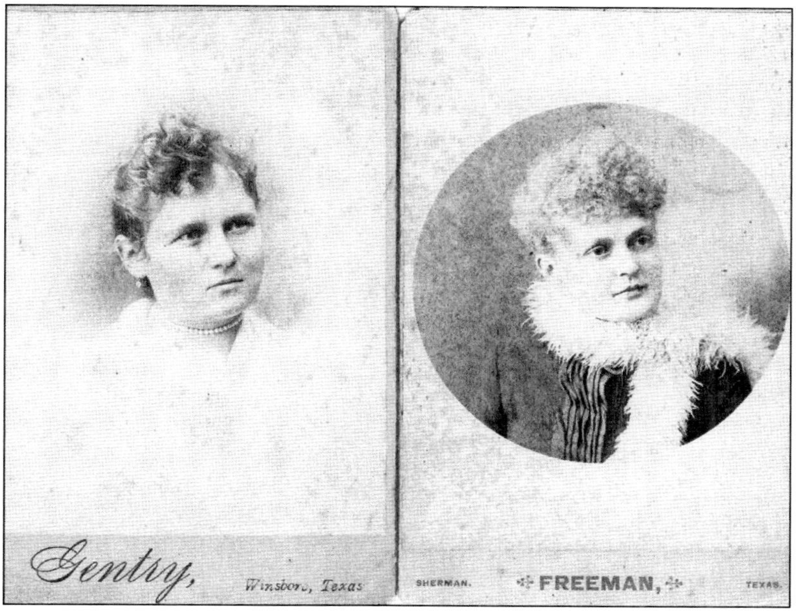

Valla Faye Robinson (left) was a piano teacher in Winnsboro, and Nolly Gorman was Will Gorman's daughter. Nolly married Dr. Claude T. Vickers, and they lived at North Main and Pine Streets in a two-story house Dr. Vickers used as an office and hospital for several years. (Courtesy of Bill Jones.)

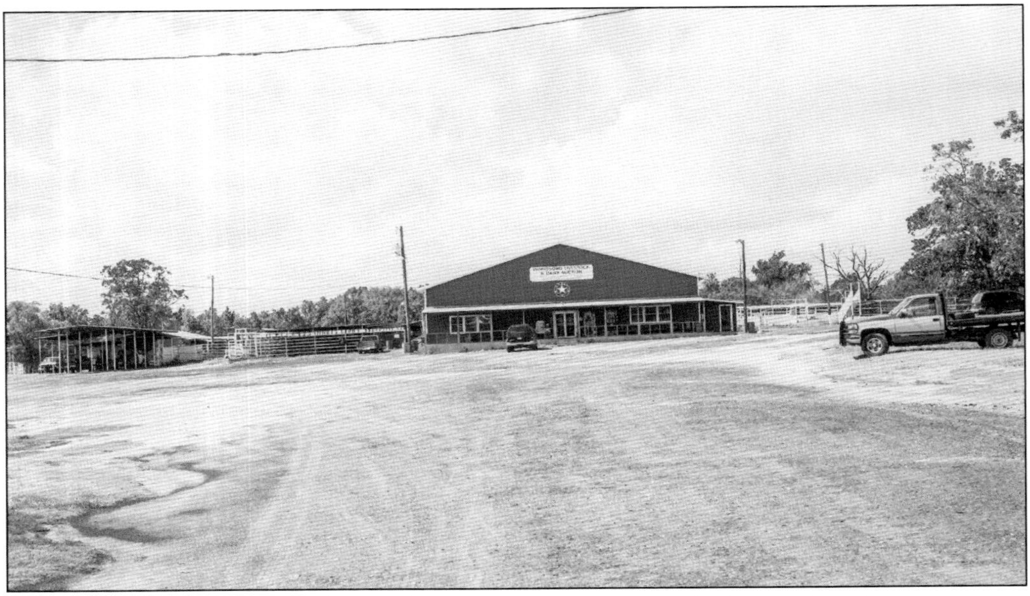

Winnsboro did not have a market for the sale of livestock until 1938. Before then, it was necessary to ship animals to markets in other cities. Ralph Robinson and Will Rushing opened Winnsboro's first livestock sale barn on Farm-to-Market 852 West. The barn changed hands a few times, and in 1952, a bigger barn was built on State Highway 11 East. The new facility, which is still operating, can handle 1,500 head of livestock and has seating for 500. (Courtesy of Bob Williams.)

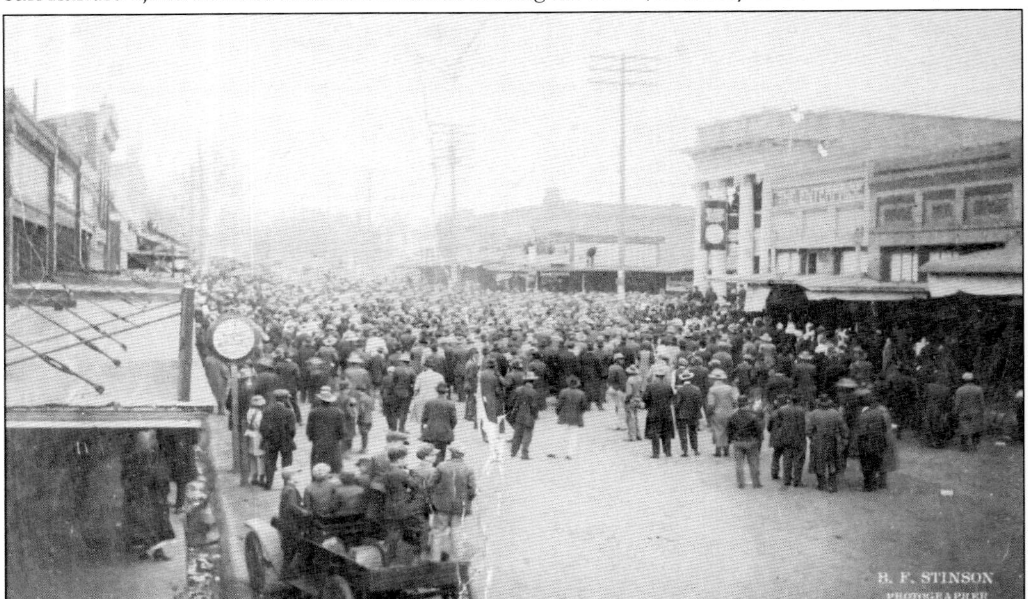

On Saturday afternoons, crowds would gather on Main Street for drawings by local merchants, who gave numbered tickets with each sale that day. The stubs were retained by the merchants and placed in a large oval hopper. Then the basket would be spun, and ticket stubs were drawn for special prizes and discounts on merchandise. This photograph was taken by B.F. Stinson, one of the early photographers to work in Winnsboro. (Courtesy of the *Winnsboro News*.)

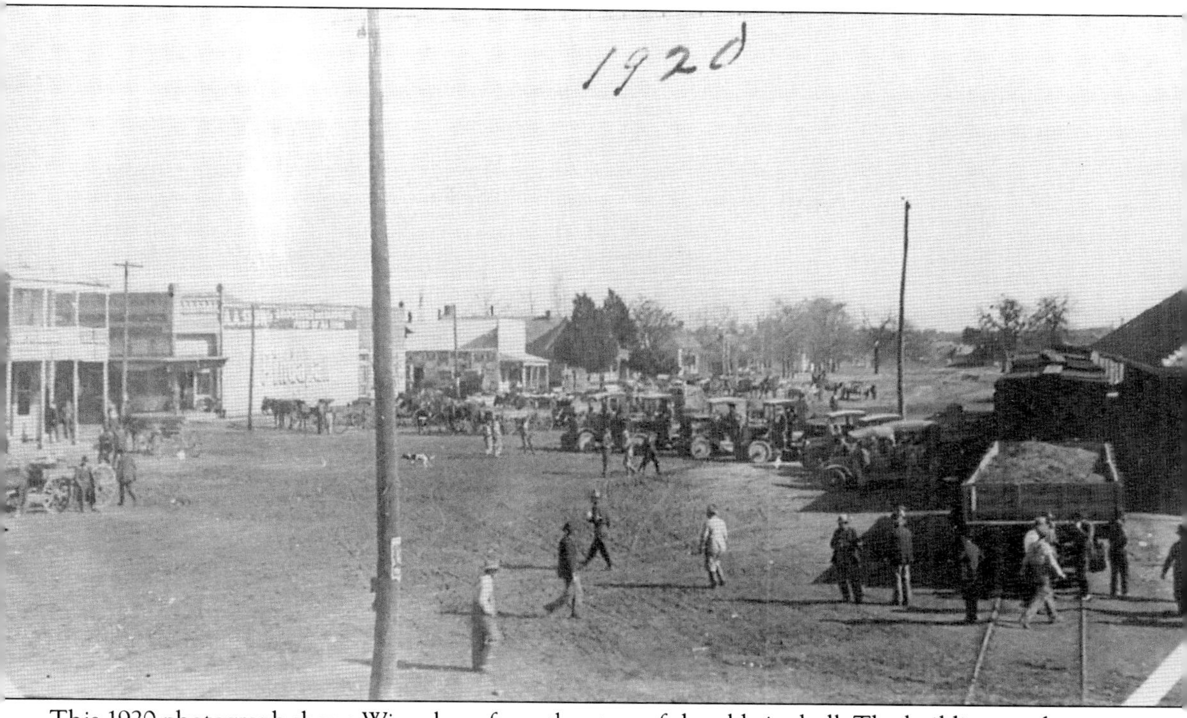

This 1920 photograph shows Winnsboro from the steps of the old city hall. The building on the far left was the Harris Saloon, which operated there until 1910. More recently, it was the home of Lou Viney Winery before it became Cibo BBQ. Between it and the next building was an alley street known as "the market street." The name was later officially changed to Market Street. The Massel Saloon was on the next corner. The building was constructed by Will Gorman, and it currently houses the Winnsboro Center for the Arts. That building backs up to Franklin Street (Smoky Row). The next building was a grocery store with a produce packing shed in the back. It later became the Winnsboro Hotel. Broadway (Highway 11) ended at the Beech Street intersection, and the open area served as a wagon yard. (Courtesy of the *Winnsboro News*.)

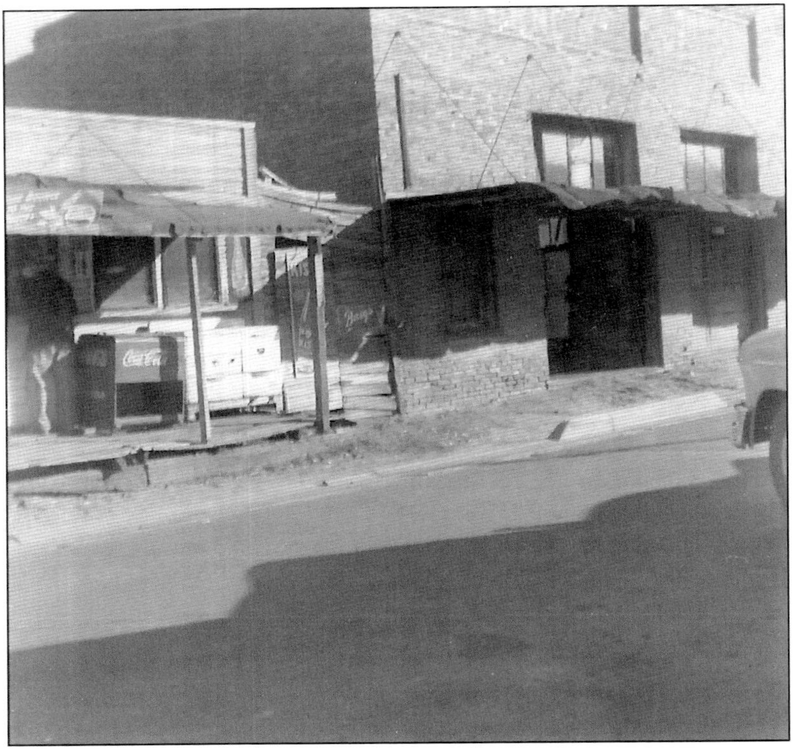

The Black Cat Café was a popular eating place in Winnsboro. It was rumored that unsavory people would sometimes hang out at the café, so other folks tended to avoid it. (Courtesy of the *Winnsboro News*.)

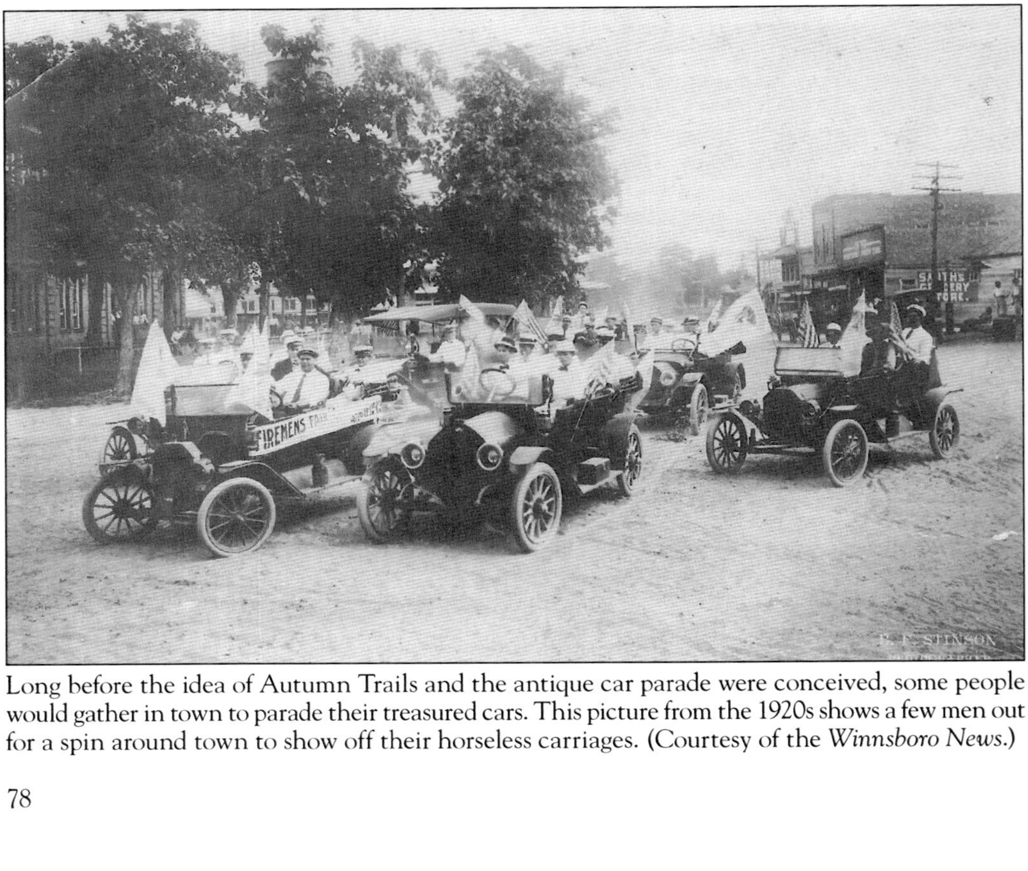

Long before the idea of Autumn Trails and the antique car parade were conceived, some people would gather in town to parade their treasured cars. This picture from the 1920s shows a few men out for a spin around town to show off their horseless carriages. (Courtesy of the *Winnsboro News*.)

Four

Then and Now

The charm of a small town can often be found in the historic old buildings that have been restored. There is something endearing about the businesses and homes that have so many memories attached to them. These are just a sampling of the old homes that have been restored to their former glory. They were once the homes or businesses of prominent Winnsboro residents, and a number of them have been purchased by people who have moved here from the Dallas area. They came to Winnsboro for the same reason the early settlers did—the town sits in a beautiful area of East Texas and offers a chance to experience the quiet rural life.

Many of the people who have relocated to Winnsboro left high-level corporate jobs for new opportunities in Winnsboro. Such was the case of artist Barbara Richert and her business partner, Barbara Hums, who purchased the old Andrews Building and restored it to open the Winnsboro Bakery in the mid-1990s.

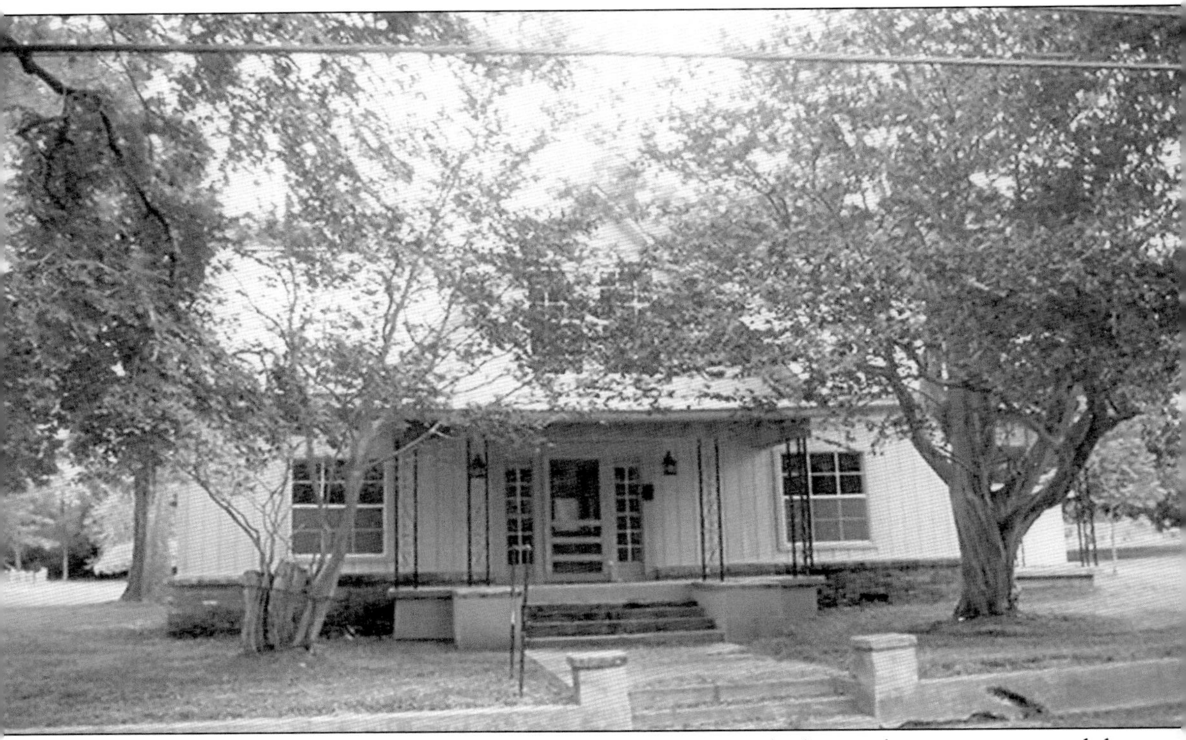

This 136-year-old home started out as a church in 1872. Several religious denominations used the building for services, and the bell was rung to announce funerals, weddings, fires, and religious and public meetings. Later, the building was purchased by Henry Mitchell and moved to 404 West Pine Street. Tom and Marie Wyatt acquired the property in 1958 and lived there until 2007, when the home was sold to Carol Snodgrass Reeves, who restored the home. (Courtesy of Bob Williams.)

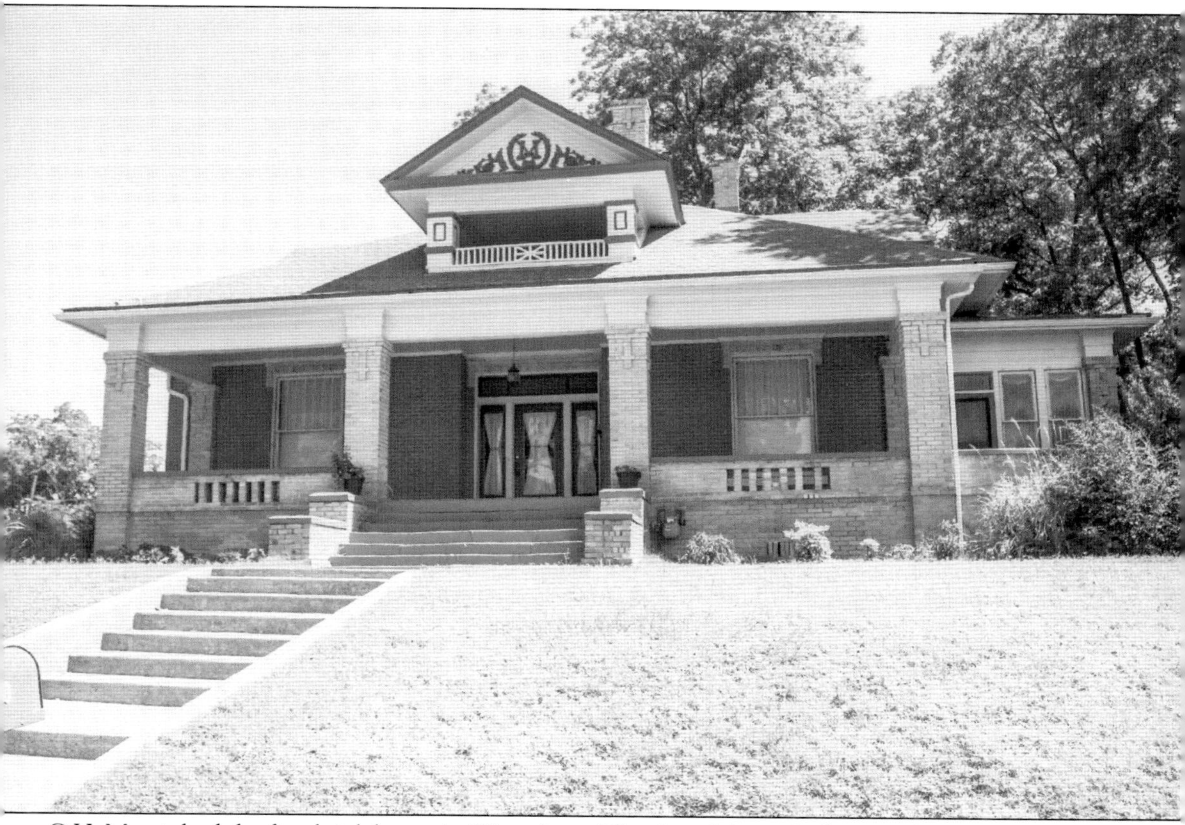

C.H. Morris had the first brick house in Winnsboro. The three Ms on the house, which is located on the northeast corner of Church and Elm Streets, stands for Me, Myrtis (his wife), and Money. S.S. Morris, from Pittsburg, Texas, came to Winnsboro in 1893 and established the M&P Private Bank, which was the first bank in town. In 1901, it was nationalized and became First National Bank of Winnsboro. (Courtesy of Bob Williams.)

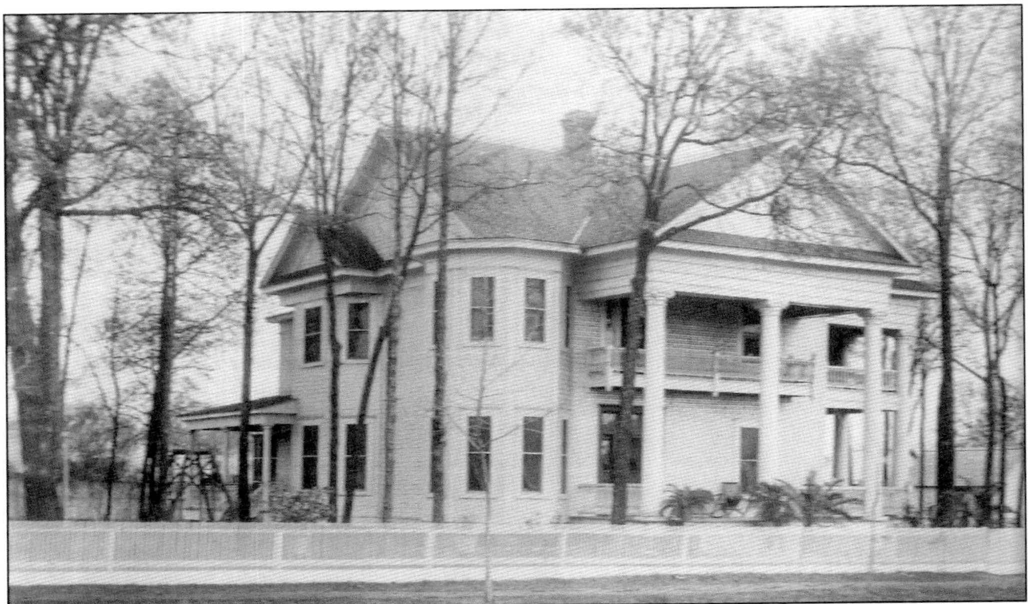

The home of Anna and M.D. Carlock Sr. on South Main Street is a familiar Winnsboro landmark. This picture was taken shortly after the lovely Victorian mansion was built in 1903. It is now the home of the Oaklea Mansion, a bed-and-breakfast owned by Norma Wilkerson. The old carriage house has been turned into a meeting room. (Above, courtesy of the *Winnsboro News*; below, courtesy of Bob Williams.)

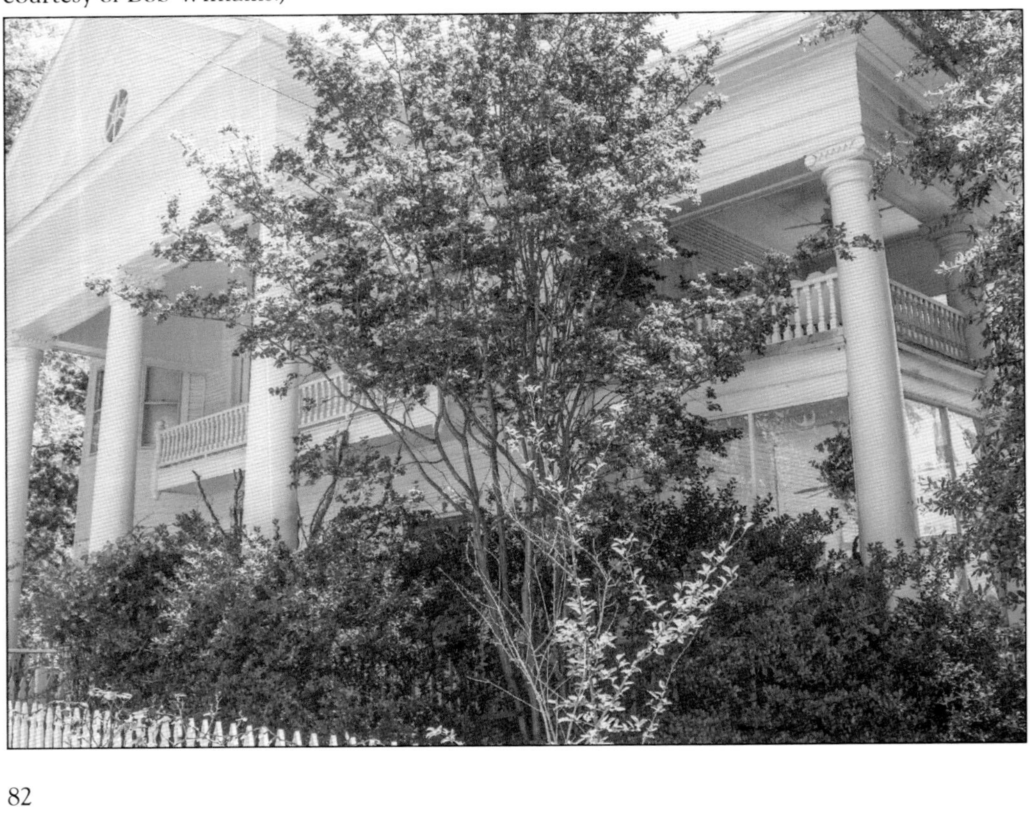

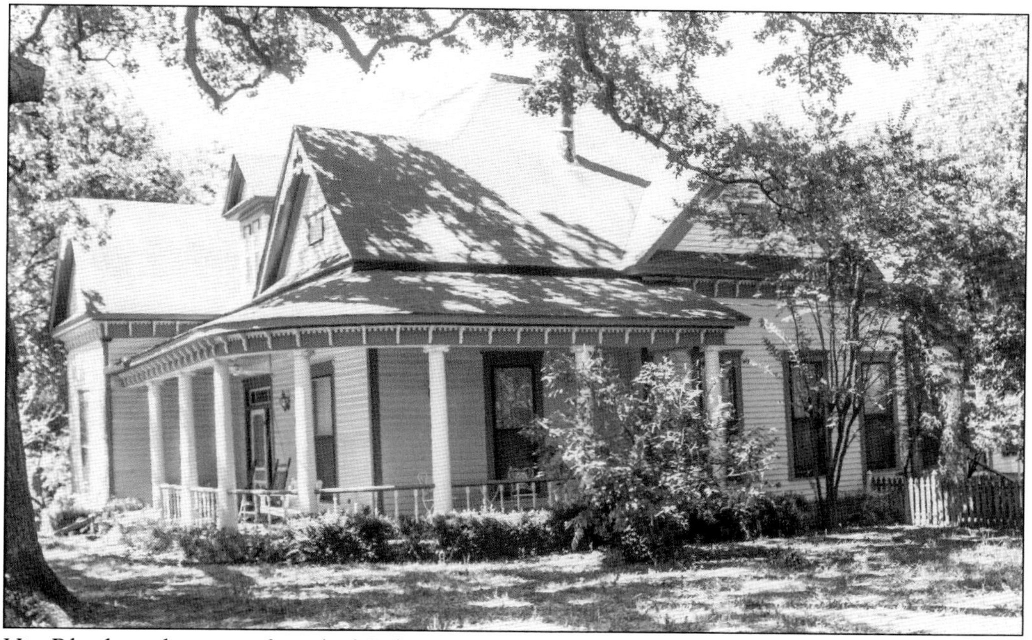

Hix Rhodes, who was a friend of Col. James A. Stinson, built this beautifully restored home in 1904. The house was the old Southerland home for many years before it was sold to Billy Joe Parnell in the 1980s. (Courtesy of Bob Williams.)

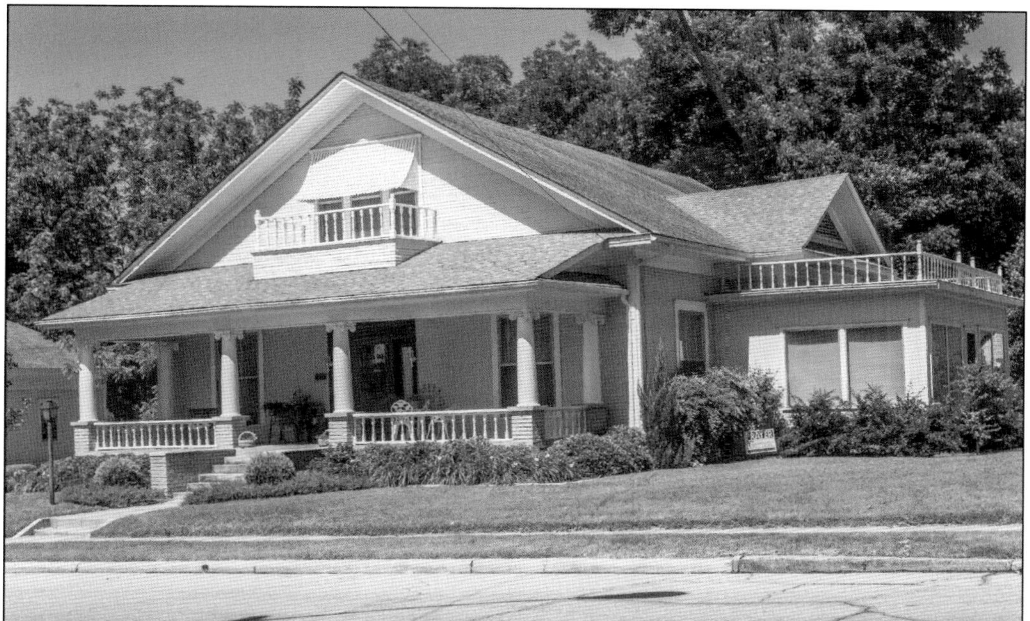

Bob Wilkinson was a hardware merchant in Winnsboro at the turn of the century. He built a home at the southwest corner of Church and West Elm Streets that was sold in 1913 to R.G. Andrews, who completely remodeled it and made it into one of the more fashionable homes in Winnsboro. James and Sallie Lucy Andrews Old lived there until the 1980s. (Courtesy of Bob Williams.)

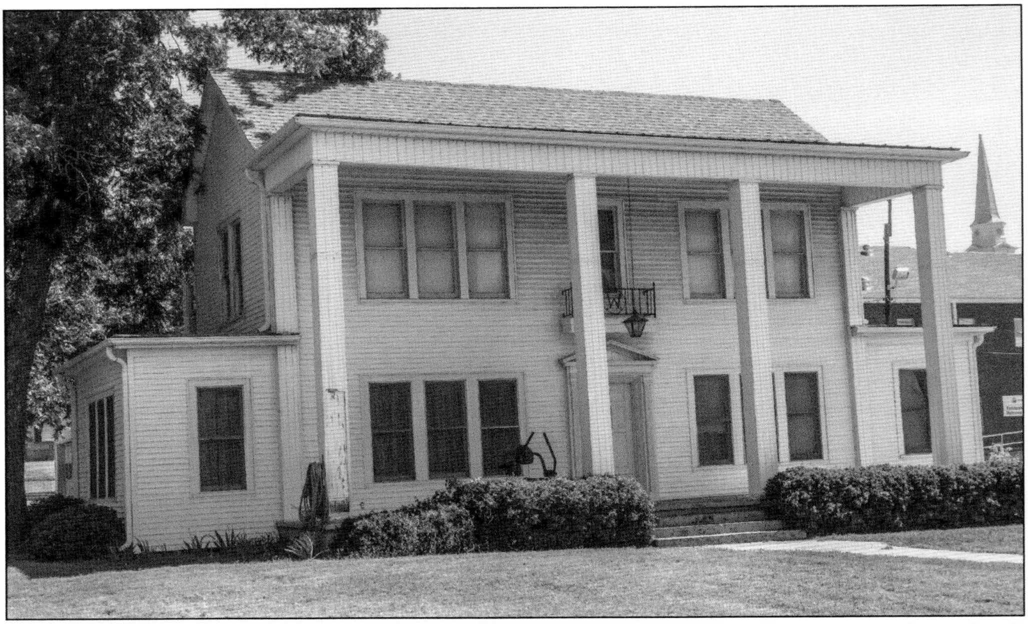

Built in 1926, this home was originally owned by Ivan Wright, who was the manager of an oil mill from 1926 to the early 1980s. His daughter Martha Wright married Dr. Bob Craddock, who had a practice in Carthage, Texas. Bob Craddock is a cousin to Sue Craddock Hamm. There used to be some beautiful 200-to-300-year-old trees out front. (Courtesy of Bob Williams.)

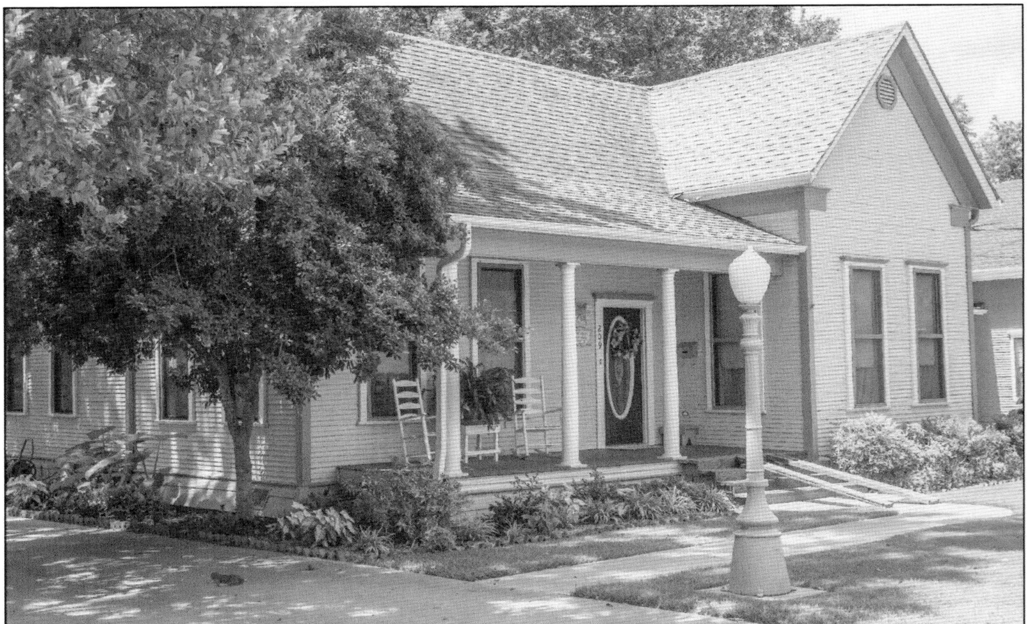

Myrtle Street was the social center of Winnsboro in the early 1900s. Many of the homes there have been beautifully restored, and the street has been declared a historical district. This home owned by Dwayne Redding, brother of Wayne Redding, is a wonderful example of the beautiful homes in this district. (Courtesy of Bob Williams.)

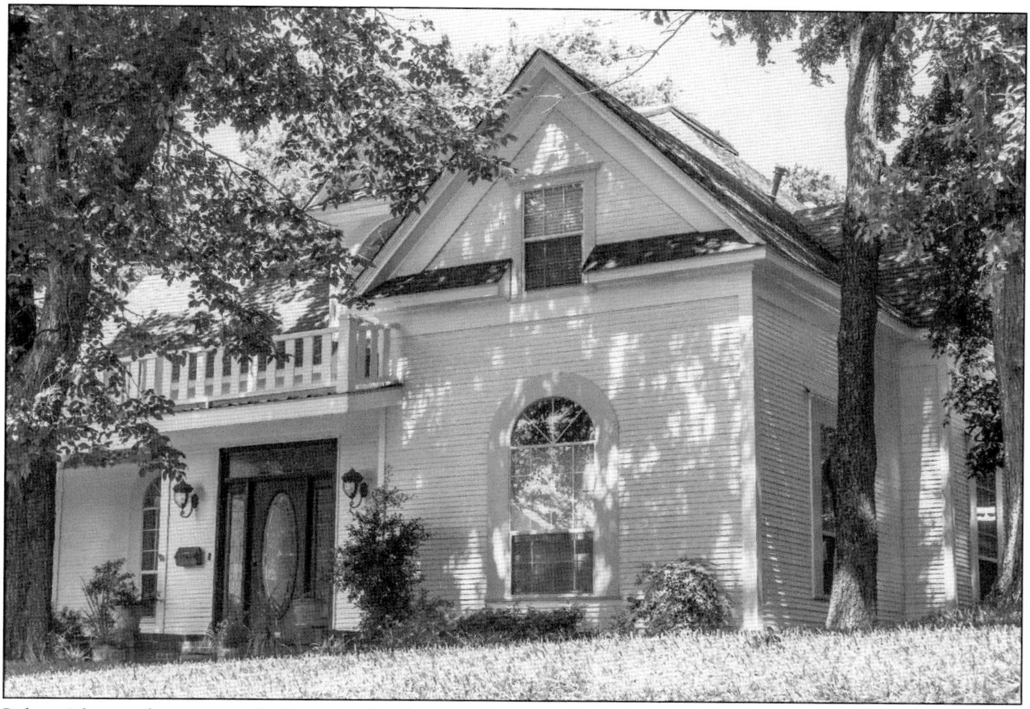

John Alexander currently lives in this home that was built by a Mr. Colquitt in 1903. His brother Oscar Branch Colquitt was governor of Texas in 1907. The home was later owned by Red Newman, and Steve Newman was raised there. John bought it early 1980s and did an immaculate job restoring it. (Courtesy of Bob Williams.)

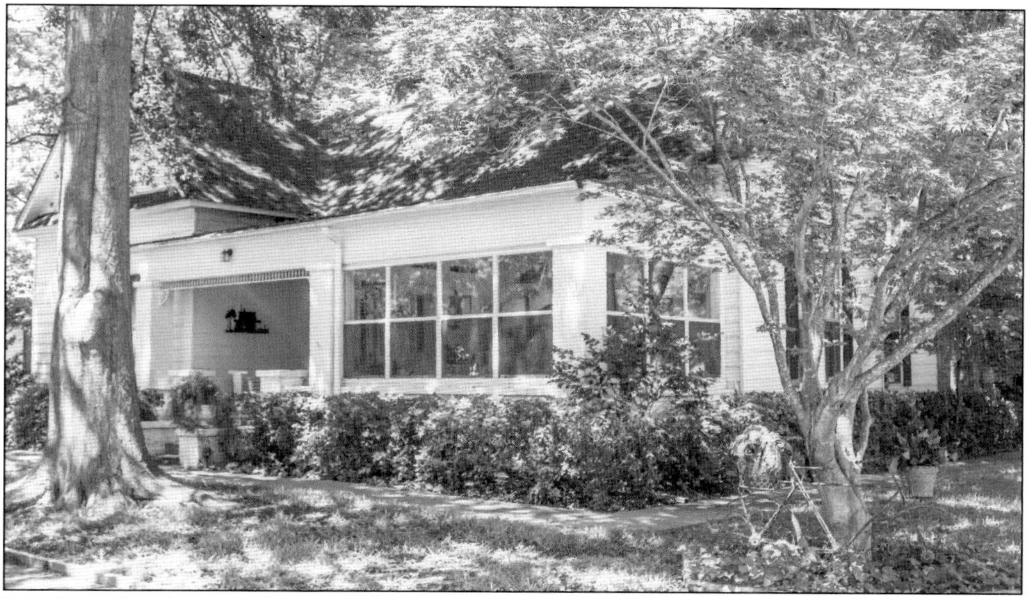

R.B. Howell, who was a lawyer and two-time mayor of Winnsboro, built this house in the early 1900s. Howell, along with Charles Morris, was largely responsible for getting the Carnegie library in Winnsboro. R.B. Howell was a town leader and greatly respected. (Courtesy of Bob Williams.)

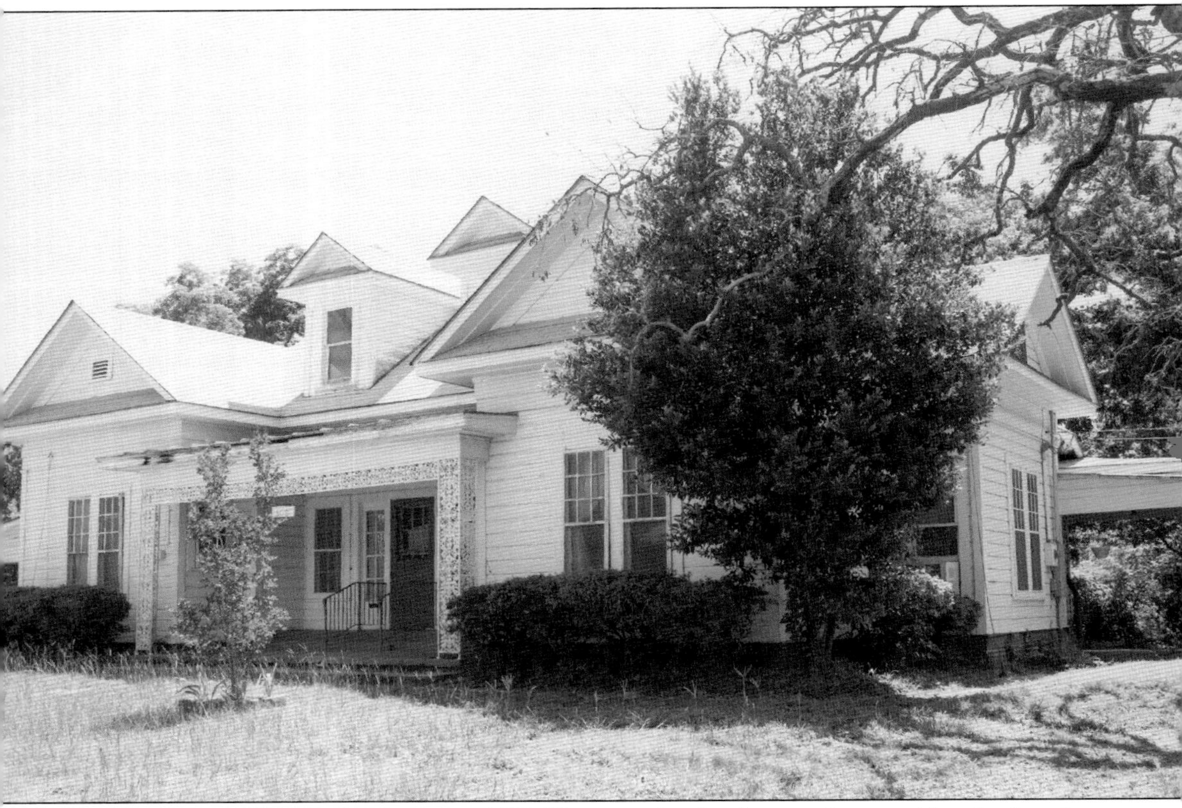

B.F. Campbell built this home in 1912. He was a lumber baron who considered education so important that he made sure his five girls went to college. They all had teacher's certificates, and one daughter, Leola, taught in Winnsboro. Locals remember going to his place on a summer day to get watermelon. (Courtesy of Bob Williams.)

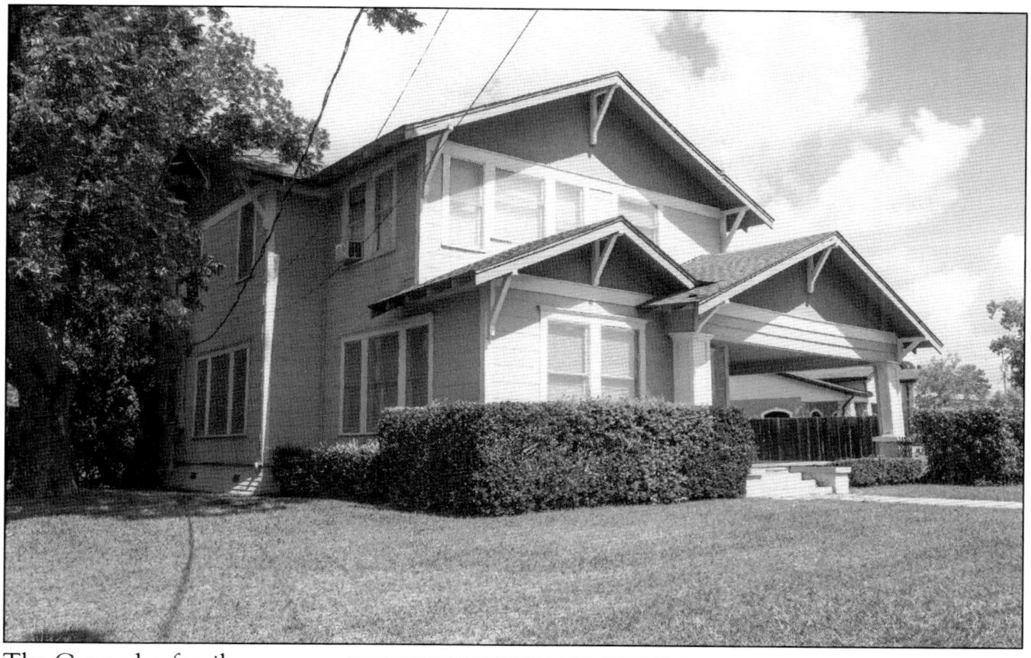

The Cannaday family came from Purly in 1879, soon after Winnsboro was settled. Henry Cannaday opened a dry goods store in 1907 and passed in on to his son Russell. This home was built in the early 1900s, and Henry F. Cannaday, DDS, lives there now. (Both, courtesy of Bob Williams.)

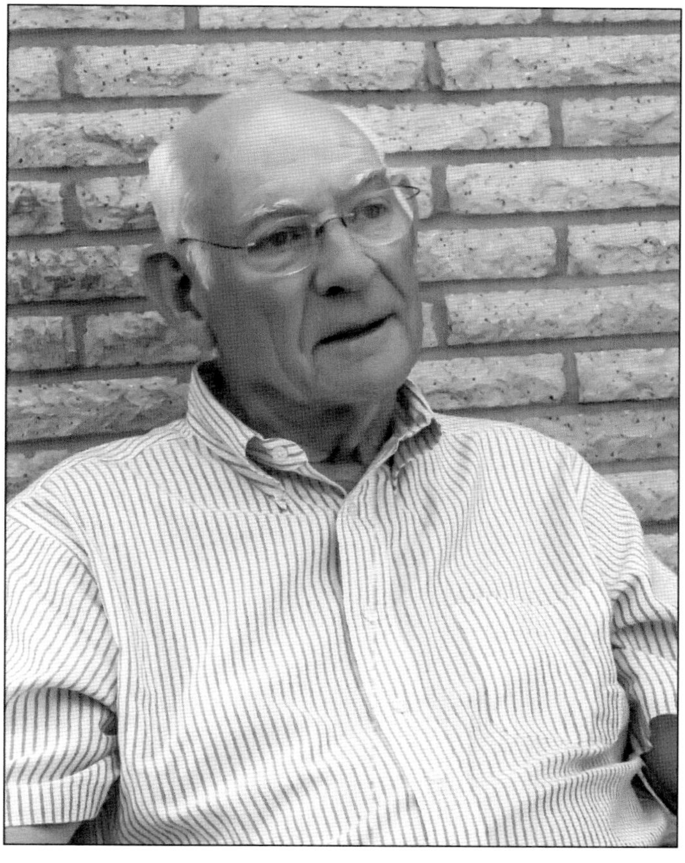

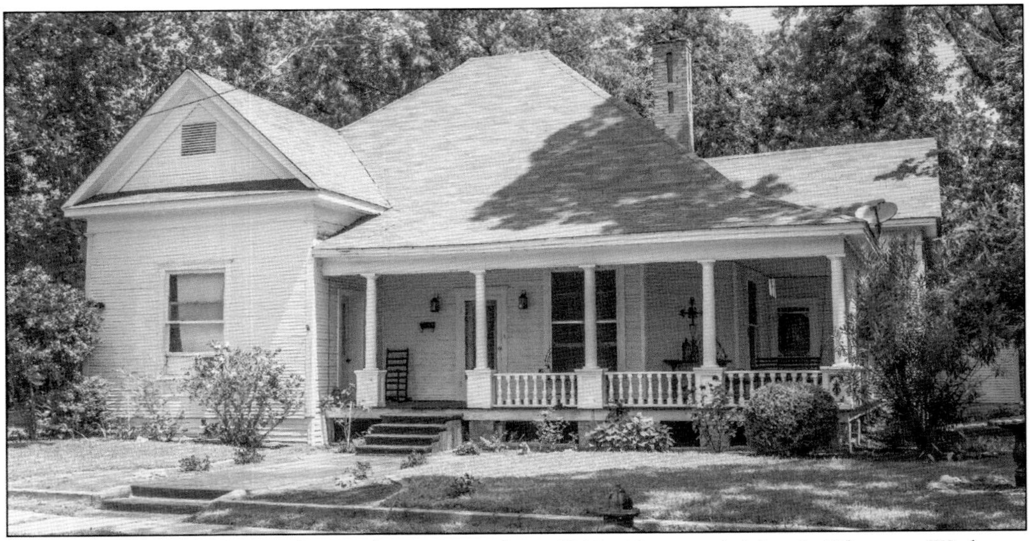

This home was built by Wick Worthington in about 1910. Along with Marvin Thomas, Wick was instrumental in starting the first chamber of commerce in Winnsboro. This house is representative of the fashionable homes around town in that era. (Courtesy of Bob Williams.)

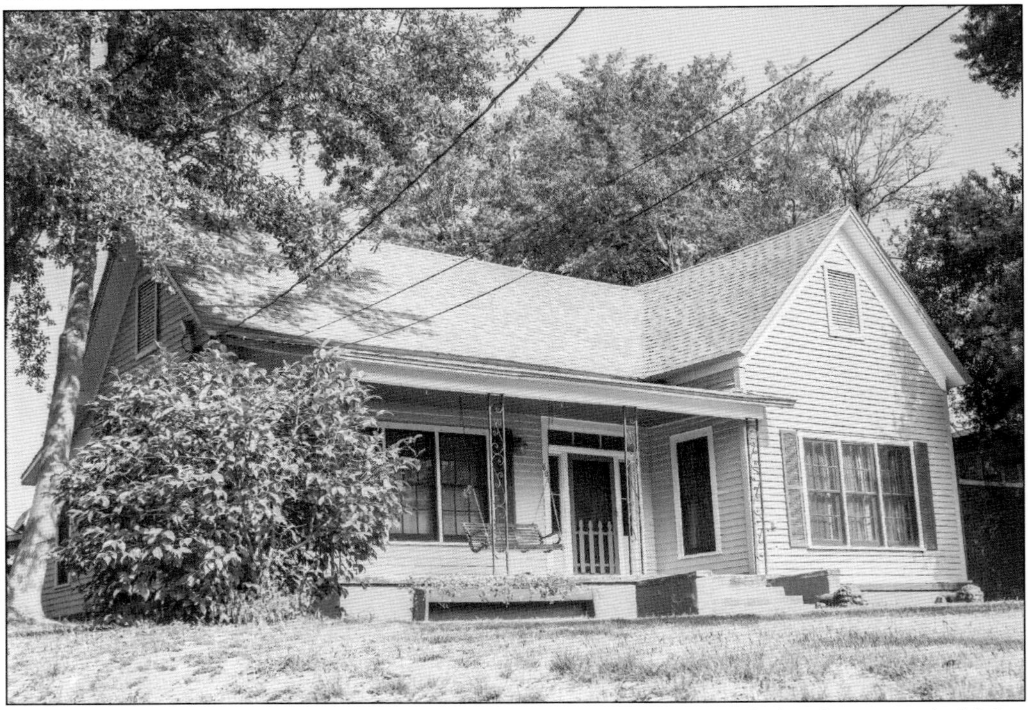

In 1909, Will Suiter was elected mayor of Winnsboro, and with the help of city marshal John Cain, Suiter closed all the saloons. During Suiter's tenure, the city saw improvements in streets, and the plank sidewalks in the business district were replaced with concrete walks. Suiter served as mayor until 1914 and then was elected as a state senator. He held that office for eight years. His daughter Elizabeth Suiter served in the Texas legislature. She had a successful law practice, was a civic leader, and also served as mayor of Winnsboro. (Courtesy of Bob Williams.)

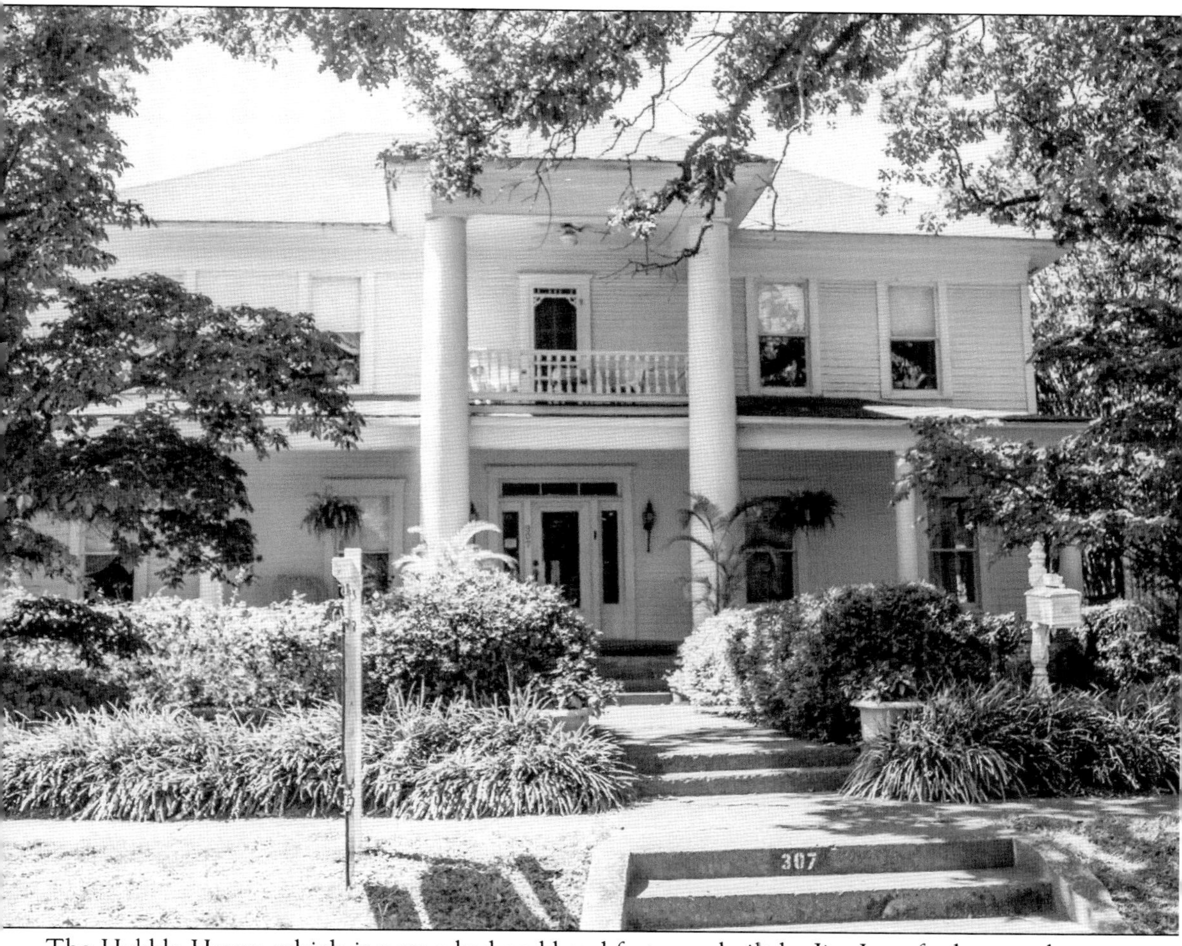

The Hubble House, which is now a bed-and-breakfast, was built by Jim Langford, an early Winnsboro merchant and developer. In 1906, Langford moved and sold the house to James Stinson. Stinson's daughter Sallie was married to James Stephen Hogg, who was governor of Texas from 1890 to 1895. After changing hands several times, the house was purchased by Dan Hubble, a Baptist minister, who turned it into a bed-and-breakfast. He later sold the bed-and-breakfast to Tim Carmichael. Dan Hubble was pastor of First Baptist Church in Winnsboro for 10 years and also served as mayor of Winnsboro. (Courtesy of Bob Williams.)

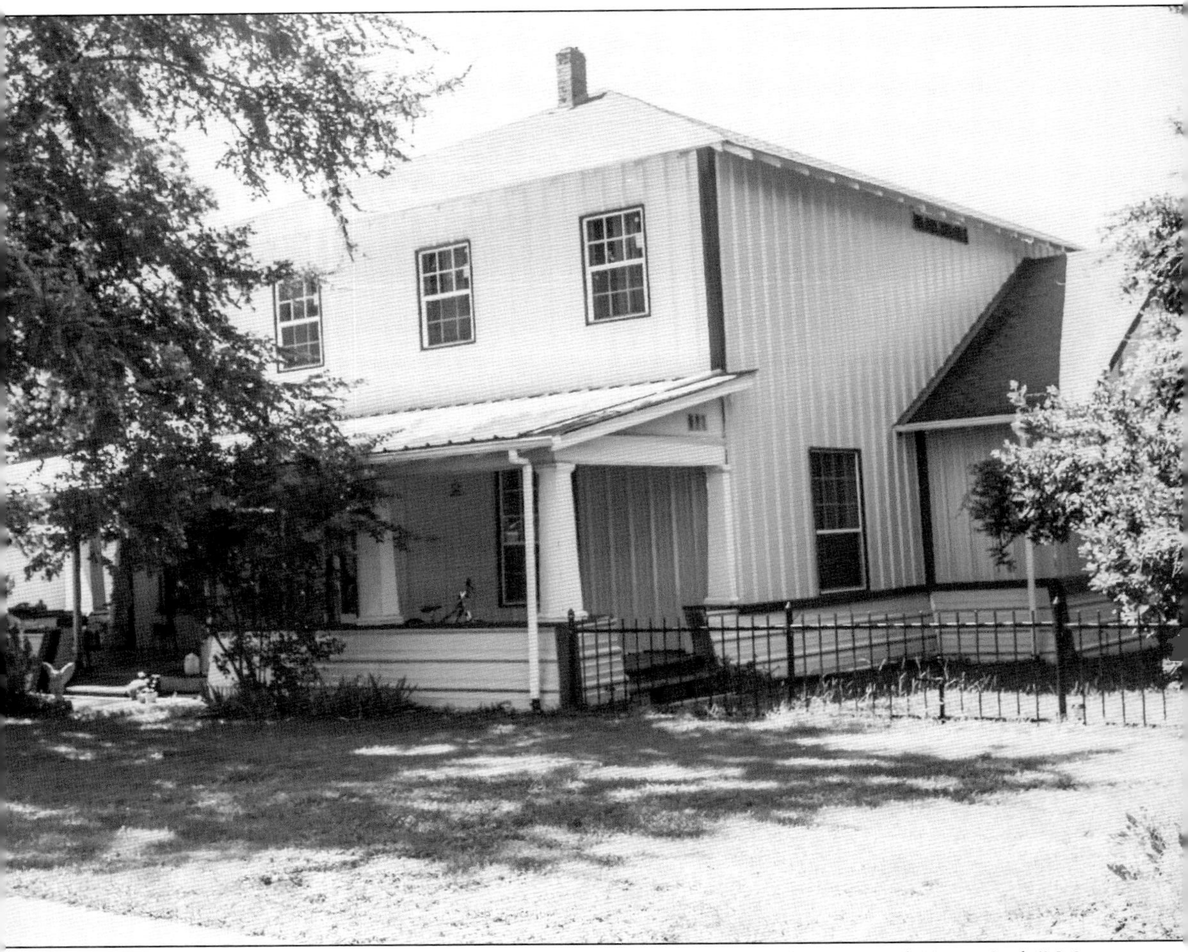

One of oldest residences in Winnsboro was the home of "Uncle Jim" and "Aunt Lula" Moore, who ran it as a boardinghouse after they sold the Moore Hotel. Rumor has it that Aunt Lula only missed serving meals three times in 44 years. Uncle Jim owned a delivery bus, and he was Winnsboro's first traffic officer, blowing a whistle at jaywalkers on Main Street. Uncle Jim died in 1943, and Aunt Lula died in 1947. (Courtesy of Bob Williams.)

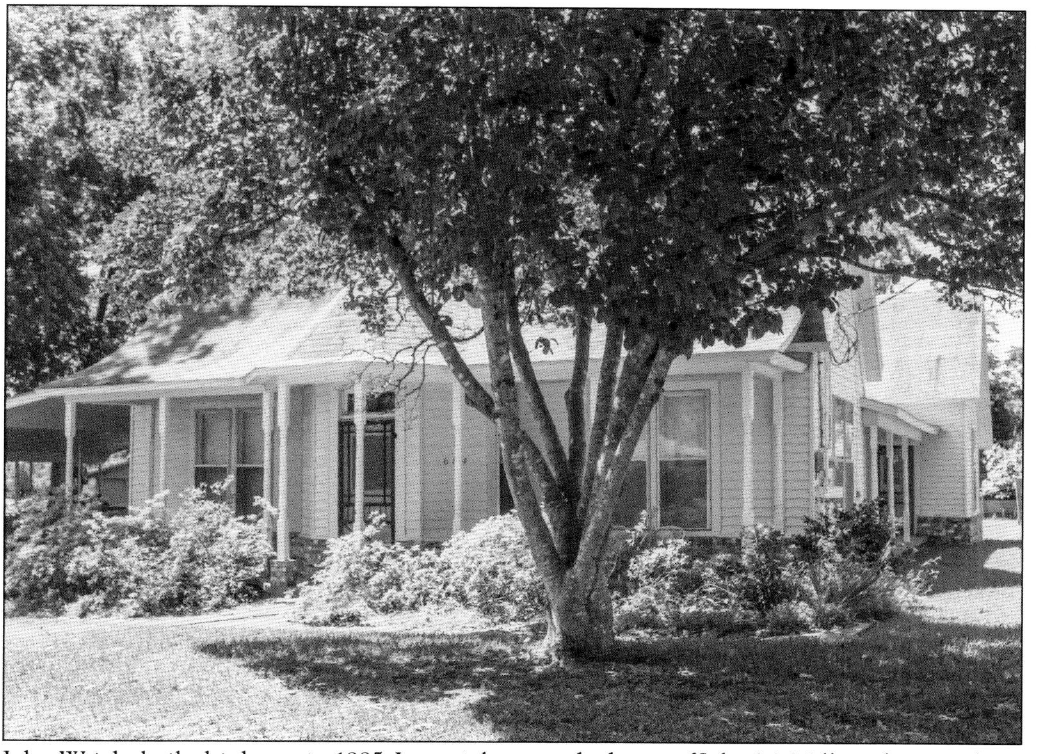

John Wright built this home in 1885. Later, it became the home of John McMillan, the son of one of the founders of Winnsboro. John lived there while he worked in Winnsboro; he later moved to Dallas. (Courtesy of Bob Williams.)

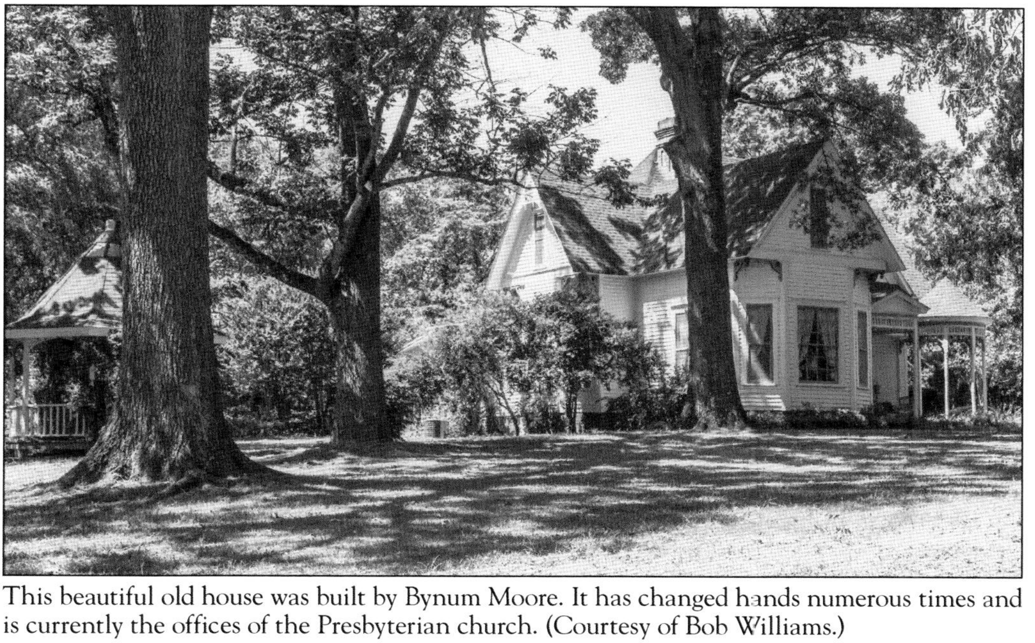

This beautiful old house was built by Bynum Moore. It has changed hands numerous times and is currently the offices of the Presbyterian church. (Courtesy of Bob Williams.)

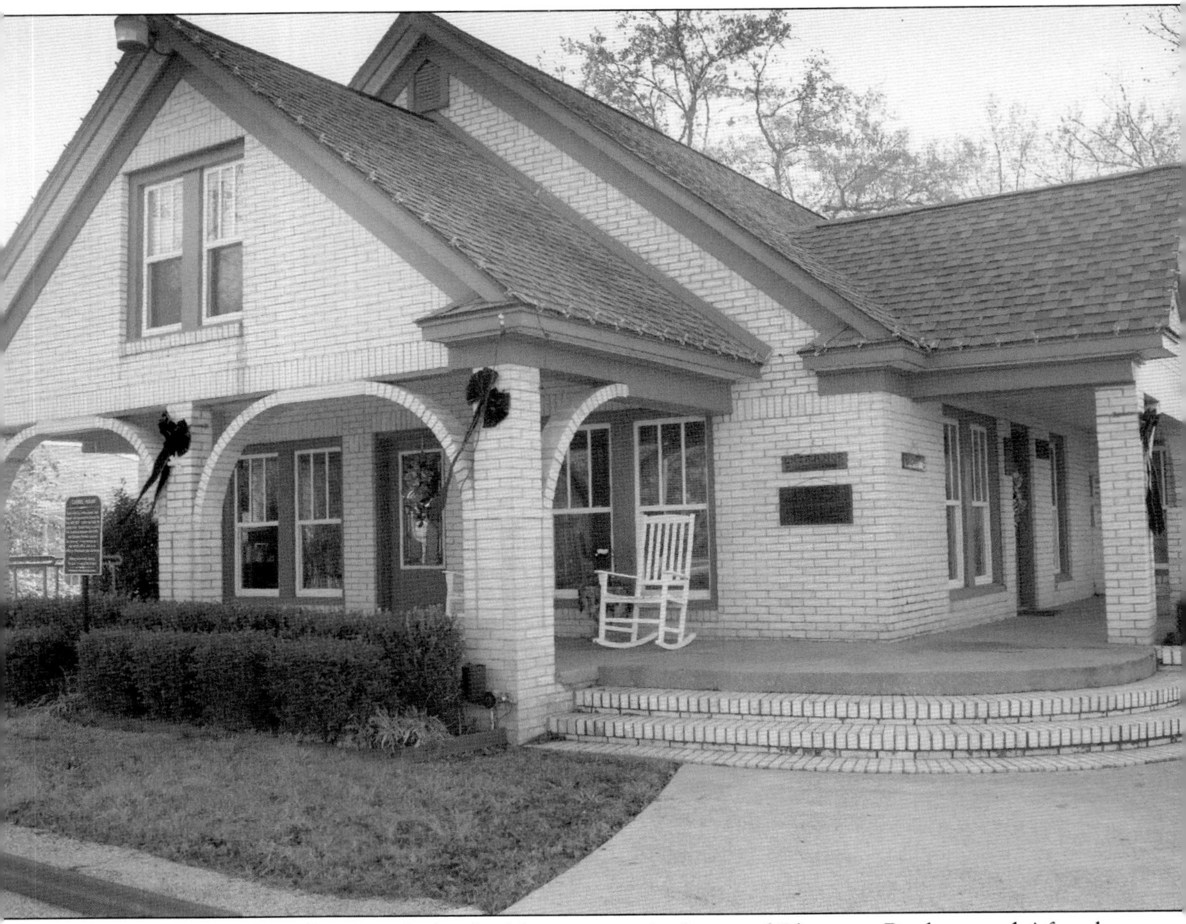

Built in 1937 by John Cassel, this building is now the home of Clements Realtors and Afterglow Productions. John Cassel operated the Cassel Gin from 1927 to 1951, a time when cotton was a major money crop in the area. The Cassel family lived in the home until 2005, when it was sold to Clements Realtors. The home was restored and refurbished and turned into offices. (Courtesy of Bob Williams.)

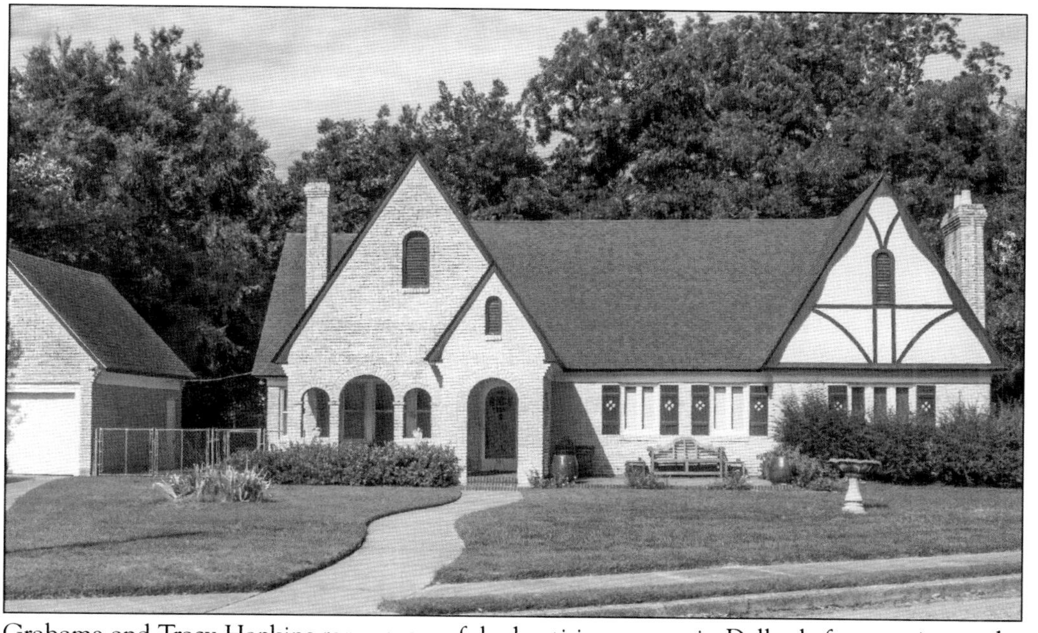

Grahame and Tracy Hopkins ran a successful advertising agency in Dallas before moving to the Winnsboro area. In 2012, they purchased this home, which once belonged to Robert Hardie (R.H.) McCrary. McCrary came to Winnsboro in 1912 and opened a hardware store on Franklin Street. Later, he bought Bob Wilkinson's hardware store, which also served as a funeral home. R.H. McCrary moved the business to its longtime Main Street location in 1932, and it was housed in that historic building until it moved to its present location at 201 East Elm Street. It is the only business in Winnsboro to have celebrated its 100th year anniversary, and the current owners, Robert and Shirley Watters, are related by marriage to the McCrary family. (Above, courtesy of Bob Williams; below, courtesy of Maryann Miller.)

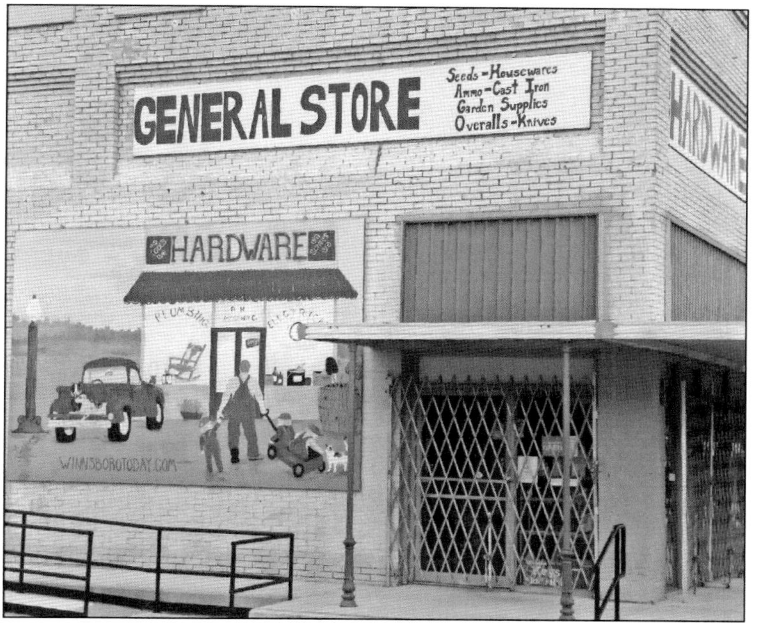

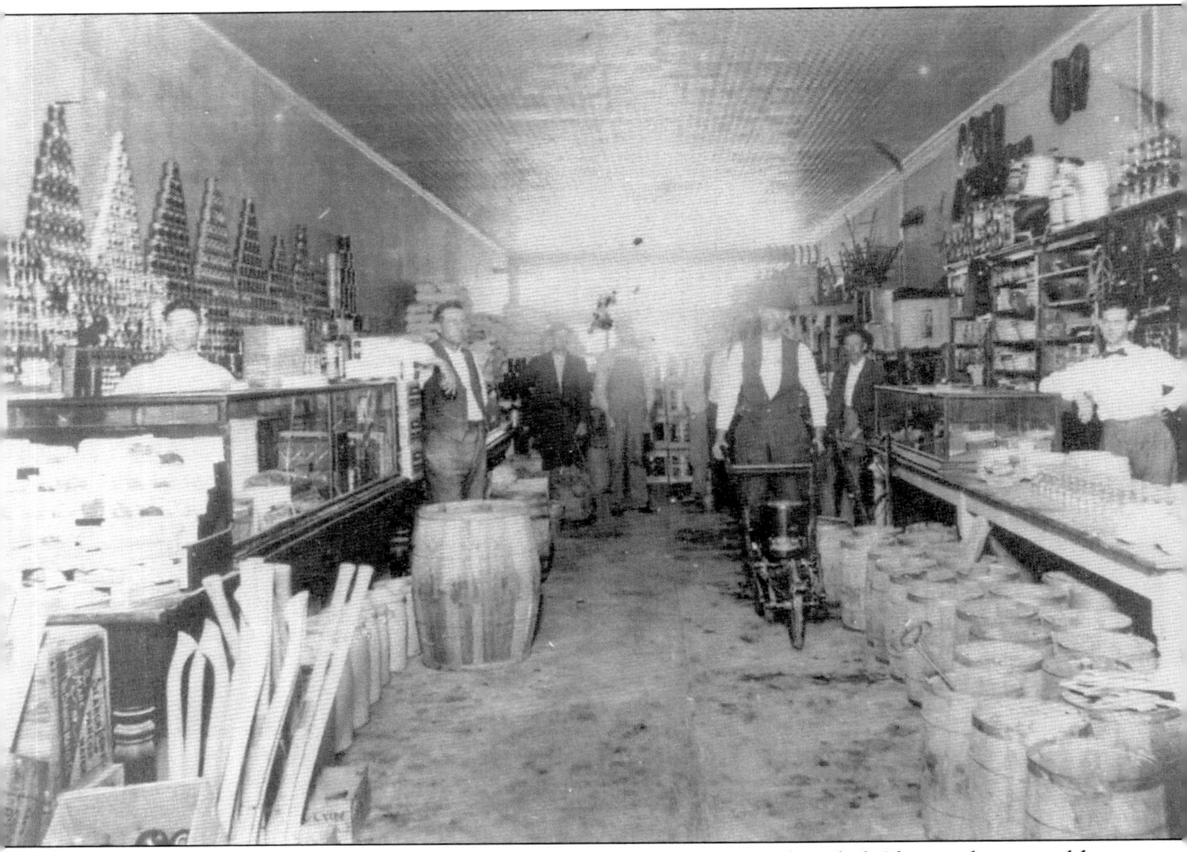

R.H. McCrary never liked to see a man leave the store empty-handed. If something could not be found at any other place in town, usually it could be located at McCrary's. In this picture of the inside of R.H. McCrary's Hardware Store, around 1912, McCrary is standing behind the counter on the right, and Charles A. Edwards is behind the counter on the left. The customers are unidentified. (Courtesy of the *Winnsboro News*.)

R.H. McCrary was noted for treating all customers the same, whether they came in the store to buy 10¢ worth of nails or an expensive bedroom suite. He would always rise from his desk in the rear of the store and greet every customer who came in. In the old days, a plow point, butter churn, harness, or wagon could be acquired at McCrary's for a reasonable price. (Courtesy of the *Winnsboro News*.)

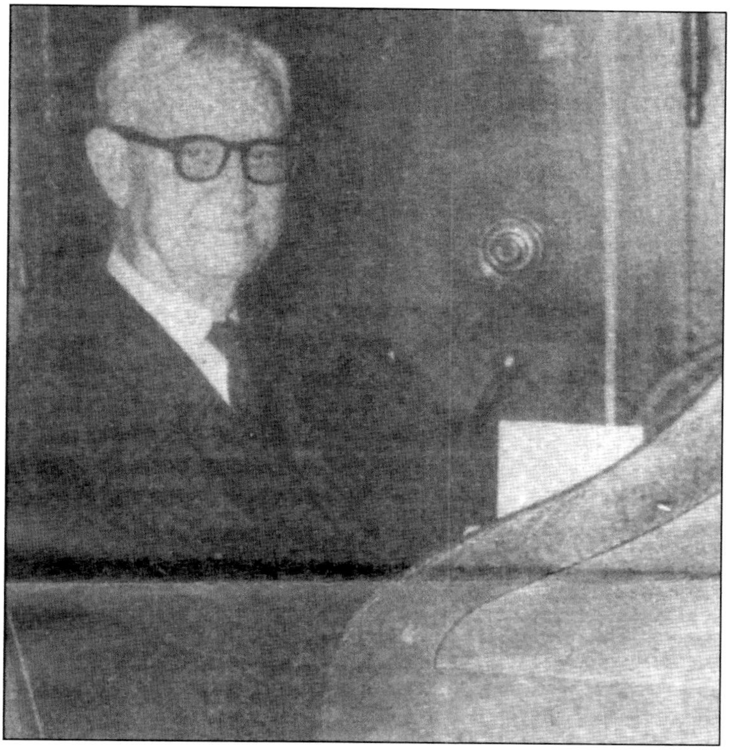

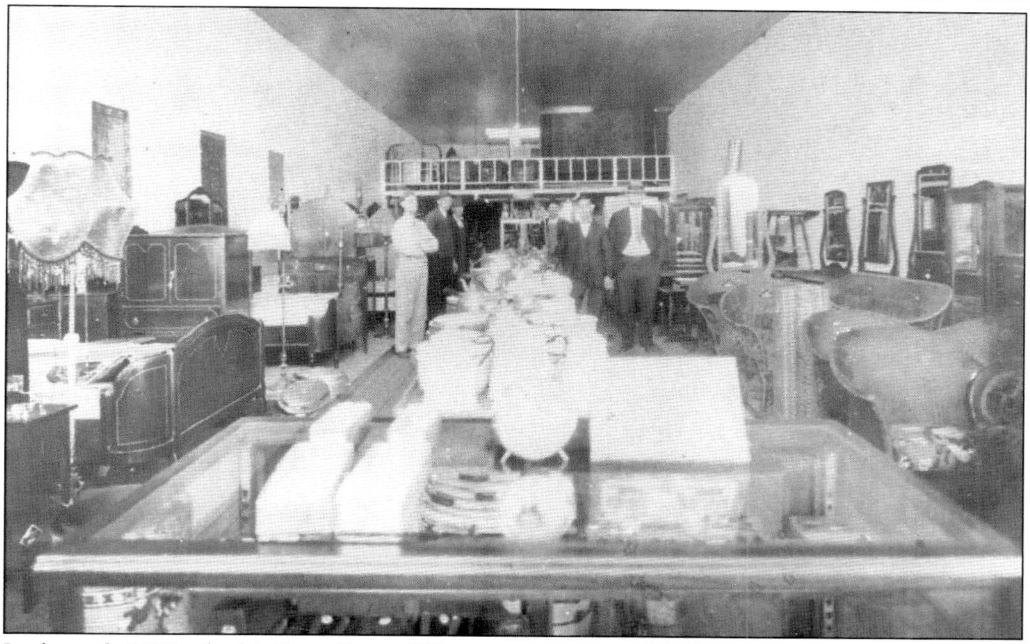

In the early 1930s, the McCrary Funeral Home operated out of the building, utilizing the upper loft while the lower floor served as a hardware business. R.H. McCrary was a longtime public servant and town leader. For over 50 years, he served as director of Farmers Cotton Oil Company, director of First National Bank, and deacon of First Baptist Church. (Courtesy of the *Winnsboro News*.)

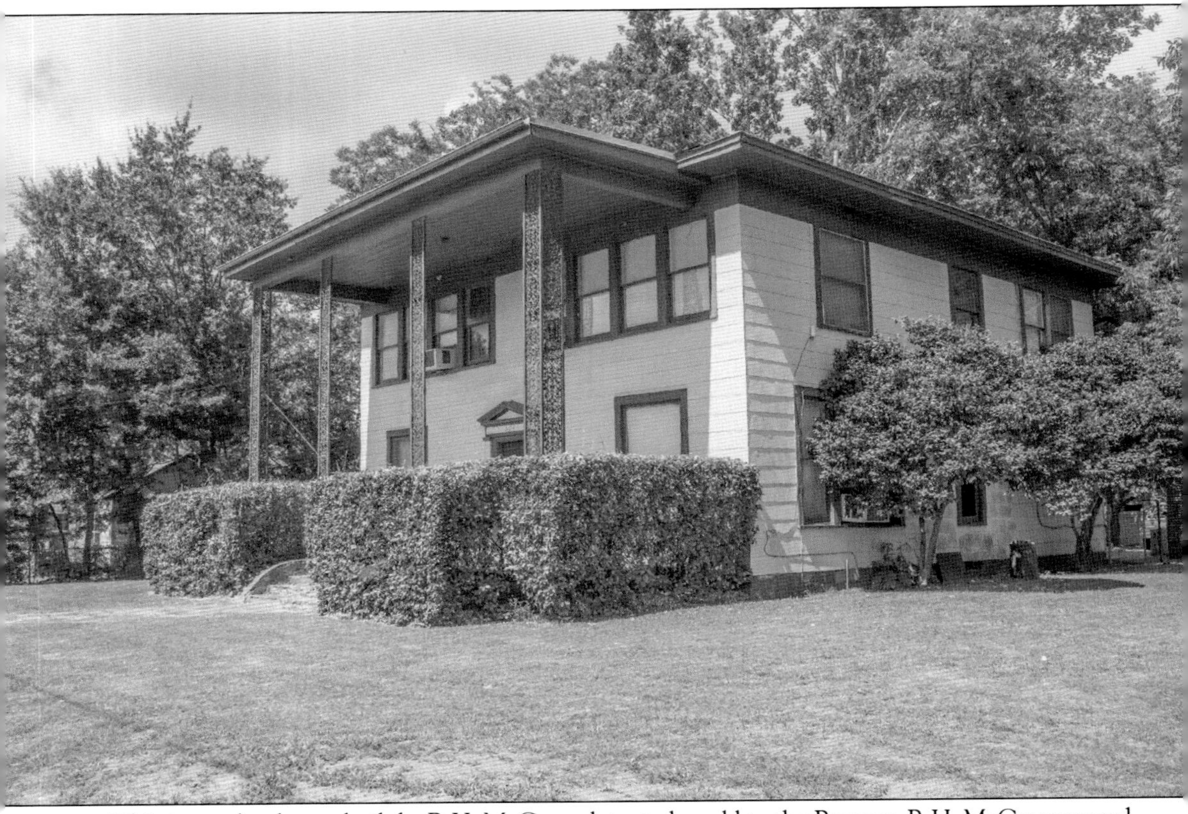

This is another house built by R.H. McCrary, later to be sold to the Brewers. R.H. McCrary served two terms as mayor of Winnsboro and was a member of the city council and the local school board. In 1958, the chamber of commerce named him Man of the Year, and in 1971, when he was 89 years old, R.H. McCrary was honored as the oldest native-born citizen of Wood County by the Old Settlers. (Courtesy of Bob Williams.)

Five

The Oil Boom

In 1942, oil was found near the community of Coke, about 15 miles from Winnsboro, and soon, wildcatters began drilling just south of Winnsboro. Oil fever was in the air, and when the first Gulf wildcat well came in 1944, the town boomed overnight. The three cafés in town became 24-hour-a-day businesses. Hundreds of people came to town, and boardinghouses sprang up everywhere to accommodate all the people who came to work in the oil industry. Legend has it that 500 people practically moved in overnight, and anyone with a room to rent could name their price. Speculators started drilling in various directions around town, hauling the heavy drilling rigs across wooden bridges, some of which broke under weight of the equipment. If a crew found itself short a man, the driller would pick a man off the street who was eager for a job.

At the time, there were no pipelines to take the oil to refineries, so the crude oil was loaded into tankers and hauled to refineries. Each day, the railroad brought in supplies and equipment needed for drilling, and the parking lot at the depot resembled an oilfield truck yard.

During the boom days, when Saturday rolled around, the town's two movie houses, all the cafés, and the skating rink were full. For the first time since the 1930s, jobs were plentiful, and locals had money in their pockets to spend. By 1947, the oil boom boosted the city coffers, enabling the city to pave streets, improve the sewer system, and extend water lines to all parts of the city. Two schools were built in this time of prosperity, Memorial Middle School in 1947 and Westbrook Elementary in 1952.

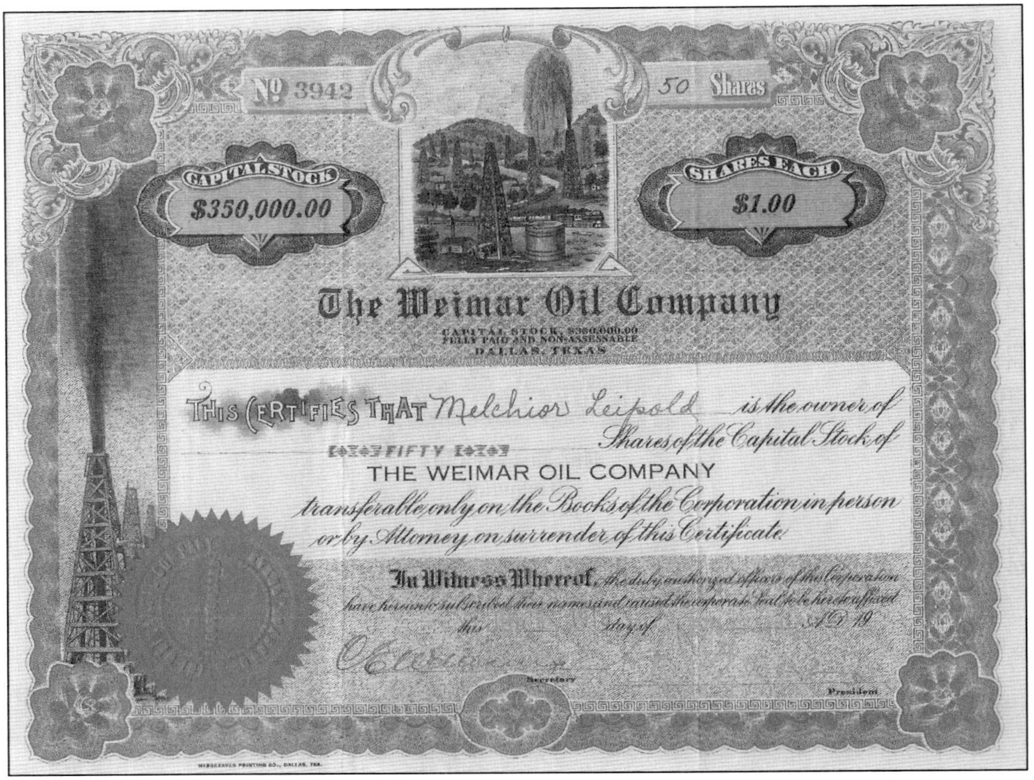

Even before drilling started near Winnsboro, oil companies sold shares in their businesses to investors. Shares were sold from $1 to $100, and a number of local businessmen, including T.G. Carlock and R.F. Taylor, invested in the early 1900s. (Both, courtesy of the *Winnsboro News*.)

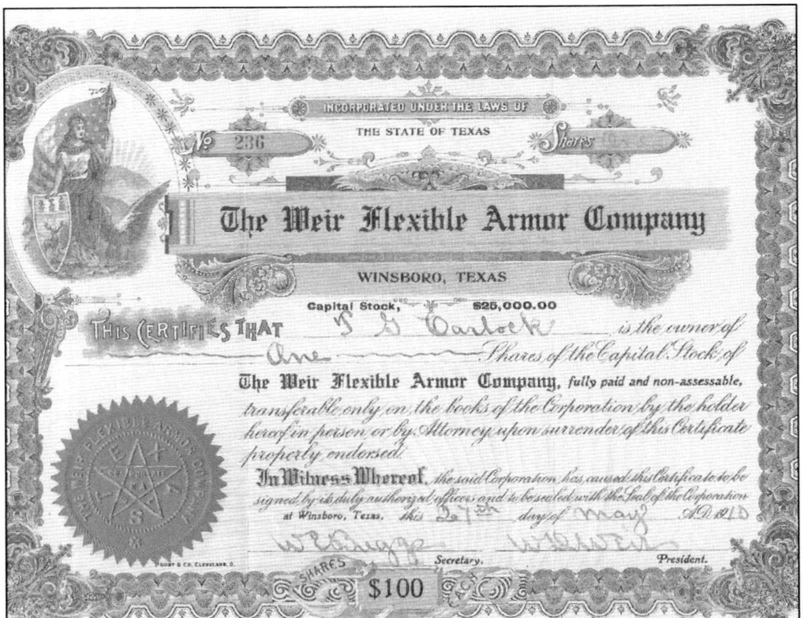

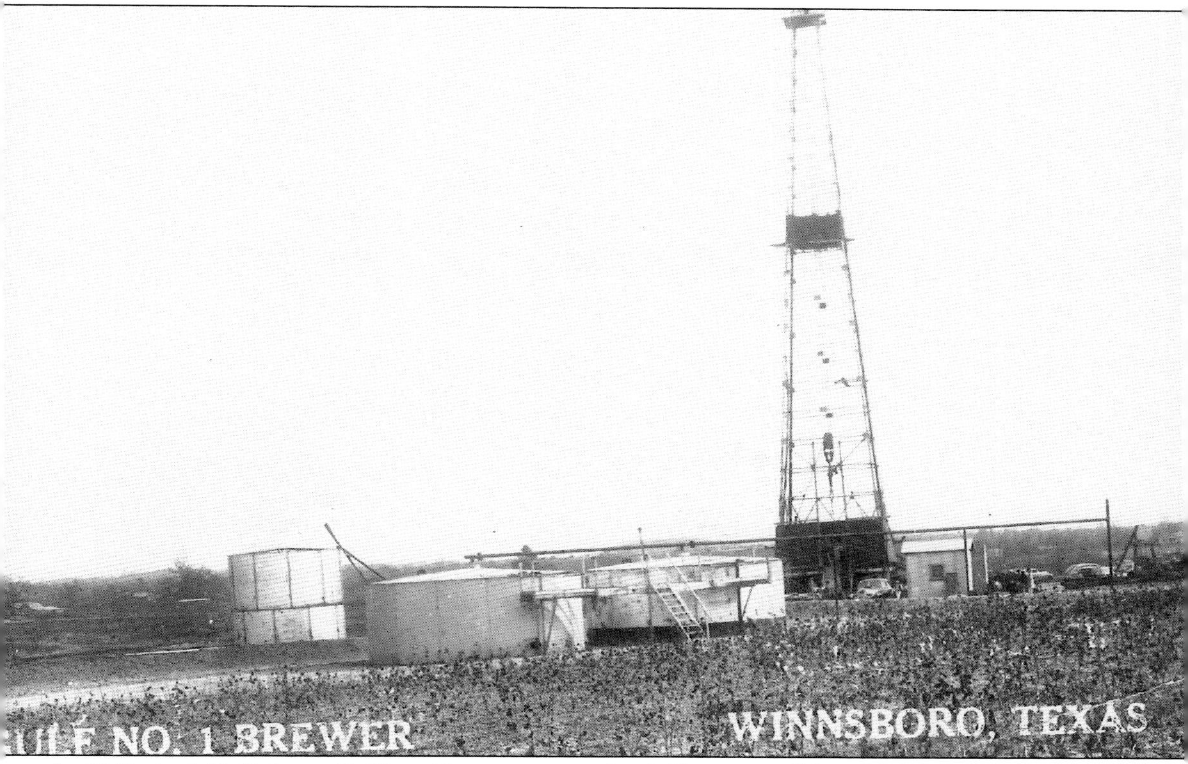

In 1943, the M.J. Delaney Drilling Company moved a drilling rig to Winnsboro. The Gulf Oil Company had a contract with Delaney to do experimental drilling south of town on the 70-acre Brewer farm. On March 9, 1944, the substance known as "black gold" began to leak from a depth of 8,400 feet. The Gulf No. 1 Brewer well initially flowed at 34 barrels per hour during testing before being placed under choke. (Courtesy of the *Winnsboro News*.)

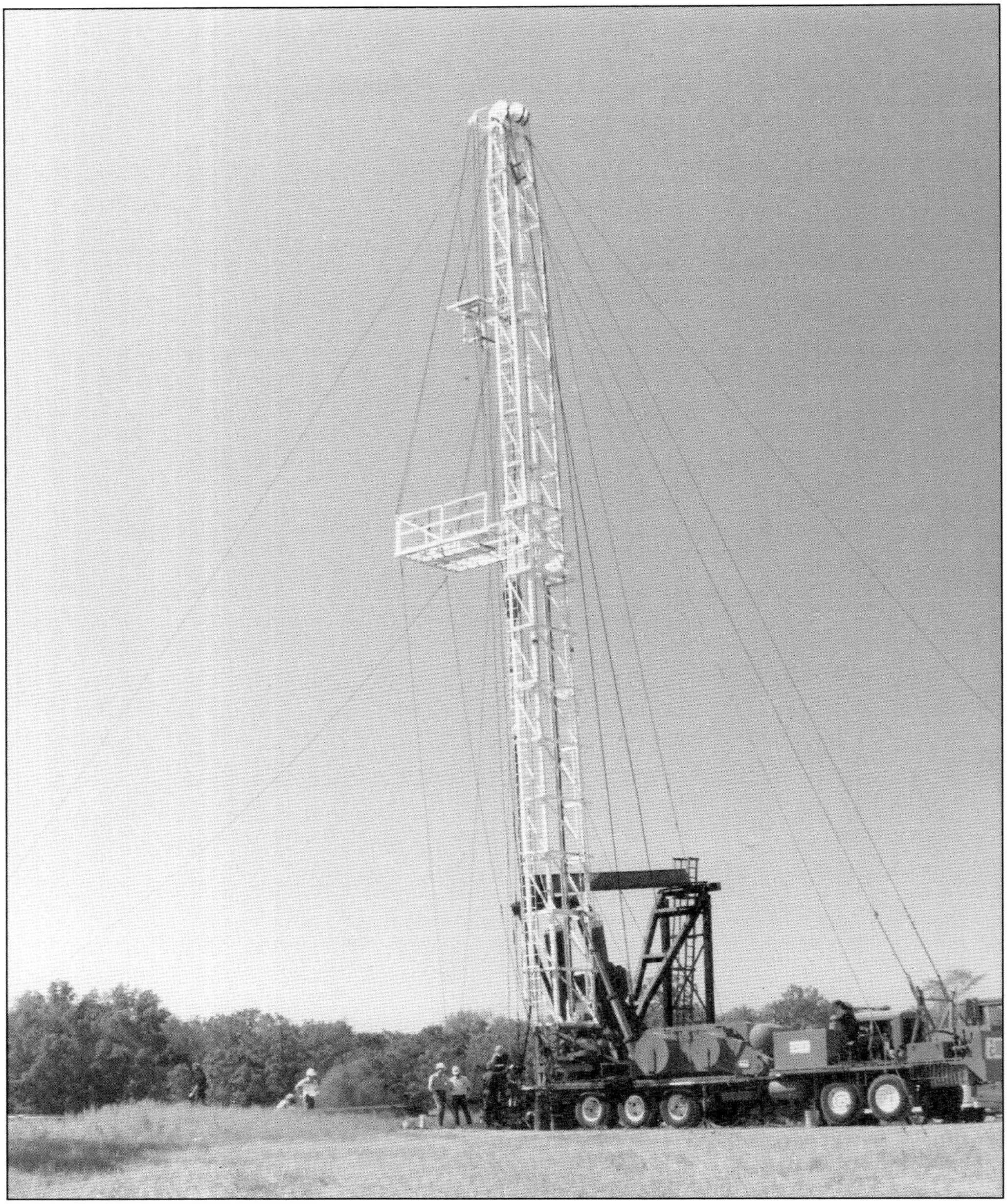

The men are working on what is called a "workover rig," and this one was owned by the Vick Well Service company in Winnsboro. The crew was drilling on land owned in the 1940s by Joe Bailey Craddock. (Courtesy of Sue Hamm.)

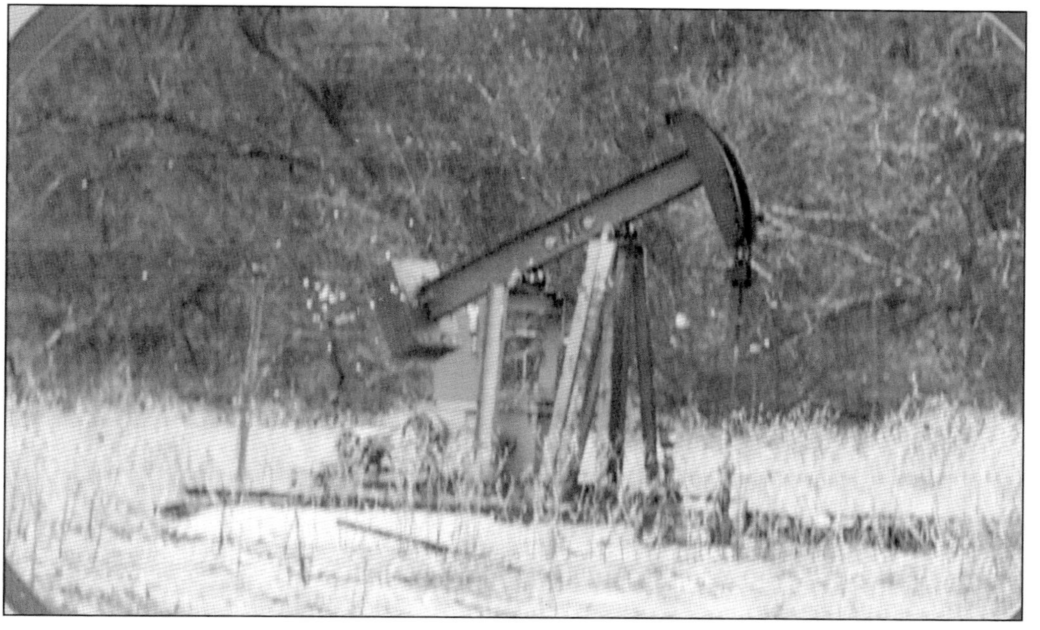

Common sights in the 1940s were these pump jacks, which pumped barrels of oil. They are still seen around town, as there are a number of wells still producing, including the one below on the Hamm property. The derrick in the background marks one of the first oil strikes actually in the town of Winnsboro. The company owned by H.L. Hunt drilled the well, and he personally supervised the drilling. The derrick still stands on property owned in the 1940s by Joe Bailey Craddock and currently owned by Jimmy and Sue Hamm. (Both, courtesy of Bill Jones.)

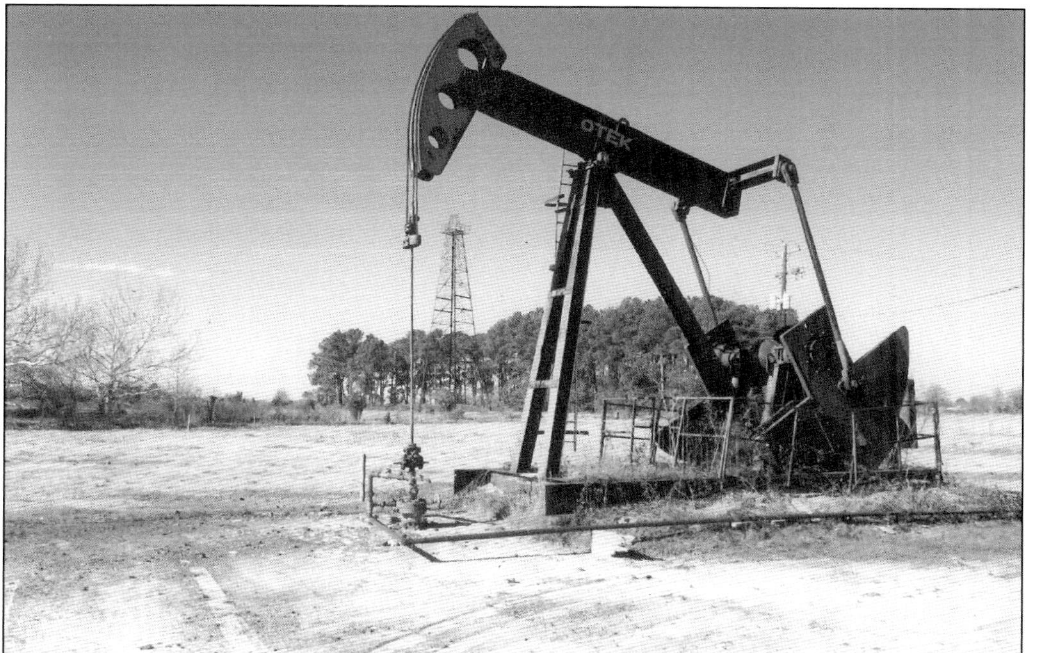

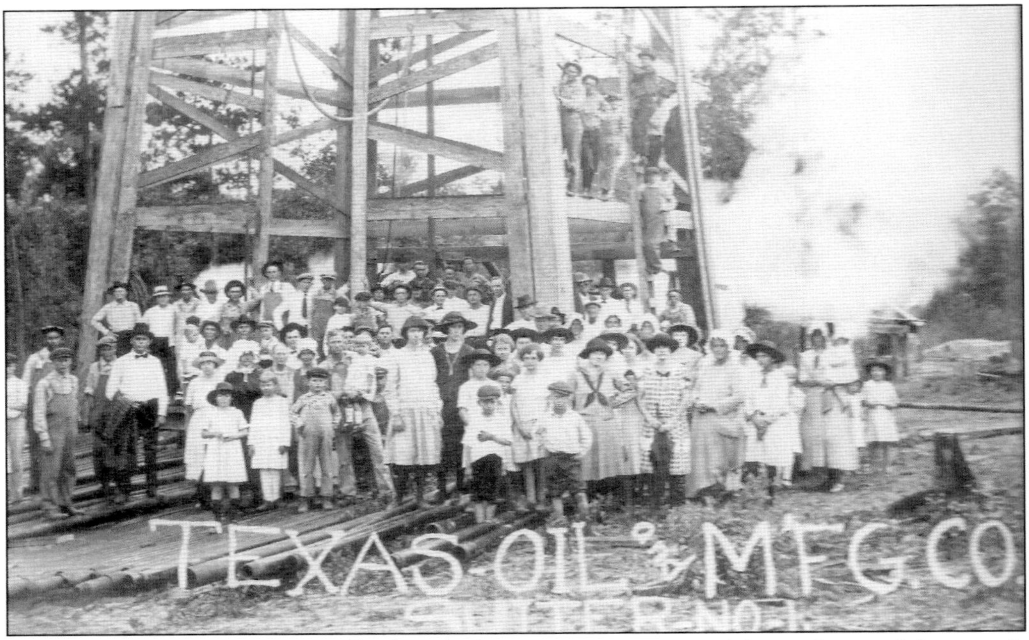

When a well came in, practically the whole town came out to celebrate the good fortune. It represented a jubilant, exciting time for everyone. Occasionally, a string of automobiles extending from the city limits to the well site carried folks out to see the new well. This is the Suiter No. 1 well, owned by Will Suiter and his family. (Courtesy of the *Winnsboro News*.)

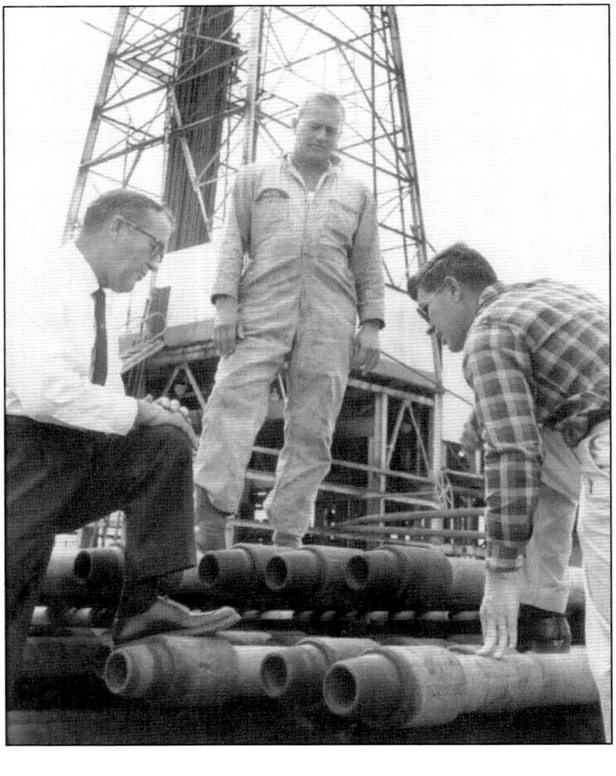

Drilling for oil was labor-intensive, as well as hard on equipment. Drilling bits had to constantly be checked and either repaired or replaced when they wore out. Two of the local people who established well service businesses were O.E. Vick and Ray Holbert. Halliburton, Continental, Arrow, National, and Bethlehem operated supply houses. The men pictured are unidentified. (Courtesy of Bill Jones.)

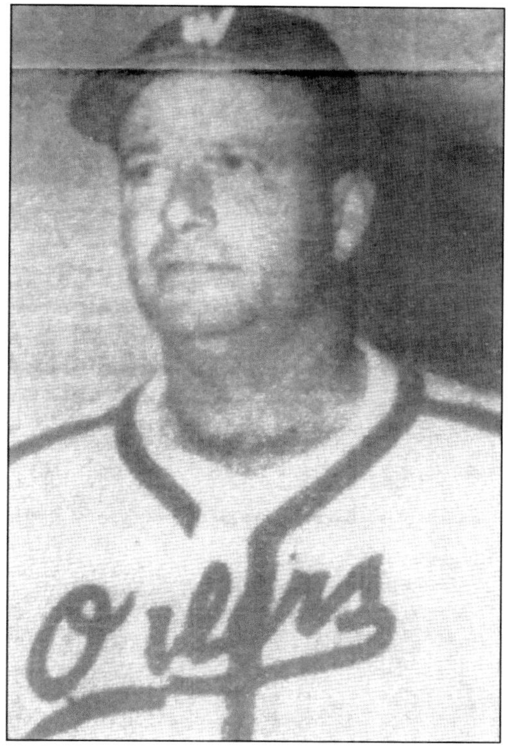

Babe Bryce was one of the of the original players on the 1947 Winnsboro Oilers baseball team that went on to win the championship title of the East Texas Amateur League that same year. When not on the road, the team played at Walker Park in Winnsboro to the delight of hundreds of fans. His teammate Carl Talbert was known as "Iron Man" to players and fans alike. Other popular players were Doyle Taylor, Tom King, and James Alford. (Courtesy of the *Winnsboro News*.)

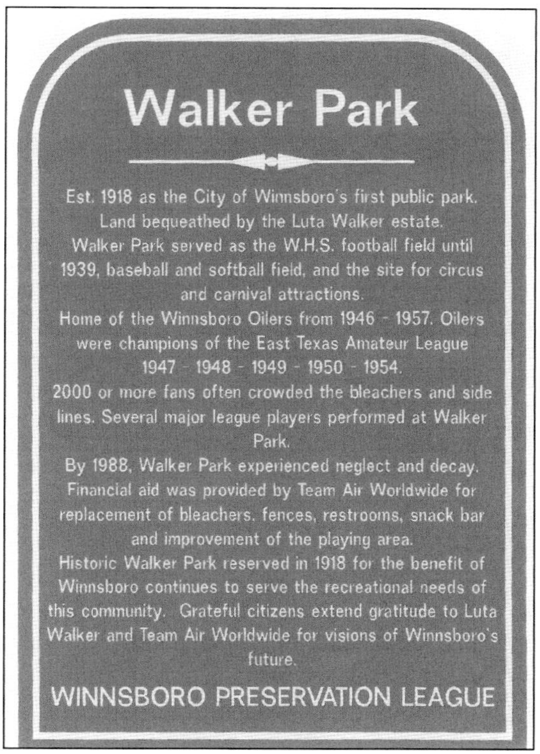

The legacy of Winnsboro's oldest park began in 1918, when Luta Walker gave the land for a public park. Walker Park served as the Winnsboro High School football field until 1939, when it hosted baseball and softball teams and was the site where the circus or a carnival would set up tents and attractions. (Courtesy of the *Winnsboro News*.)

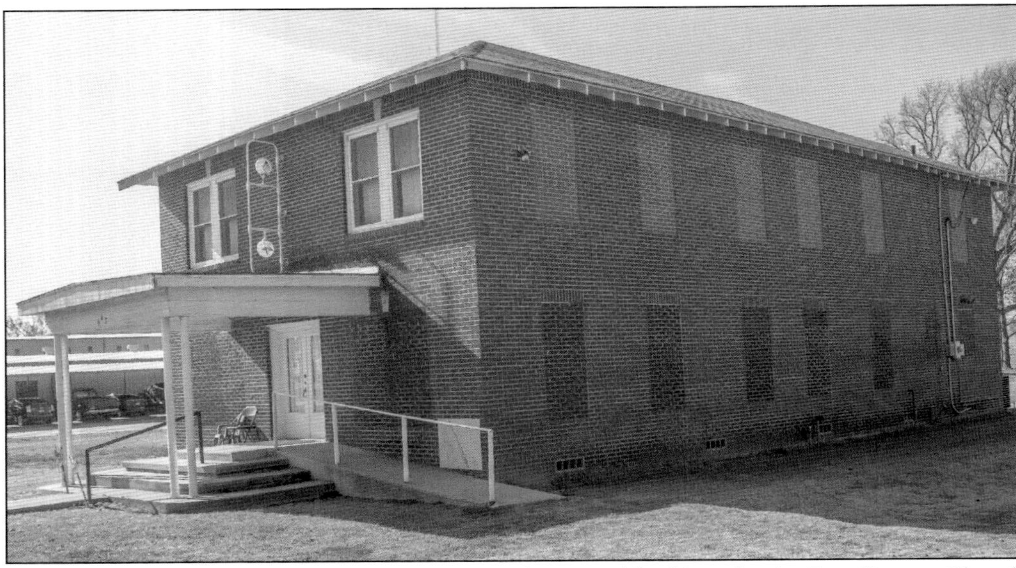

The Masonic lodge on West Broadway was an educational building for the First Baptist Church until the Masons bought it in 1952. To ensure the privacy of their meetings, they bricked over all the windows on the sides of the building so people passing by could not look in. When the Masons acquired the building, they put in a new cornerstone, establishing a record of when they moved into the site. From the time the Masons came to Winnsboro from Cypress in the late 1800s, there were as many as six lodges in and around Winnsboro. (Both, courtesy of Bob Williams.)

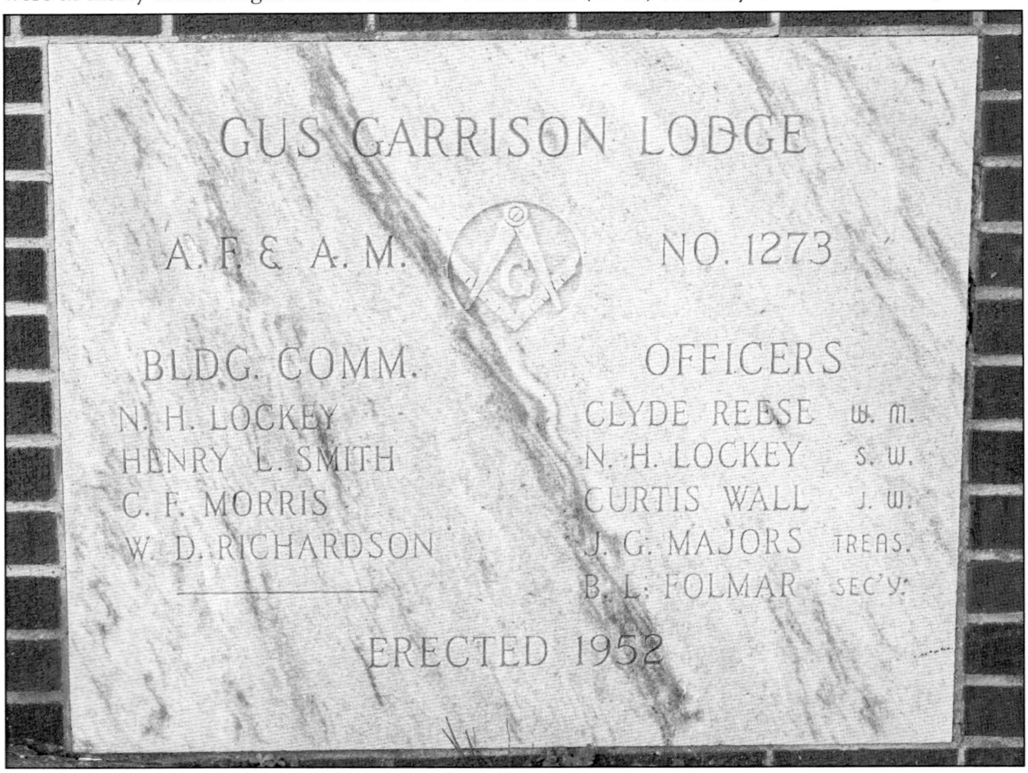

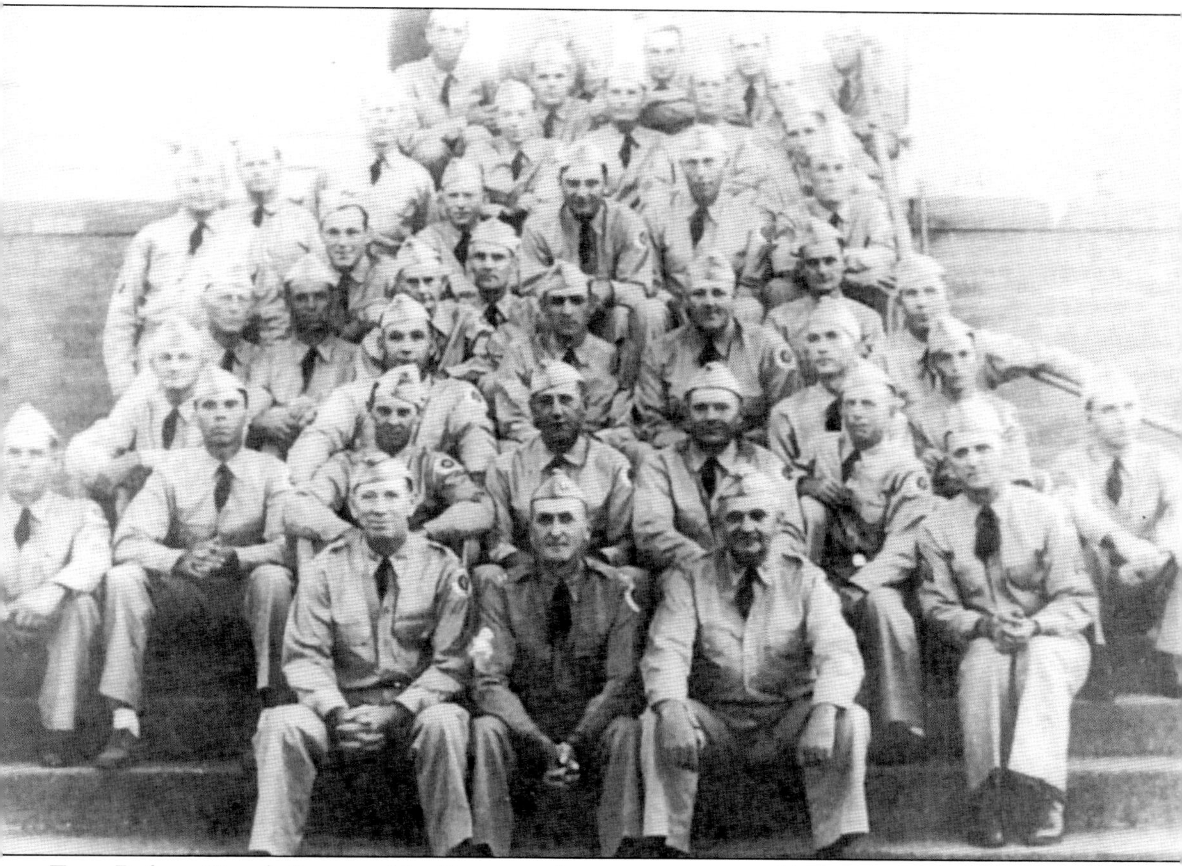

Texas Defense Guard, Company No. 42, was a volunteer unit organized by local citizens to perform the duties left by the mobilization of the National Guard in 1940. Weekly drills were held in the Army hall, located in the R.G. Andrews Building. Members of the guard are, from left to right, (first row) Leroy Hawkins, Don Rawlings, and Joe T. Ivey; (second row) Pete Laminack, J.C. "Bud" Junior, R.H. "Bob" Rymes, Vernon Stanley, Carl Raley, Con Jordon, Asa Dickson, and Paul "Skeeter" Mitchell; (third row) Curtis McNair, Tommy McLeroy, Houston Nickelson, three unidentified, and R.C. Martin; (fourth row) unidentified, Tommy McLeroy, Sam Harp, J.D. Arrington, R.A. Wilson, R.G. Jarred, Loye Richardson, and Vertie Sanford; (fifth row) Wimp Woodard, Mink Morris, Ralph Ayers, Plez Tedford, Jim Bob Beard, Buford Folmar, A.C. Beard, Joe Benard, Fred Bithell, and Arvil Anders; (sixth row) James H. Hughes, Tommy Heart, Willie Watkins (the last surviving member of the Texas Defense Guard), Tilly Brewer, and Nathan Shirley. (Courtesy of the former Myrtle McAfee Studio.)

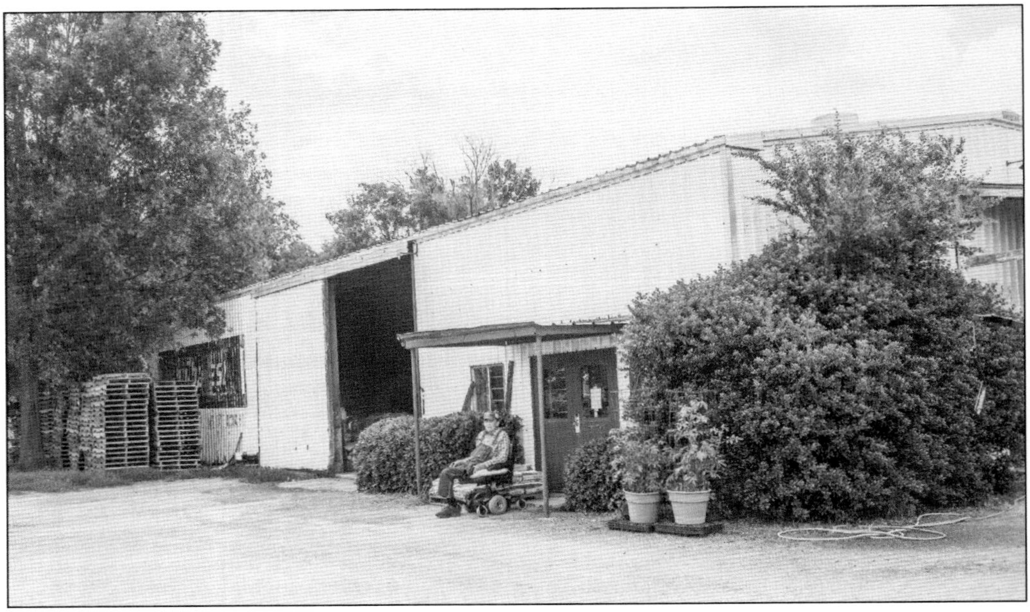

Wayne Redding owned a feed store on West Coke Road from 1978 until he retired in 2012. Even when activity was limited due to health issues, he went to the store every day and was highly respected by his customers. He could answer questions about crops, livestock, and anything else a customer cared to ask. For many years, he was the trail boss for the annual trail rides in the spring and the fall. (Both, courtesy of Bob Williams.)

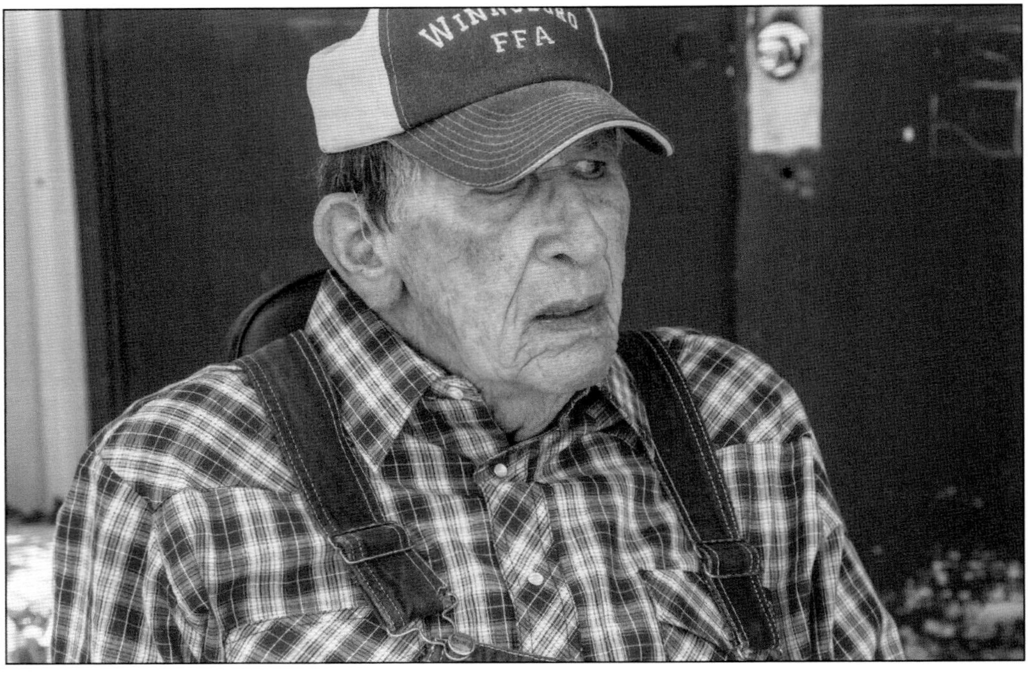

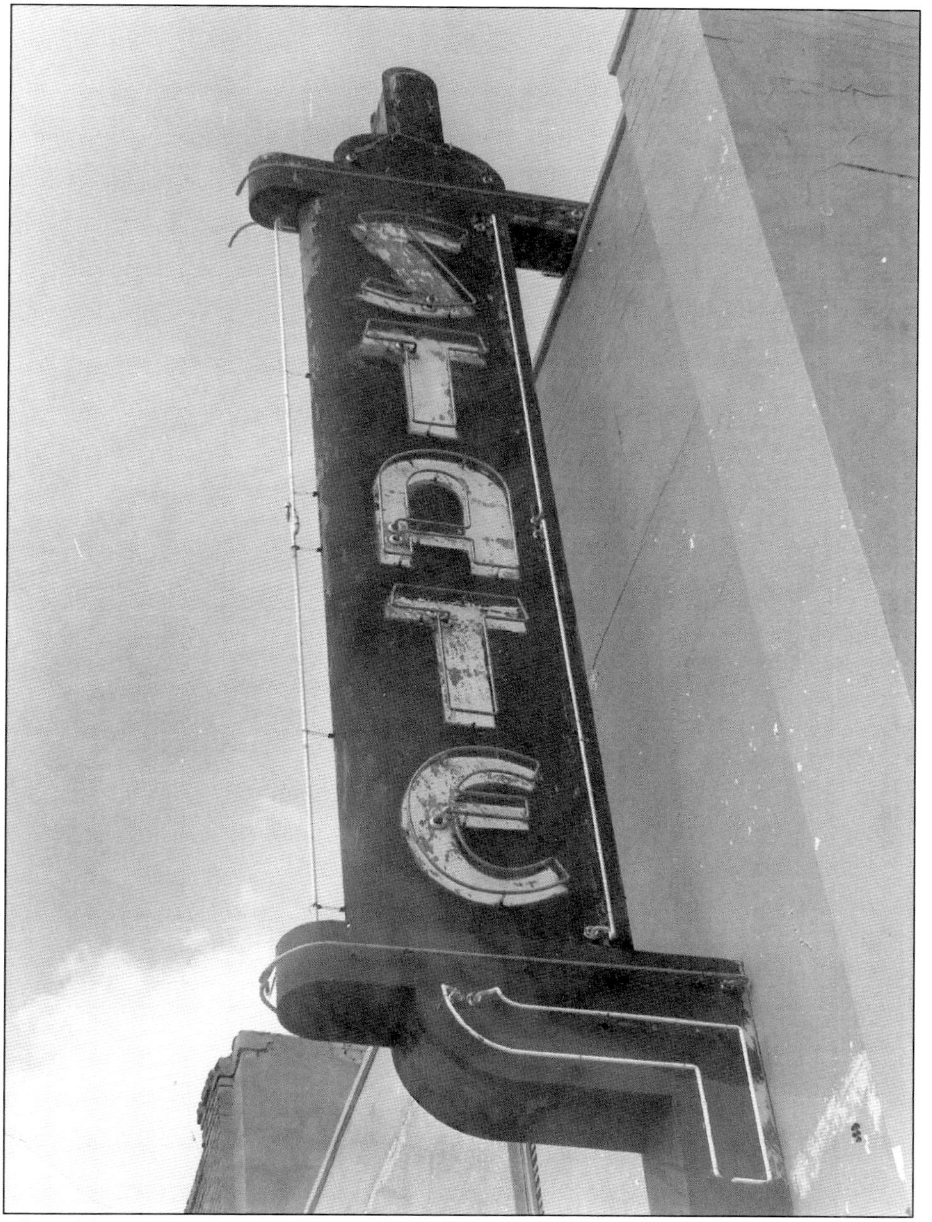

With the oil boom came a new prosperity in Winnsboro, and people had more money in their pockets. Some of that money went to the State Theater on North Main Street, where movies cost a quarter and popcorn could be purchased for a nickel. Many young couples did their courting at the State Theater, which first opened as the Star Theater in 1915 showing silent moves. Then, it became the Queen Theater. When talking pictures came about 1932, the theater was called the Amusu. In the late 1930s, Gordon McClendon, who owned the Tri-State Theater Company, bought the Amusu and named it State Theater. Gordon McClendon was originally from Atlanta, Texas, and had about 20 theaters in East Texas. The State Theater closed in the 1960s, and the building housed the Ivy Garden Restaurant for several years. Most recently, it has been the home of the Varsity Diner. (Courtesy of Bill Jones.)

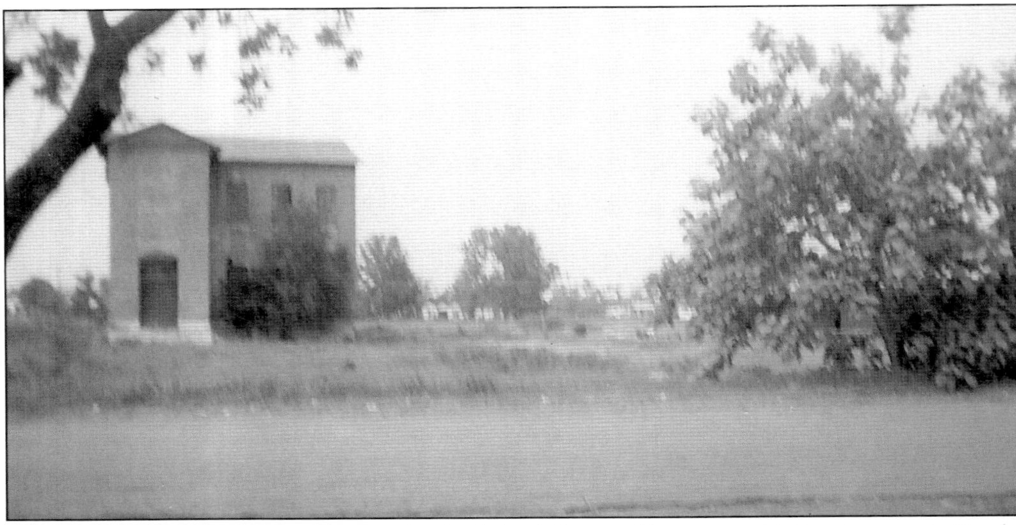

Locals referred to this old building as the Little Red Gin, and kids named it Frankenstein's Castle. A gin and sawmill operated here from the early days of Winnsboro's history until the early 1930s. The first oil mill was located here. Bill Jones, who used to play in the field around the building with his boyhood friends, took this picture in 1956. (Courtesy of Bill Jones.)

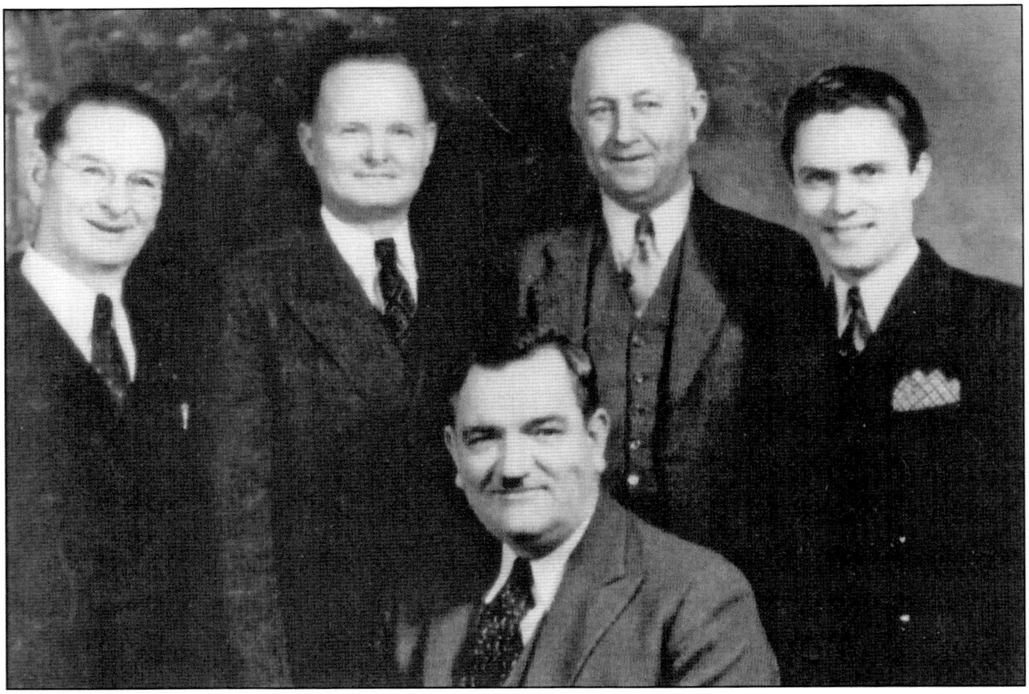

The original Stamps Quartet had an annual tri-county singing convention out in City Park in the late 1930s and into the 1940s. Thousands of people came to the events. At first, people came in wagons, and when cars started coming, the National Guard had to handle the parking of vehicles. The members, from left to right, are Jim Gaither, baritone; Walter Rippitoe, first tenor; Bob Bacon, lead; and Marion Snider, pianist. Seated is V.O. Stamps, who sang bass and was president of Stamps-Baxter Music. (Courtesy of the *Winnsboro News.*)

Six

Notable People, Places, and Events

The most infamous people connected to Winnsboro were Bonnie and Clyde, the notorious couple who spread a reign of terror from Dallas to Shreveport from 1932 to 1934. Winnsboro was one of the places the couple traveled through on their way from Dallas to Louisiana. According to old-timers, the outlaws were seen around town quite often but were never known to break the law.

Other names of note include Jonan Brown, a local girl who had a promising career as a theater teacher in the Dallas area before she contracted polio. She moved back to Winnsboro to live with her parents, John and Bee Brown, and was director of the Autumn Trails Queen's Pageant for 17 years.

Author Claudia Cranston was also from Winnsboro, and she was a respected journalist in the 1920s and 1930s.

Henry Marshall and his wife, Alabama "Bama" Gist Marshall, could not make a living farming in Winnsboro, so they went to Dallas, where Bama cooked at a Woolworth diner. One of her specialties was a little pie that eventually led to a successful business, the Bama Pie Company.

Perhaps the most important event in Winnsboro is the annual Autumn Trails Festival, which is held each October. It started in 1958 and continues to this day. Each weekend of the month is dedicated to special attractions that draw visitors from all over.

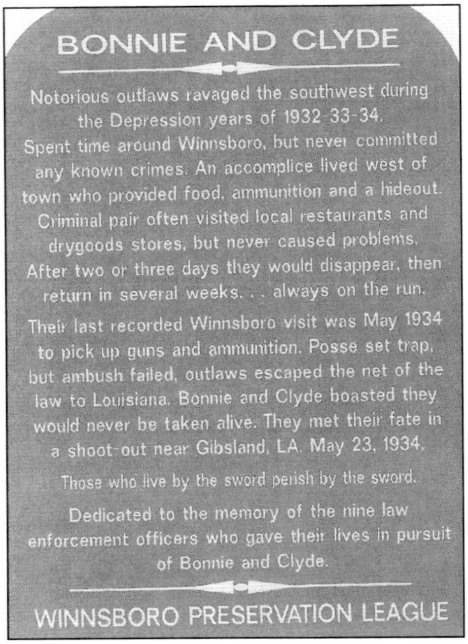

Bonnie and Clyde would often visit their friend Jack Nichols, who was born at Pleasant Grove near Winnsboro and went to Dallas as a young man. He met Bonnie at the restaurant where she worked, and they became friends. When he came back to Winnsboro and Bonnie and Clyde started their crime spree, Jack would offer them food and shelter. On one trip, they stopped to pay Jack Nichols money they owed him, and had the sheriff from Dallas come that day, he could have caught them. One local woman said the following of the pair: "Even though they were mad-dog killers, they were always polite to us." (Courtesy of Bob Williams.)

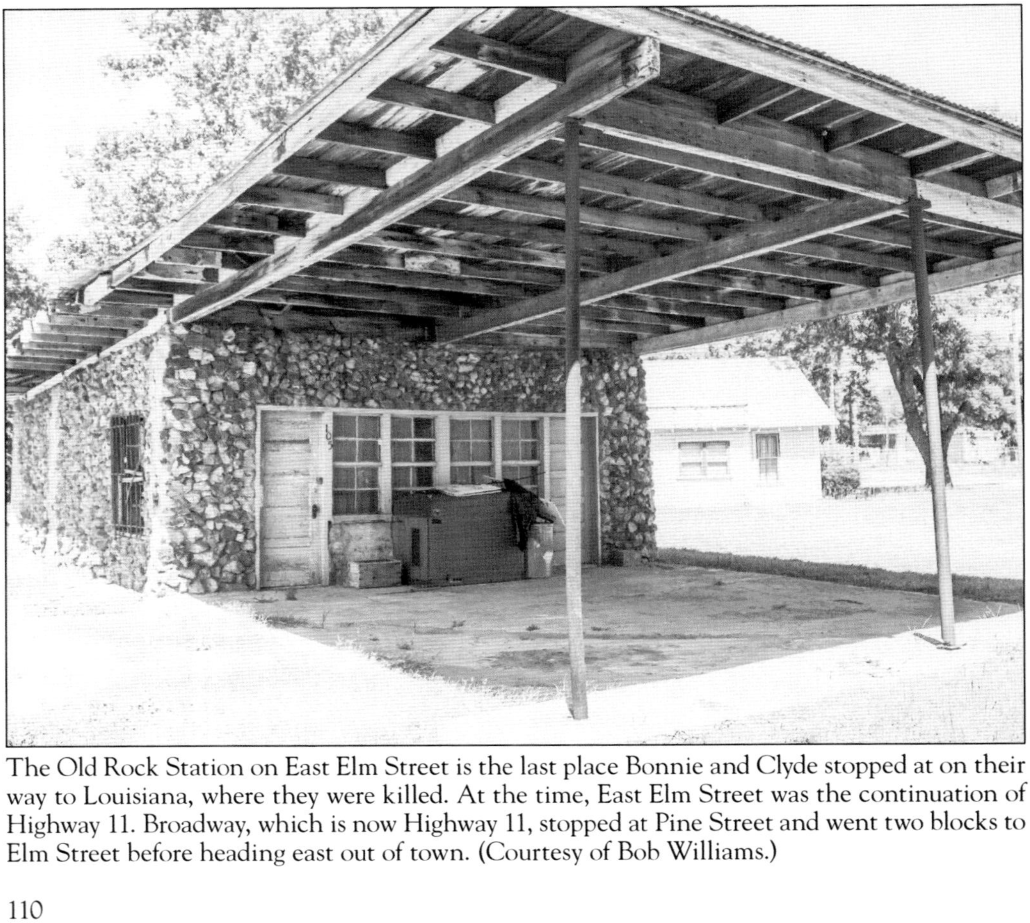

The Old Rock Station on East Elm Street is the last place Bonnie and Clyde stopped at on their way to Louisiana, where they were killed. At the time, East Elm Street was the continuation of Highway 11. Broadway, which is now Highway 11, stopped at Pine Street and went two blocks to Elm Street before heading east out of town. (Courtesy of Bob Williams.)

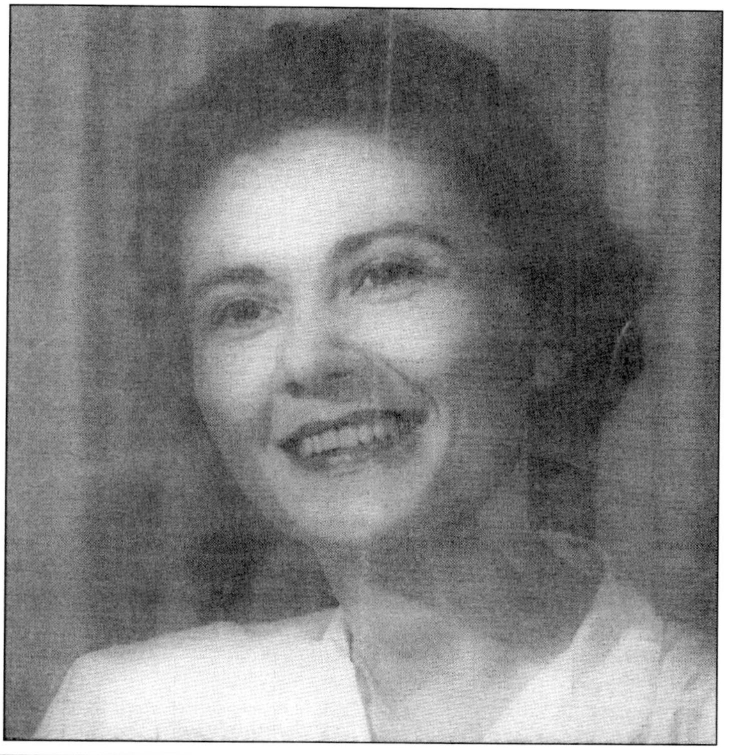

For 21 years, Jonan Brown was the editor and writer for the Autumn Trails Brochure. In 1962, at the fourth Autumn Trails Festival, Jonan presented her play *The Cabin*, a story that touched on the history of East Texas from 1850 to the present. Drama critics from the *Dallas Morning News* hailed her play as exceptionally good, and after the Winnsboro production, the play was performed at Texas Women's University in Denton and received good reviews. (Courtesy of the *Winnsboro News*.)

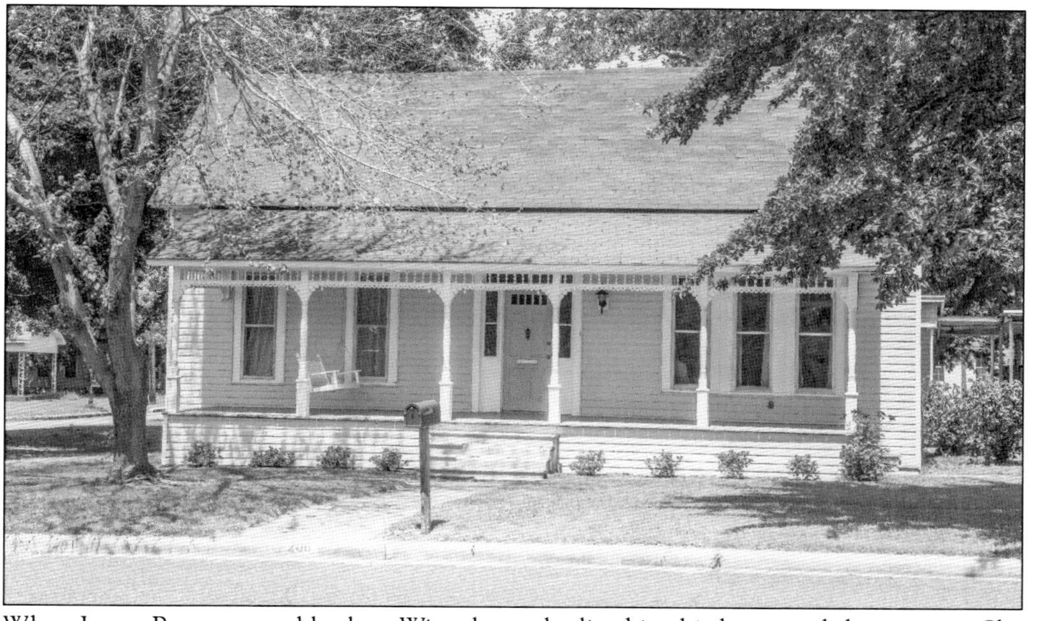

When Jonan Brown moved back to Winnsboro, she lived in this home with her parents. She spent 30 years of her life confined to a wheel chair, with only the use of two fingers to paint and write, but she produced a wonderful collection of work, including a book of her poems and essays called *Reflections*. Her daughter said that she never thought of her mother as disabled, only inconvenienced. (Courtesy of Bob Williams.)

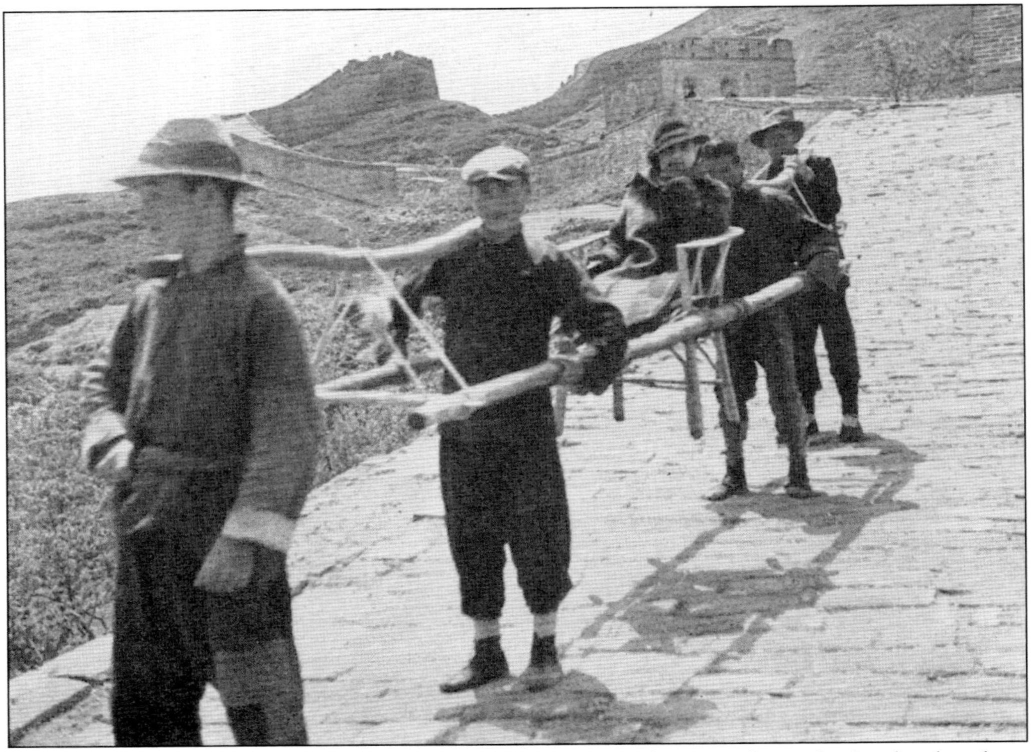

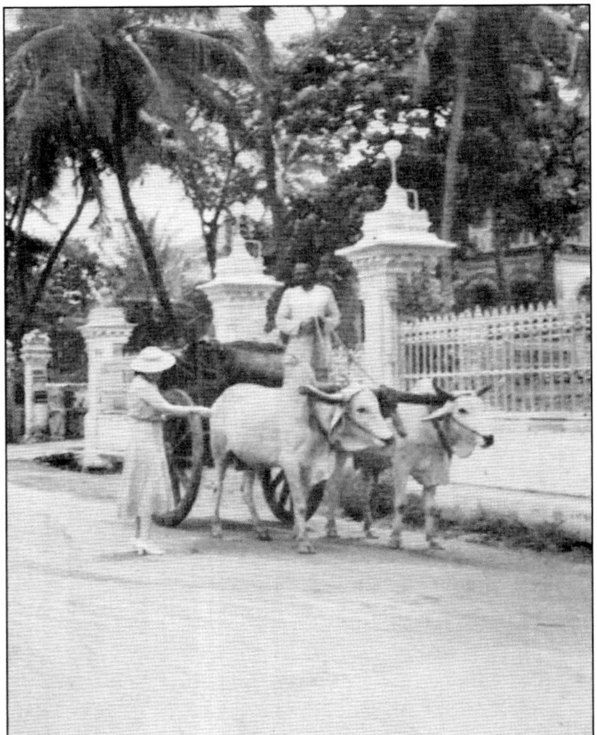

After completing high school and college, Claudia Cranston worked for a time in Washington, DC, then moved to New York to work as a copywriter for *Vogue* magazine. In 1922, her work was also featured in *Atlantic Monthly*, *Ladies Home Journal*, and *Good Housekeeping*. She is pictured here at the Great Wall of China and on a street in Bombay. Claudia's most famous work was her novel *Rosiki the Rose*, which MGM made into the 1949 movie *It's a Big Country*. Cranston did not live to see the movie, which was shown at the State Theater in Winnsboro. She returned from international travel in 1946 a sick woman and died in 1947. (Both, courtesy of Anita Thompson.)

The nonfiction book *I've Been Around* was based on Claudia Cranston's extensive travels. Working for *Vogue* and *Good Housekeeping*, she had accepted commissions to tour Europe and write about people, places, and the different cultures and customs. She visited all the countries in Europe except the Soviet Union. The book was published in 1937 by the J.P. Lippincott Company in Philadelphia and London. (Courtesy of Anita Thompson.)

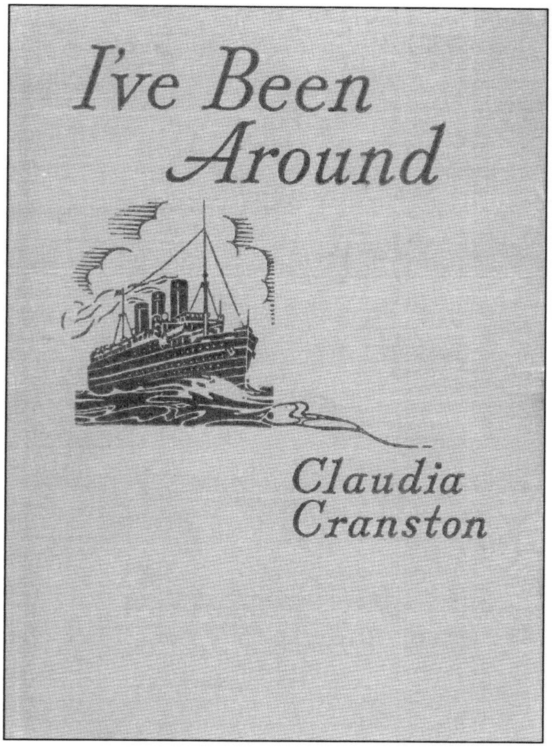

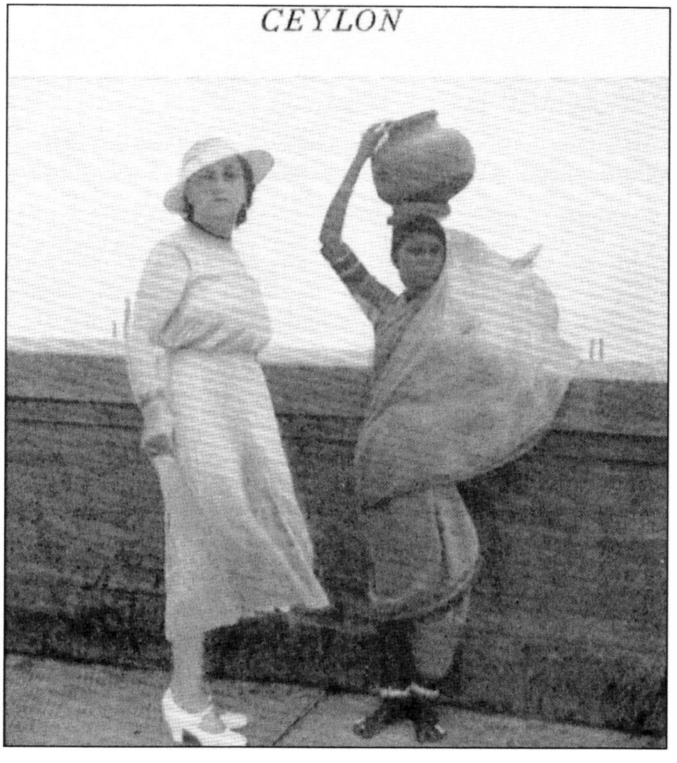

As indicated in her Author Note for her book, Claudia treasured her encounters with local citizens in her travels. "*I've Been Around* is the account of things seen and heard circling the globe in six months—the unforgettable glimpse—the first impression—the friendly word—the passing picture as it presents itself to a world cruiser who must leave to historians, political economists, and prophets, all inner explanations, apologies, and hopes." The young girl she is with here in Sri Lanka is unidentified. (Courtesy of Anita Thompson.)

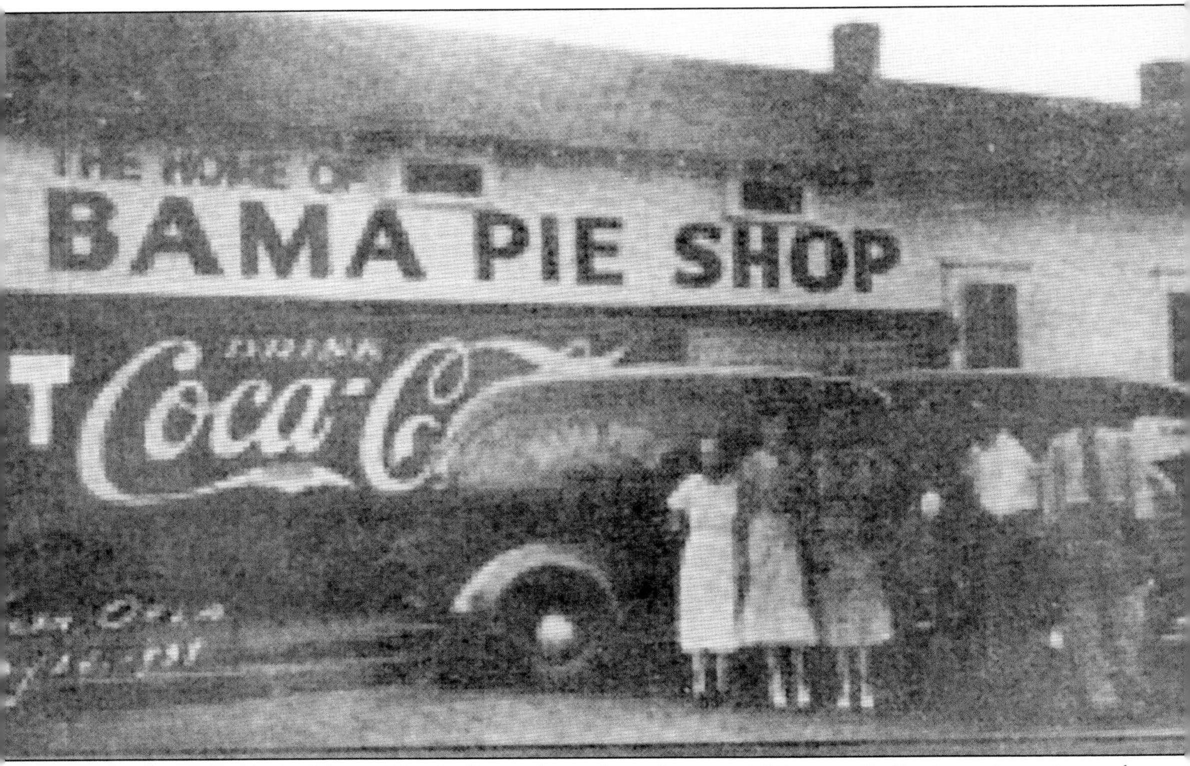

In the early 1900s, Henry Marshall sent his wife and seven children to Dallas in an iron-rimmed wagon. Henry stayed behind to sell his stock, tools, and anything else he had to pay his debts. Then he, too, headed for Dallas, walking and picking cotton and hitching rides. In Dallas, Bama cooked at a Woolworth diner, and one of her specialties was a little pie that customers loved. In about 1930, Henry urged her to make the pies at home so he could sell them door-to-door, which he did to great success. As the business grew, Henry bought an old Ford car that became the Bama Pie Company's first delivery car. Bama quit her job at Woolworth and, with the help of the children, started producing hundreds of the little pies a day. An agreement with McDonald's to supply pies to the various franchises launched the Bama Pie Company into prominence. (Courtesy of the *Winnsboro News*.)

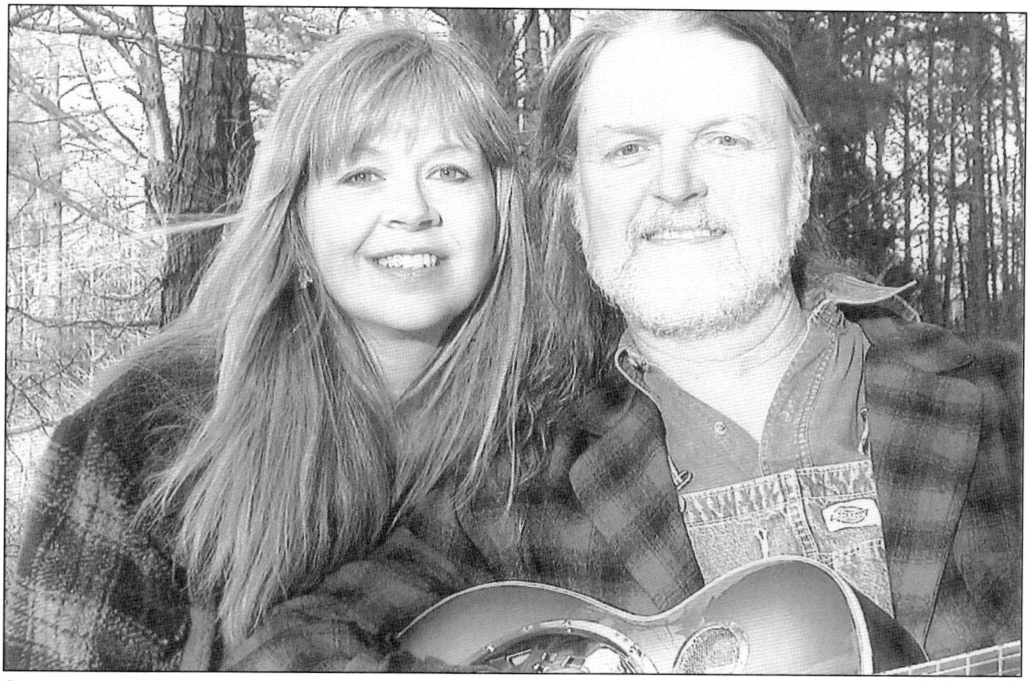

Singers-songwriters Lynn Adler and Lindy Hearne came to Winnsboro in 2001 and bought property that had been owned by Joseph and Mary Germann. They love their Piney Woods home, which they call the Spring Hollow Organic Song Farm, and have written a number of songs celebrating Winnsboro and East Texas. In November 2005, they established the live music venue, Crossroads Music Company, hosting national touring artists weekly, which was instrumental in the resurgence of Downtown Winnsboro as a shopping, dining, and arts destination. Lindy is also a talented photographer and shared this picture of the small lake on their property, immortalized in the song "Goolsby's Pool." (Both, courtesy of Lindy Hearne.)

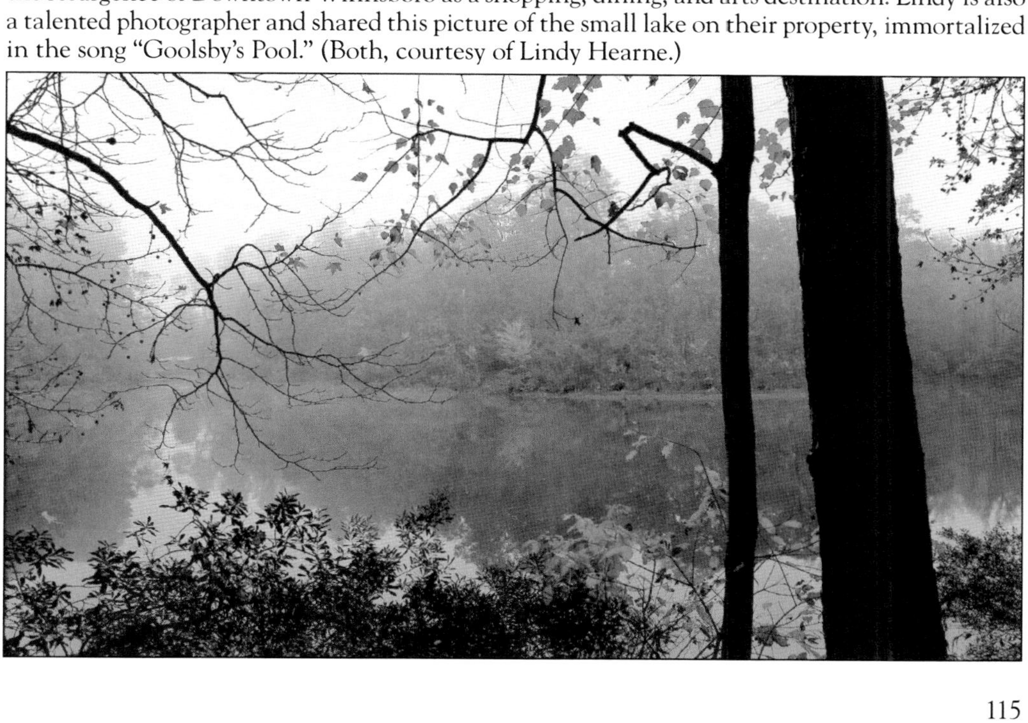

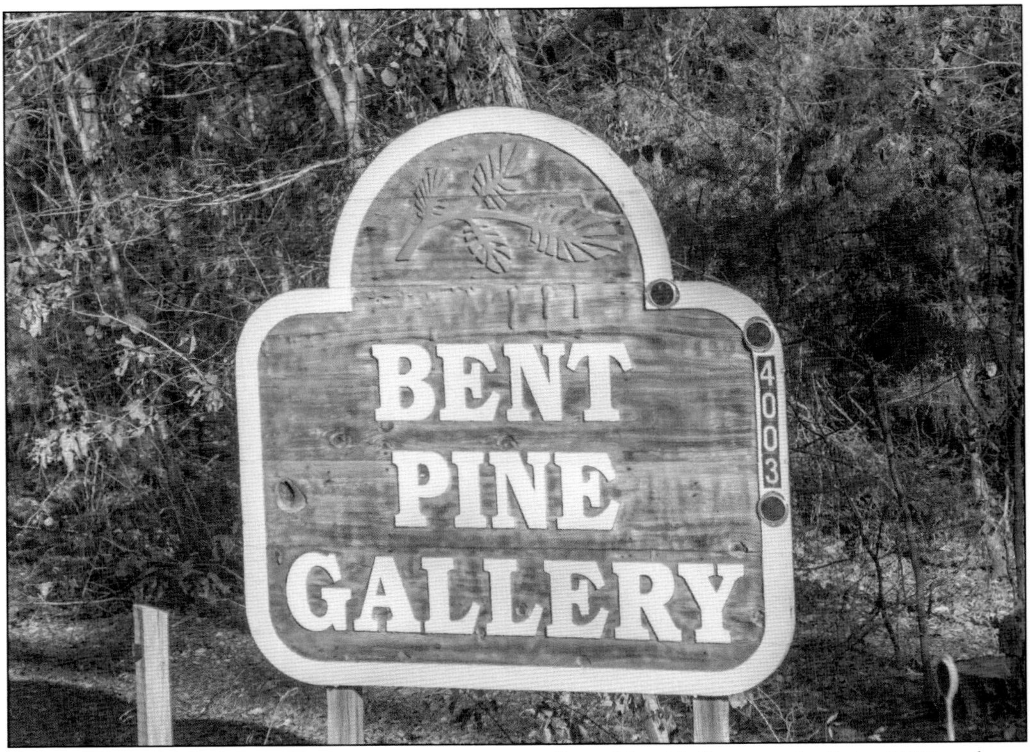

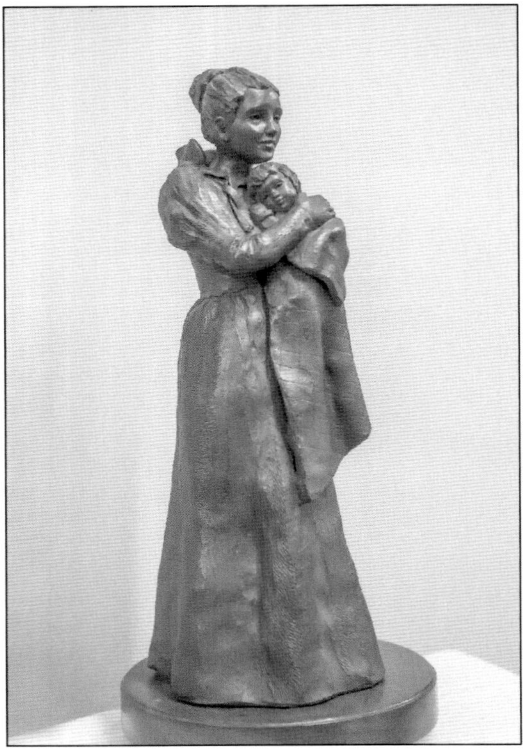

Bent Pine Gallery was built in 1983 and was the studio for Georgia Lange Moore for a number of years. Georgia is a well-known sculptress who has lived in Winnsboro since 1980. In addition to creating pieces on commission for her clients, she has taught art in her studio, as well as in schools in Dallas and East Texas. In 2003, she closed the gallery and devoted most of her efforts to working as a community volunteer, primarily with nonprofit service organizations. Her specialty is women and children, and the Wood County Historical Commission commissioned this statue, owned by Bill Jones. The intent was to have a life-sized stature depicting a Wood County pioneer woman that would stand on the grounds of the Wood County Courthouse. The artist made this replica, and when the project was halted, Bill Jones purchased the small statue from the historical commission. (Both, courtesy of Bob Williams.)

M.D. Carlock Jr. and his wife, Rhea, were instrumental in starting Autumn Trails, along with Howard W. Rosser and several other prominent Winnsboro people. The concept of a month-long festival was first conceived in the mid-1950s, and the first official weekend was in 1958. It has been said that Autumn Trails added a new dimension to the economic life of Winnsboro. This photograph was taken in the late 1990s. (Courtesy of Bill Jones.)

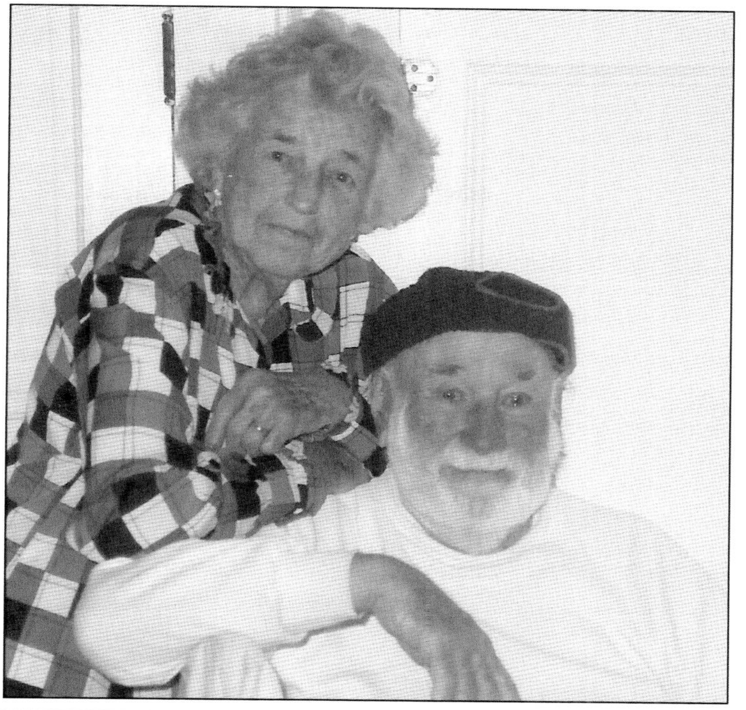

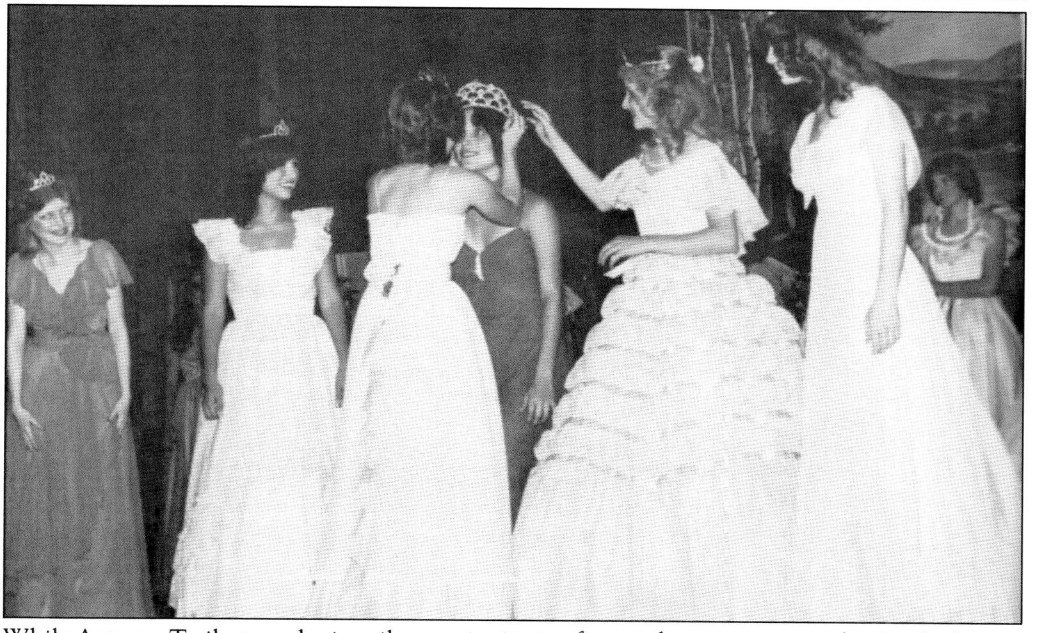

While Autumn Trails started primarily as an invitation for people to come out and enjoy the beauty of the fall colors in and around Winnsboro, specific events, such as the Autumn Trails Pageant, became more and more popular. Each succeeding year brought more pomp to the event, such as the coronation ball held at the City Park Auditorium. In 1979, Camille Goodrich, Autumn Trails Queen XXII, was crowned by Lisa Lindly, Queen XXI, and attended by, from left to right, Jana Duggins, Ria Decker, Shareece Brewer, and Jane Metcalf. (Courtesy of the *Winnsboro News*.)

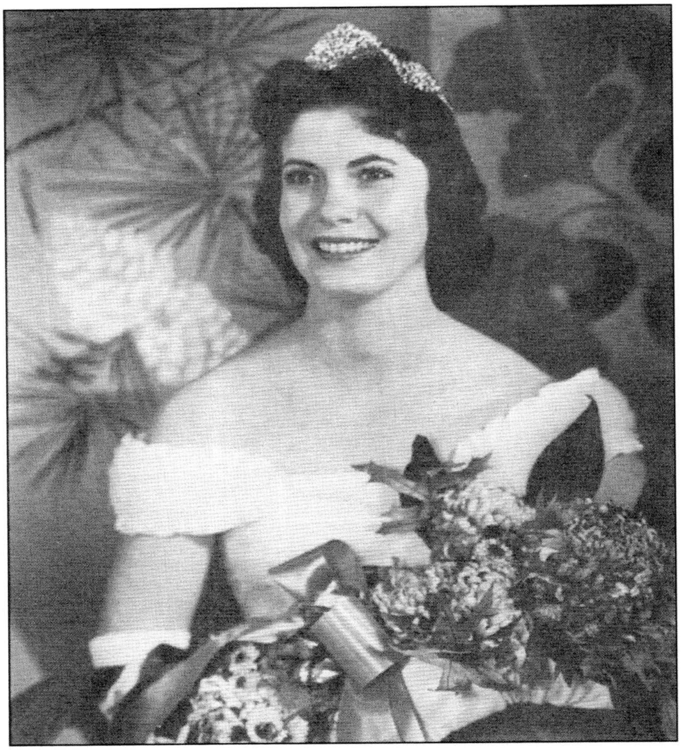

Claudia Mullinax, daughter of Claude and Hailey Mullinax, was crowned Autumn Trails Queen II. The queen was always an official representative of Winnsboro at various community activities, especially during the month of October. (Courtesy of the *Winnsboro News.*)

Miss Autumn Trails in 1967 was Mary White. (Courtesy of the *Winnsboro News.*)

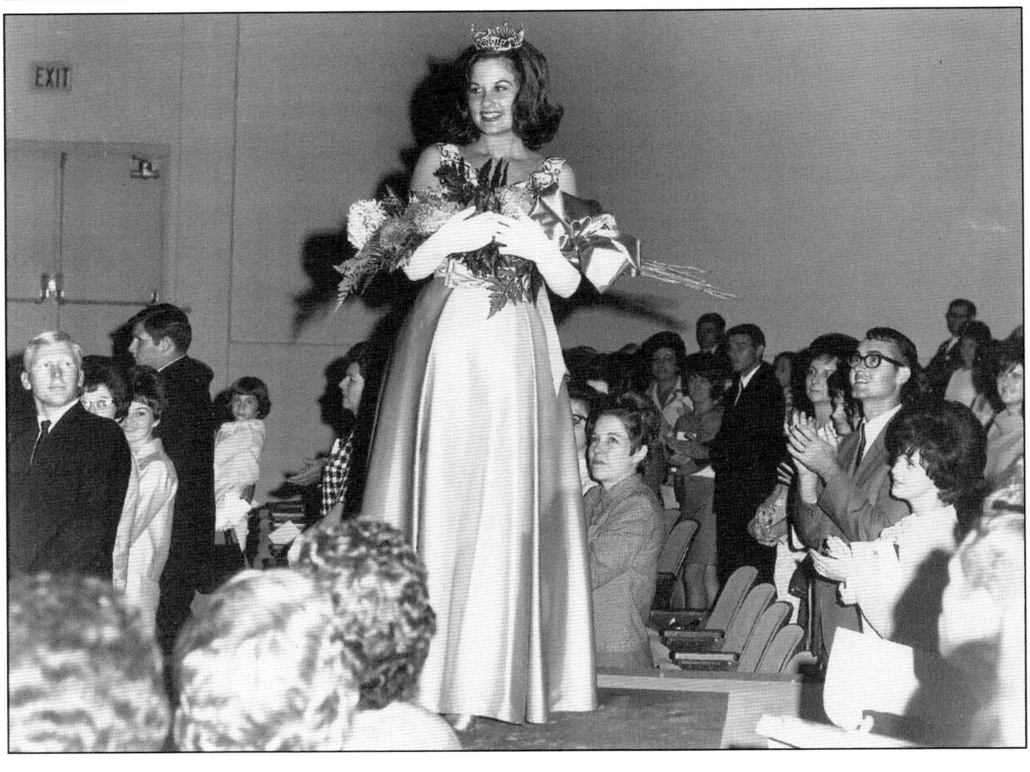

One of the biggest events for Autumn Trails, in terms of sheer numbers, is the annual Trail Ride. It was one of the original Autumn Trails events and had been going on informally for two years prior. The first ride was in 1957, and legend has it that it was so cold that year that the natural gas lines of Lone Star Gas blew up. The original group, led by trail boss Wayne Redding, rode about 35 miles. (Courtesy of the *Winnsboro News*.)

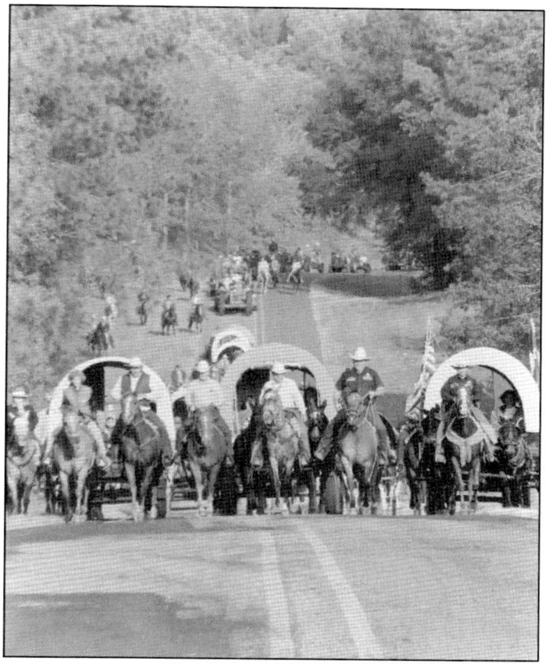

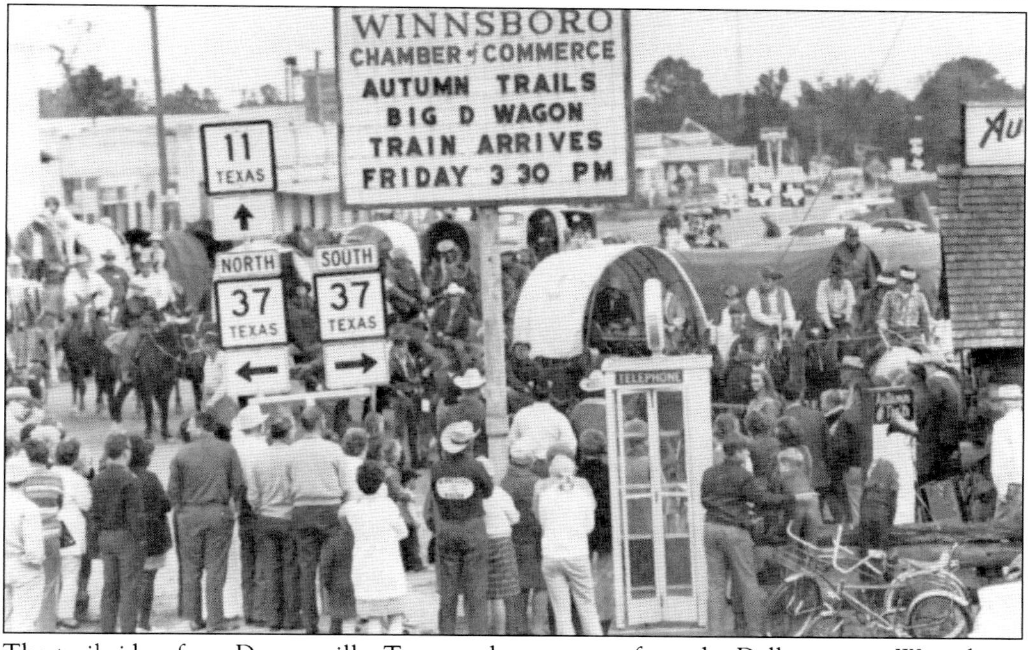

The trail riders from Duncanville, Texas, rode every year from the Dallas area to Winnsboro, taking a week to travel the 90 miles to join the annual trail ride. When other Dallas-based riding clubs joined them, they became "the Big D Wagon Train," and their arrival on a Friday afternoon was quite an event. By the late 1970s, the trail ride was so popular that 4,000 to 5,000 participants would come to town, some on horseback and some in wagons. They camped at Reid Park for the weekend, sometimes longer, and would take day rides along scenic trails. Evenings were times for campfires, cookouts, and sometimes a barn dance. (Courtesy of the *Winnsboro News*.)

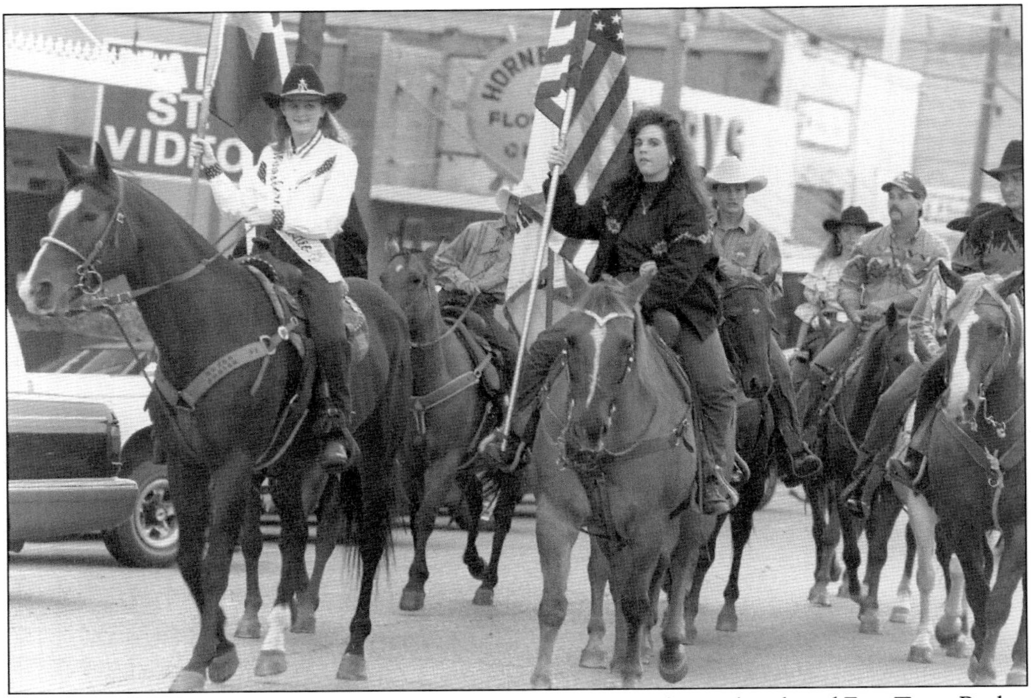

The parade on Friday afternoon officially kicks off the Trail Ride Weekend, and East Texas Rodeo queens still lead the parades, holding the flags. (Courtesy of the *Winnsboro News*.)

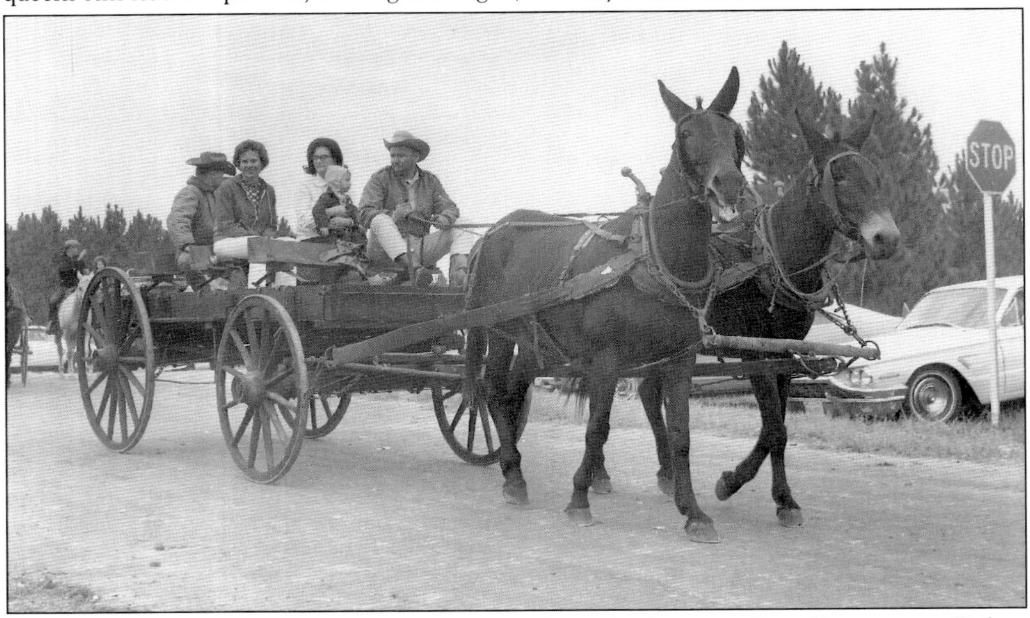

There are often almost as many mules as horses in the trail ride, especially pulling wagons. Riding in this wagon is Dinah Dodgen Nix, holding her daughter; Jerry and Clara Zeigler are in the back. The driver, who has not been identified, was a member of a trail riding group that would ride from Texarkana to Duncanville, a suburb of Dallas, and join the ride from there to Winnsboro. This picture was taken in 1966 or 1967. (Courtesy of the *Winnsboro News*.)

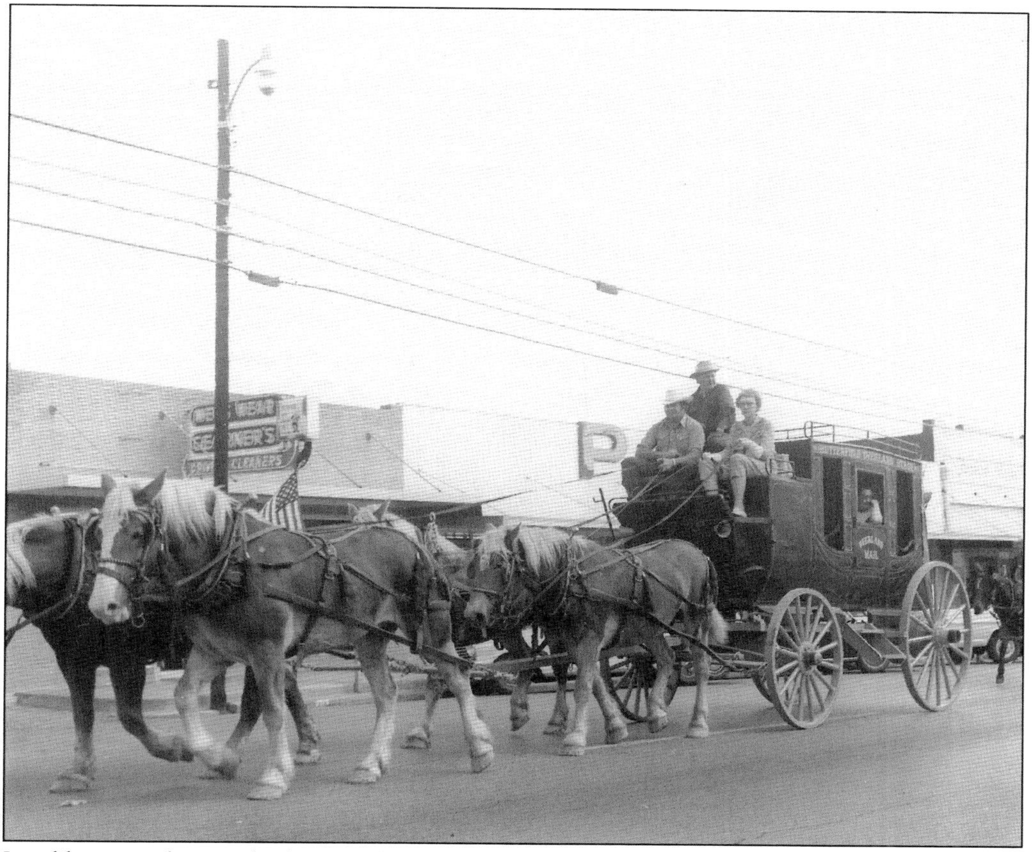

In addition to the standard covered or open wagon, some people came to the trail ride weekend in restored stagecoaches. The people in these pictures were not able to be identified. (Both, courtesy of the *Winnsboro News*.)

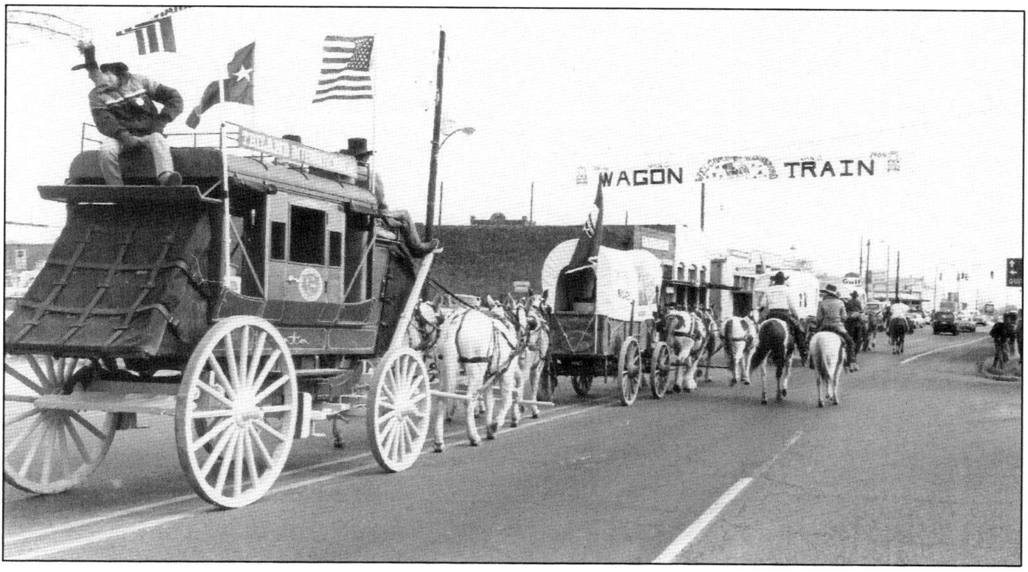

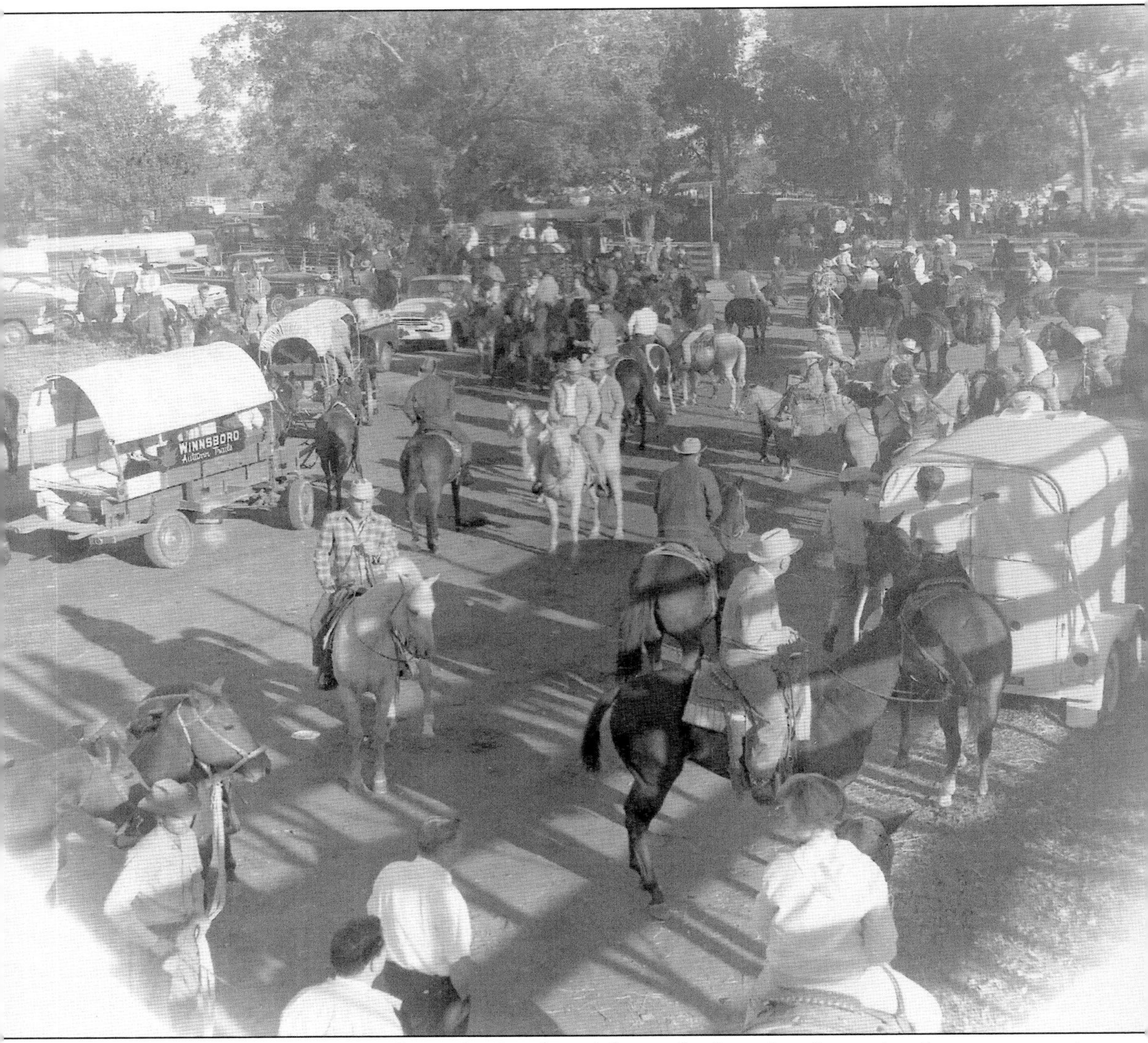

Riders and drivers get up early on the Sunday of the trail ride and gather to head out on a scenic ride. There are a number of tours that can be taken heading out of Winnsboro City Park. One takes riders past Winnsboro Municipal Airport, Cater's Lookout, McGee's Little Red Schoolhouse, 4-D Guest Ranch, a nature trail park, the old iron bridge, and Bent Pine Gallery. (Courtesy of the *Winnsboro News*.)

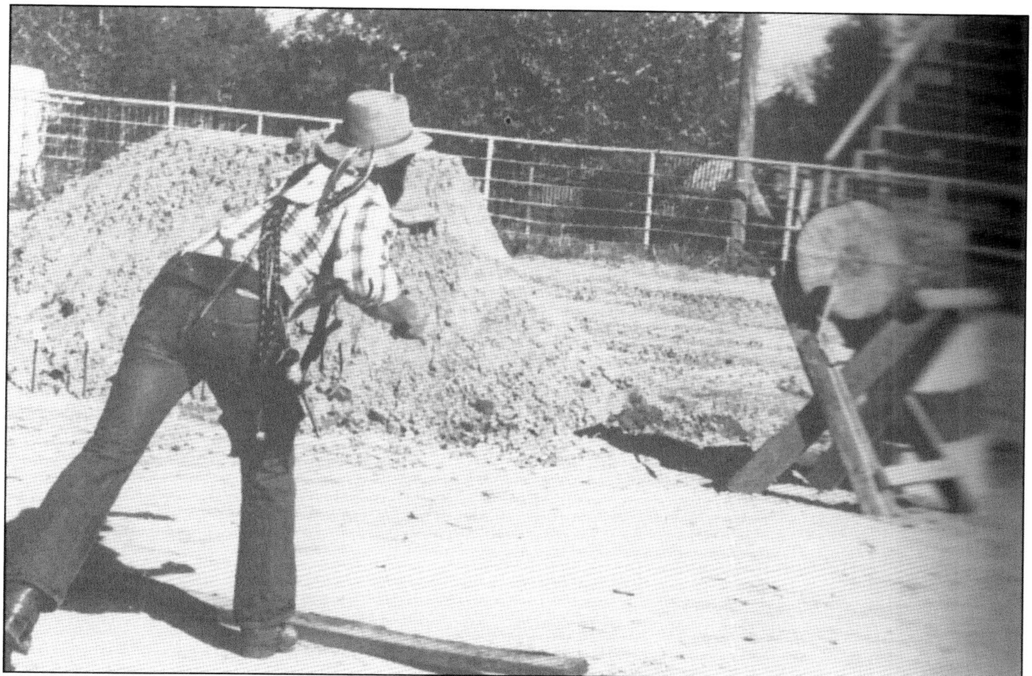

The Tomahawk Throw is part of the Black Powder Rendezvous, held at the Winnsboro gun range. When the Black Powder Rendezvous became part of Autumn Trails in the 1970s, it was like the frontier came alive again. Most participants dressed in authentic costumes and used the same weapons mountain men used in the 1800s. A number of shooting competitions are held at the Winnsboro Gun Club throughout the year, but this weekend is devoted to black powder muzzleloader flintlock muskets and pistols. (Both, courtesy of the *Winnsboro News*.)

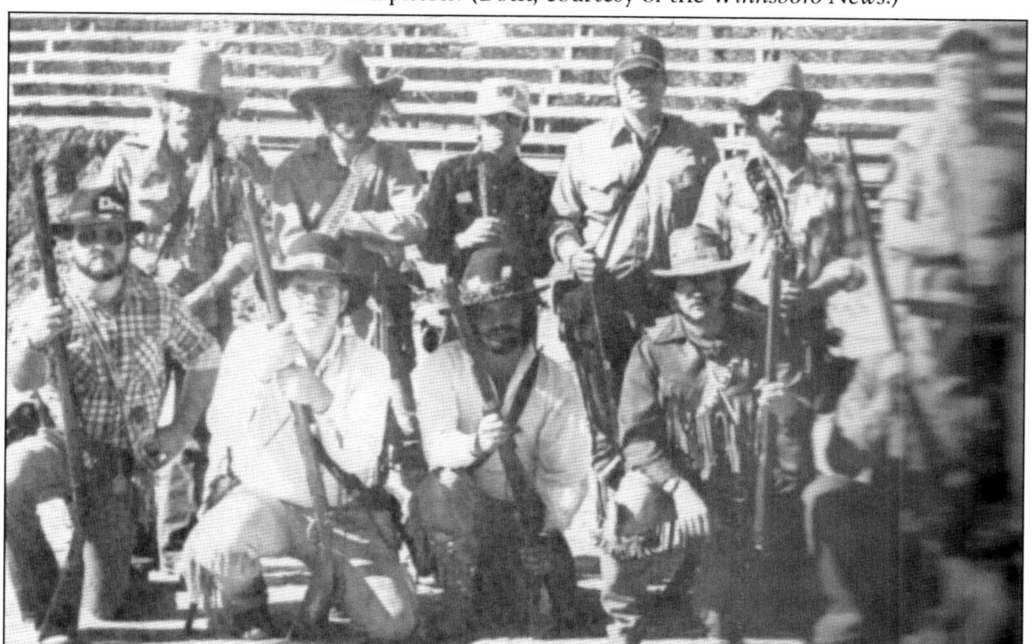

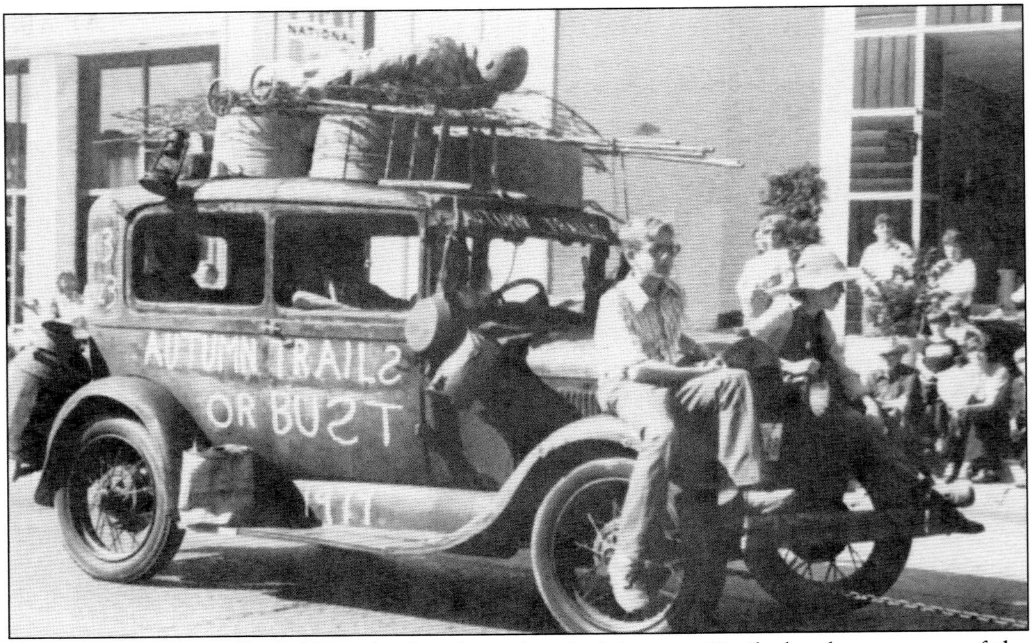

The Antique Car Rally, held on the fourth weekend of Autumn Trails, has become one of the most popular weekends of the festival. It all started with Bob Willis back in the early 1960s, when he restored an antique car as a member of the Dallas Model A Club. Driving the old car he decorated with washtubs, old mattresses, milk cans, and other "old-timey" items, Bob came to Winnsboro to visit his brother John Willis. On a lark, he decided to drive the old car through town and had so much fun that the next year he persuaded a friend, J.B. Vaughn, to join him. The following year, they talked the Dallas Model A Club into sponsoring a tour to Winnsboro. The first tour had 15 cars, and now the tour numbers over 200 cars. They parade through town before going on one of the scenic drives. (Both, courtesy of the *Winnsboro News*.)

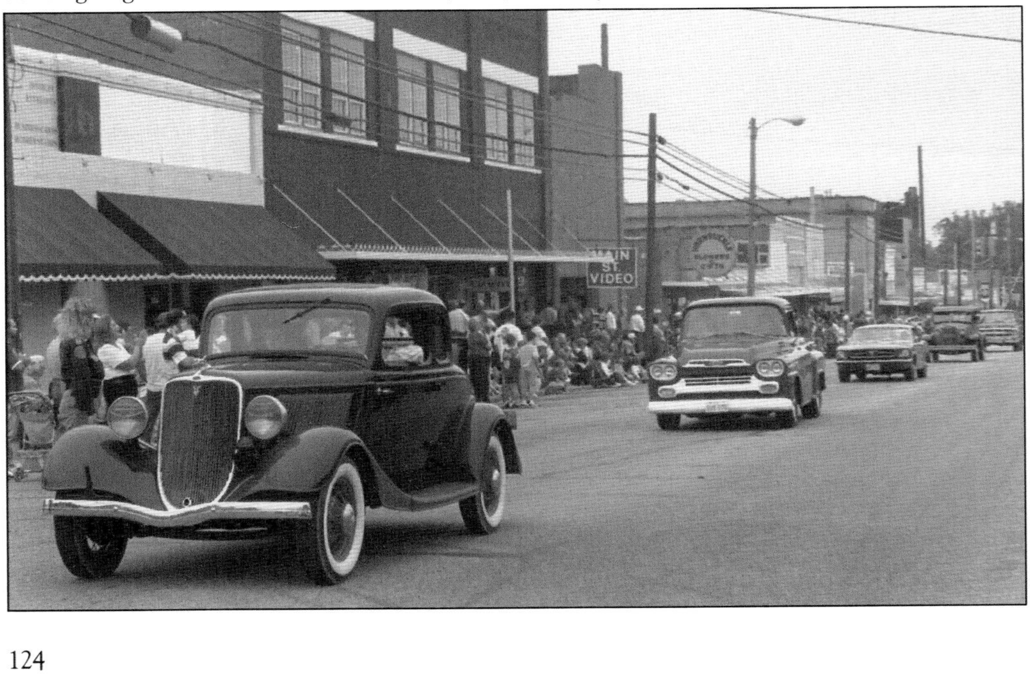

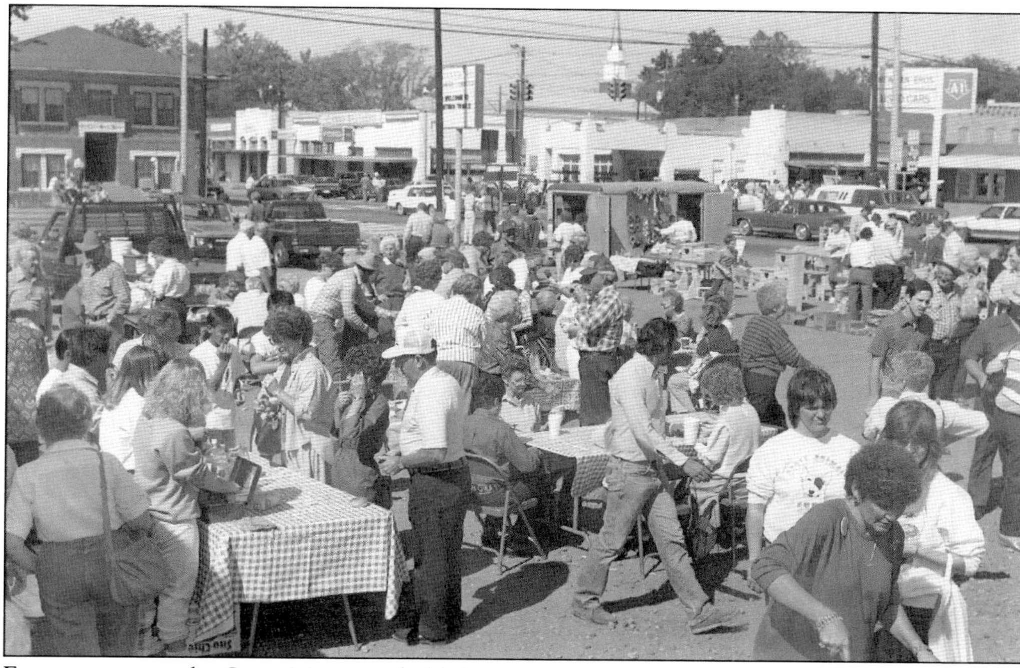

For many years, the Swap Meet was held downtown during Autumn Trails. People could shop and trade and enjoy chili and stew prepared by local churches. Later, the Swap Meet was moved to City Park (Reid Park). (Courtesy of the *Winnsboro News*.)

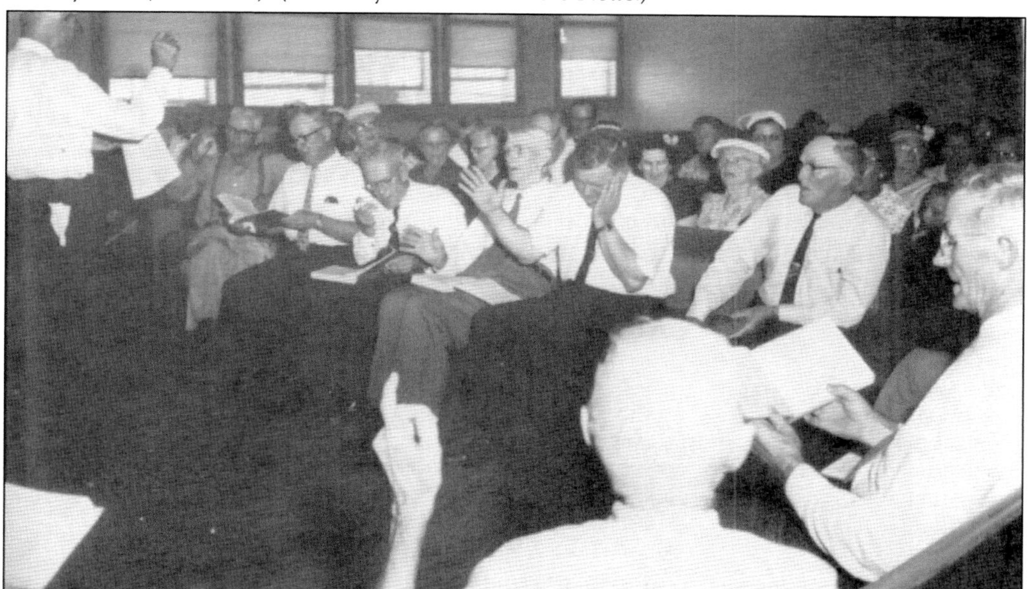

Religion is an important element in the lives of East Texas residents, and Winnsboro is no exception. Area-wide gospel and religious songfests have long been an integral part of the community, with the Wood County Songfest an annual event since 1894. The competition first met in Winnsboro in 1926, and later, it was incorporated into the annual Autumn Trails Festival. (Courtesy of the *Winnsboro News*.)

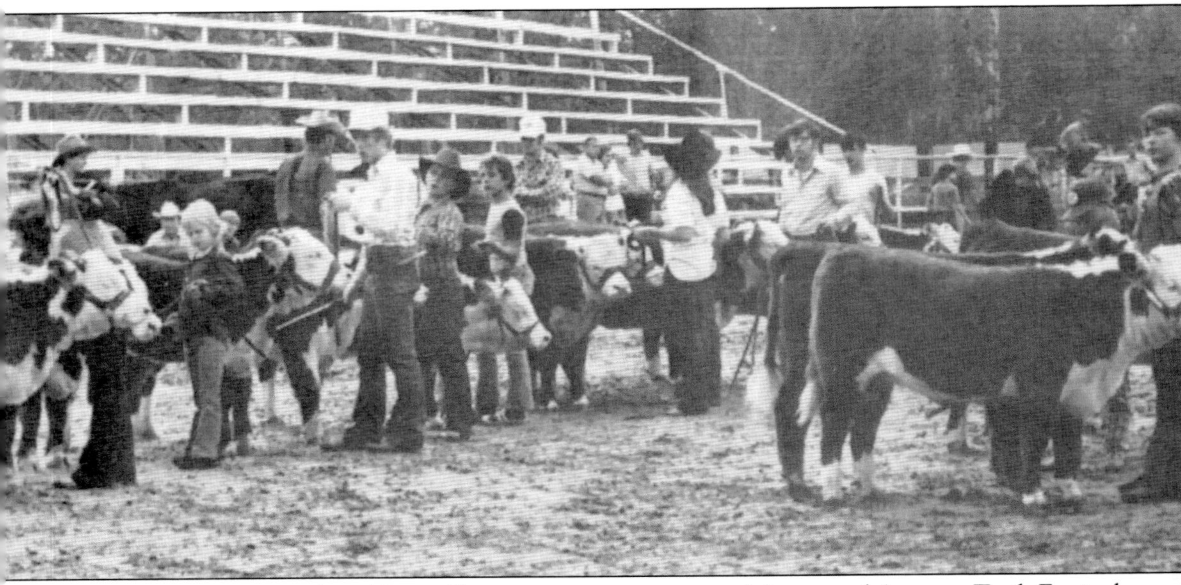

The Junior Livestock and Dairy Show is an important part of the annual Autumn Trails Festival. This picture, taken in the mid-1970s, shows some of the local young people from the Future Farmers of America (FFA) clubs and school agriculture departments who annually take part in the show. Traditionally held on the fifth weekend of October, this is the concluding event of the festival and was started in 1970. (Courtesy of the *Winnsboro News*.)

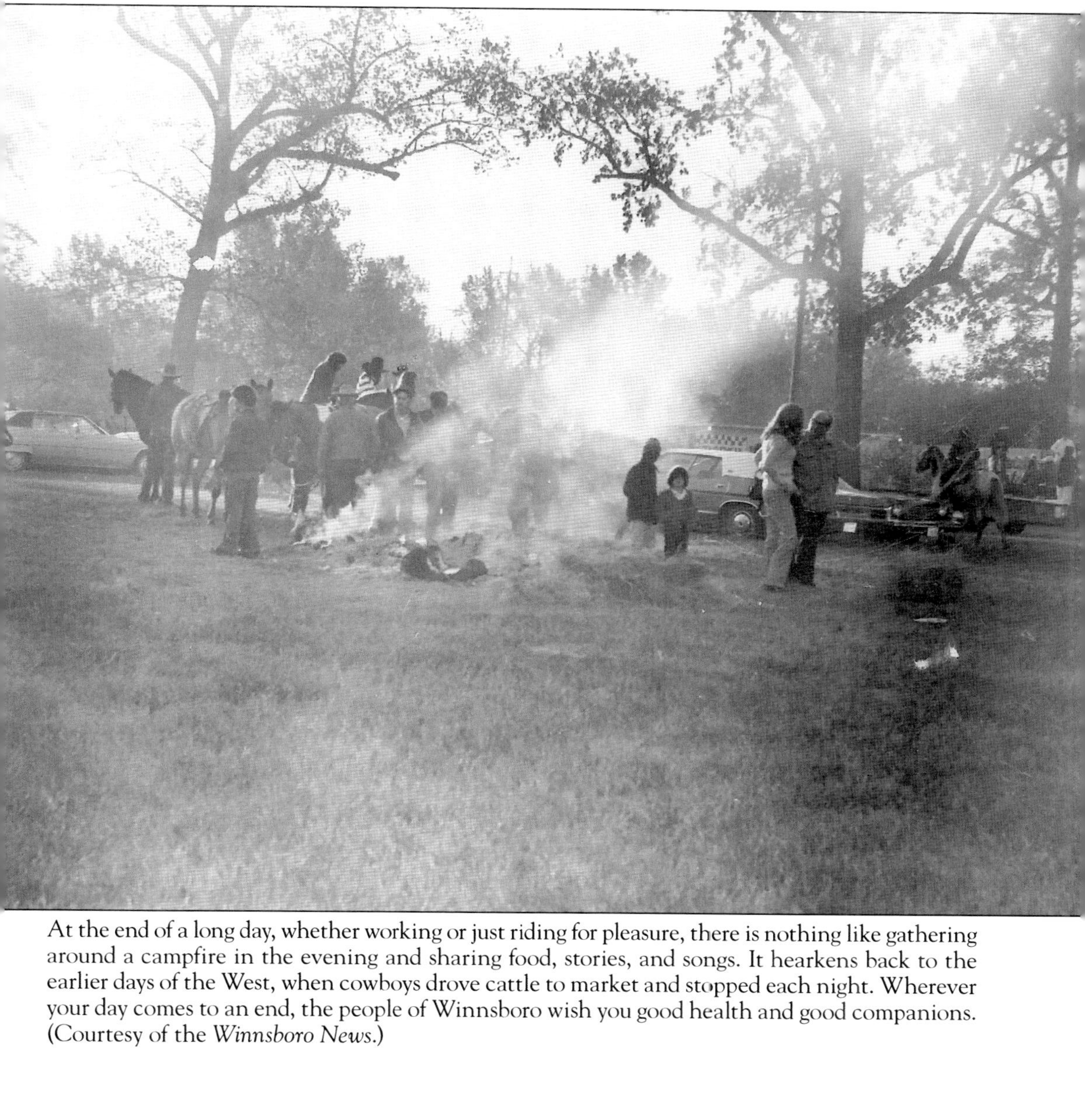

At the end of a long day, whether working or just riding for pleasure, there is nothing like gathering around a campfire in the evening and sharing food, stories, and songs. It hearkens back to the earlier days of the West, when cowboys drove cattle to market and stopped each night. Wherever your day comes to an end, the people of Winnsboro wish you good health and good companions. (Courtesy of the *Winnsboro News*.)